War wick University Caribbean Studies

Caribbean Families in Britain and the Trans-Atlantic World

Edited by

Harry Goulbourne and Mary Chamberlain

CARIBBEAN

Abbreviations

EC($)	Eastern Caribbean(dollar)
ED	Enumeration District
EEC	European Economic Community
BDTC	British Dependent Territories Citizens
BOC	British Overseas Citizens
BVI	British Virgin Islands
CUKC	Immigration lawyers' term for clients who lost UK citizenship as the Caribbean gained independence
CARICOM	Caribbean Common Market
DOMs	Departements d'outre-mer (French Overseas Citizens)
EEC	European Economic Community
ESRC	Economic & Social Science Research Council
EU	European Union
LFS	Labour Force Survey
NGO(s)	Non-governmental Organisation(s)
NSPCC	National Society for the Prevention of Cruelty to Children
PIS	Policy Institute Survey
PNC	People's National Congress (of the Union of South Africa)
PPP	People's Progressive Party (of Guyana)
PSI	Policy Studies Institute
SSD(s)	Social Services Department(s)
STATIN	Statistical Institute of Jamaica
UNIA	United Negro Improvement Association
WICP	Women in the Caribbean Project
WISC	West Indian Standing Conference

Acknowledgements

We wish to thank the Economic & Social Research Council (ESRC) for their financial support and the academic guidance of their (anonymous) referees of the three-year research project Living arrangements, family structure and social change of Caribbeans in Britain (Award L3152 53 009) under the *Population and Household Change Programme 1995–8* co-ordinated by Professor Susan McRae of Oxford Brookes University. We are also grateful to the ESRC for supporting (from our original budget) the weekend conference in 1998 at which nearly all the papers in this volume were presented.

We remain grateful to Roger Whittingham, who is conducting research for his doctorate (under the supervision of Harry Goulbourne and Harry Cowen) into minority ethnic communities and housing in Gloucester, for administrative support for the conference at which the papers in this volume were presented.

We are also grateful to our editor at Macmillan Publishers, Shirley Hamber, and to the co-editors of the Warwick University Caribbean Series, Professor Alistair Hennessy and Professor Gad Heuman for their support in bringing this venture to fruition.

Preface

Nearly all the contributions in this volume were first presented at a weekend conference at the Gloucester Suite, Francis Close Hall, Cheltenham & Gloucester College 26–29 March 1998. This was an international gathering of scholars working on Caribbean families in North America, Continental Europe, Britain and the Commonwealth Caribbean. Other participants came from the Barbados and Jamaica High Commissions in London, charitable foundations and the Commission for Racial Equality. The conference marked the first attempt to bring together academics, policy makers and charitable organisations in the Atlantic world around a common set of issues that Caribbean families confront. The conference was made possible by the Economic & Social Science Research Council (ESRC), who kindly permitted us to use a small research surplus from a three-year project on Caribbean families to be used to finance the participants from within Britain and abroad who were presenting papers. Support was also provided by individual participants who either paid for themselves or were funded by their institutions or employers who saw the conference as relevant to their work. The conference and papers by Chamberlain, Goulbourne, Owen and Plaza are outputs from the Living arrangements, family structure and social change of Caribbeans in Britain research project conducted between 1995 and 1998 and financed by the ESRC under their *Population and Household Change Programme*. The Caribbean family project was led by Goulbourne and Chamberlain, with Plaza as Research Fellow (18 months) and David Owen (six months).

It is hoped that this volume will serve the purpose of stimulating empirically based discussion about the wide range of issues and challenges that Caribbean families face both in Britain and the wider Atlantic world.

Harry Goulbourne
Mary Chamberlain
November 1999

Introduction

1 | Caribbean families in the Trans-Atlantic world

Harry Goulbourne and Mary Chamberlain

Introduction

The papers in this volume provide a critical introduction to a number of key aspects of Caribbean families, kinship systems and living arrangements as they have evolved in the triangular Atlantic world of Europe, North America and the Caribbean. Whilst the British situation constitutes the hub around which discussion revolves, contributors raise academic and policy concerns which transcend the national boundaries within which such issues are normally addressed in academic and policy circles. The papers offer much needed fresh empirical data and reflection on features of the relatively neglected experiences of Caribbean families in the cross-Atlantic world in which they have lived, particularly during the last half century since the docking of the *Empire Windrush* at Tilbury in 1948. This volume, therefore, constitutes a critical but empirically based contribution to academic and policy debates about crucial aspects of Caribbean family life in and outside the region. However, in these brief introductory remarks, we deliberately restrict ourselves to a few general observations in the conviction that it is best to leave the contributors to speak for themselves in the chapters offered.

The general themes

Contributors to this volume are not overly concerned with formal structures, typologies of Caribbean families, or a unified disciplinary perspective. To be sure, some chapters, such as those by St Bernard and Owen, are more closely focused on formal structures, but in the main, the general concerns of contributors are with meaning and interpretation of social processes, and the understanding and recognition of historical and new patterns of, and issues about, living arrangements. The wide range of disciplines represented here – including sociology, anthropology, history, social geography and social policy – enriches the overall contribution. The problems, issues and opportunities associated with Caribbean families both in the region and in Britain necessitate the combined efforts of researchers in more than any one field of academic and intellectual inquiry. The centrality of the institution of the family in public, policy and academic debates underlies the need for collaborative multi- if not inter-disciplinary collaboration. We are of the view that this volume is an important contribution in that direction. Accordingly, the volume emphasises three main closely related themes that we regard as central to an empirically informed understanding of Caribbean families in the Atlantic world. These themes are the general context of research into Caribbean living arrangements, the transnational characteristics of Caribbean families, and some of the problems faced either in the Caribbean or in Britain by these families. The collection is therefore divided into three broad sections about the Atlantic context, the demographic and transnational characteristics within which Caribbean families live and, finally, some of the issues around the practicalities of living arrangements, social provisions and policy in Britain and the Caribbean.

Part One sets out three broad contextual chapters by Chamberlain, Goulbourne and Smith. Goulbourne outlines the general socio-political framework of the transnational relations across the Atlantic within which Caribbean families live their lives – a theme to which he returns in the concluding chapter. The chapter by Chamberlain gives a general description, and points out the relevance of the migration experience of Caribbeans in the Atlantic world. Raymond Smith's contribution draws upon long experience of research in the Caribbean and the USA to highlight some major features in the research and policy debates about Caribbean and Black families in the three points of the Atlantic with which this volume is concerned. His observations about these debates in the USA and the Caribbean are apposite to the British situation, as is made clear in a number of later chapters.

While these contextual chapters emphasise different perspectives and suggest new directions for future research in this multi-disciplinary field, they also agree on two important points. These are, first, that there is a need to adopt a more nuanced and sensitive approach to the study of Caribbean families, and second, that there is a need for empirically verifiable data about family matters where Caribbeans, particularly Black Caribbeans in Britain, are concerned.

Part Two of the book picks up and develops the theme of the demographic and transnational characteristics of Caribbean families and kinship. First, quantitative analyses outlining the demographic profiles of Caribbean families and households in Britain and the

Caribbean by David Owen and Godfrey St Bernard commence the discussion about these substantive aspects of Caribbean families across the Atlantic. Taken together, these descriptions reveal broad commonalities between Caribbean family patterns in Britain and the region, such as rates of marriage. Chamberlain's contribution in this section takes us back to the theme of meaning and interpretation as partly expressed by social actors themselves. This theme is followed through by Reynolds in her chapter on fathering in Caribbean families in Britain, and by Abenaty, who discusses the developing phenomenon of 'return' migration from Britain to the Eastern Caribbean, focusing particularly on the St Lucian experience. Trevor Noble concentrates on Guyanese middle-class kinship networks within and outside the Caribbean and relates his findings to broader considerations of middle-class kinship irrespective of ethnicity and spatial distribution.

Part Three continues with the general theme of living arrangements, but places emphasis on the nature of social and welfare provisions where Caribbean families are concerned. Chapters by Ravinder Barn and Dwaine Plaza focus on specific issues about child adoption and ageing, and welfare policies relevant to these areas of social and family life and debates in Britain. Elsie Le Franc and her colleagues, Don Simeon and Gail Wyatt, draw our attention to the disturbing issue of domestic violence within families in the Caribbean. These issues, like others addressed in this section of the book, receive less attention than they deserve both in the Caribbean and in Britain.

But, as Goulbourne (1998) has suggested, these problems are relatively 'new' on the public agenda where new minority ethnic communities in Britain are concerned, and this observation may also be relevant with regard to Caribbean societies. In Britain, 'new' issues and concerns may be distinguished from what he calls the 'old' (but continuing) problems of education, employment, housing, police-community relations and the criminal justice system which dominated debates about Caribbean entry, settlement and consolidation in Britain over the past fifty years. Articulation and recognition of these 'new' problems reflect the growth and maturity of the Caribbean presence and confidence about transnational links across the Atlantic. Many of these issues and problems may be unpalatable, but in a Durkheimian sense they must be regarded as sociologically normal and must therefore be subjected to critical social analyses like any other aspect of social action.

The attention being given to these issues today also marks the shifts in the social policy paradigm away from public to private (mainly family and household) responsibility for social ills and needs over the last decade or so. Despite this shift, however, it must be noted that perhaps far more than with other communities in the Atlantic world, domestic problems confronted by Black families are highly charged public, and therefore, political affairs. For example, in Britain Caribbean families, like American Black families in the USA, are at the centre of public discussions about the marginal role of fathers, lone motherhood, and low educational performance of children from single parent households. In this respect, Tracey Reyonlds' chapter is of particular relevance in questioning the nature of public perception about Black fathering across the Atlantic, an issue that is again at the centre of public discussion in the USA following Orlando Patterson's (1998) recent intervention.

As noted in the Preface to this volume, nearly all the chapters here were presented at an international conference on the Caribbean family in March 1998. Given that the event marked the formal end of the large scale research (that is, the collection and collation of data) into the Living arrangements, family structure and social change of Caribbeans in Britain by Goulbourne, Chamberlain, Plaza and Owen, it may be in order briefly to explain its general aims and preliminary findings; the range of quantitative and qualitative research methods used in the research may be seen in chapters in this volume by Chamberlain, Goulbourne, Owen and Plaza. It may also be noted that our preliminary findings have particular resonance for findings by others, some of whose researchers are reported in the chapters that follow.

The Caribbean family project

The principal aim of the research, Living arrangements, family structure and social change of Caribbeans in Britain, was to examine the evolution of living arrangements of Caribbean communities in Britain through an investigation of family, kinship and household relationships and patterns and relate these to historical and contemporary Caribbean situations. The intellectual and academic, policy and general public concerns which provided the background for this project included the paucity of verifiable empirical knowledge about families in Caribbean communities in Britain and the dynamic links they have established and maintained between Britain and the Caribbean. These concerns led us to advance four hypotheses to guide our search for new empirical data about this second largest and by far the most visible new minority ethnic community in Britain.

The first hypothesis asserted that it has been the strength and resilience of Caribbean family ties that have enabled their communities to maintain themselves in the less than favourable conditions found in

Britain upon entry and settlement. In formulating this general assertion we followed the lines of investigations suggested by Driver (1982) and Barrow (1982) about the resilience and adaptation of Caribbean families and thereby questioned the more generally held view that these families suffer from the demise of traditional support systems (see, for example, Dench, 1992; Rampton, 1981) as a result of such factors as migration and a supposed vulnerability to changes in British society, such as the increase in liberal tolerance of family types and the strength of feminism.

Second, we hypothesised that several of the key patterns associated with Caribbean families are also those identified with the process of modernisation in classical sociology where a working, not an absolute, distinction is drawn between traditionalism and modernity characterised respectively by custom and choice. This hypothesis arose partly from Mintz's contention that Caribbean societies were at the forefront of the construction of the modern world (see, Mintz, 1993 also, Mintz & Price, 1992) and Goulbourne's (1991, 1998) analysis of Caribbean community action in Britain from this perspective.

We made two further assertions. First, that successful Caribbean families in Britain tended to re-migrate either to the Caribbean or North America, thereby inhibiting sizable accumulation of material and less tangible social resources in Britain. We thought that this probably conformed to historical and cultural models of Caribbean migration suggested by Richardson (1985), Thomas-Hope (1992, 1980) and Chamberlain (1997, 1998). Second, we asserted that Caribbean families in Britain have adapted to British conditions by evolving new patterns of household and kinship solidity through new identities (Hall, 1988; Goulbourne, 1999a) and multiple memberships of associations (see, Goulbourne, 1990). During the research and analysis of our data these hypotheses expectedly were modified, but in general they proved useful as initial guidelines and have helped us to arrive at understandings about Caribbean families that may not be easily induced from the bare statistics, often proffered in public debates.

It is not necessary, of course, to detail our findings here, particularly as we are still in the process of analysing our considerable data which include a series of sophisticated statistical profiles drawn from both British and Caribbean datasets, in-depth interviews of officials in the Caribbean and in-depth, life-story, interviews of three members of sixty families with backgrounds in Barbados, Jamaica and Trinidad & Tobago. The last set of interviews amounts to what must be the single largest data set on Caribbean people in Britain, and in due course will be available to the general research community in the region and Britain.

It is useful, however, briefly to mention some of our preliminary conclusions because they are consistent with many of the findings reported in this volume by colleagues working on independent research projects. In our final report to the ESRC we summarised our preliminary findings under seven broad points, and we wish to abbreviate these here.

First, we found that the living arrangements that Caribbean people have established in Britain provide the necessary care and affection, the reproduction of family and communal values, customs and traditions generally associated with the institution of the family and its role in socialising the individual into a wider social order. However, the tendency to focus on family structures (typified in the main by nuclear but sometimes extended units, legal marriages and paternal headship of homogenous households) has generally obscured these functions of Caribbean living arrangements and family patterns. For example, the relatively fluid or loose structures and apparent absence of many fathers feature prominently in academic and policy discourses about Caribbean families while fathering functions are often hidden. Our data suggest that exclusively focusing on structures may therefore distort our understanding of how Caribbean families provide the care, affection, spiritual and material necessities for their lives and how, outside the public gaze, they negotiate the conditions or minutiae of their lives. Inadequate understandings of these tend to encourage too strong a focus on the public provisions which accrue to this element in the British population. The excessive focus on structures may also encourage unfavourable comparisons between Caribbean patterns of living arrangements and those of other communities in Britain (particularly South Asians whose family structures conform to the normative values associated with the nuclear family). Such unfavourable comparisons tend to give rise to the perception that Caribbean communities suffer from a degree of 'dysfunctionality' as a result (see, for example, Dench, 1993; also, *Daily Mail*, 23 July, 1993).

Our second main finding suggested that Caribbean living arrangements in Britain have been reproducing Caribbean norms. Traditional commitment to lineage (or blood) remains stronger than commitment through affinal (marriage) commitment, and obligations and responsibility within and across generations remain primary values. Paradoxically, these traditions exhibit strong modern (or as some commentators would say, post-modern) features, including a strong emphasis on the individual's autonomy within the family, high incidence of lone mothers, an apparently low, but often hidden, participation of men in family and household matters (such as child-rearing, emotional, financial and other material support to the collective unit). This second major feature of Caribbean living arrangements in Britain also reflected Caribbean norms in terms of what may be called serial parenting, diversity of family structures and high participation of women in the workforce that has long been noted by the various Policy Studies Institute (PSI) reports on Britain's new minority ethnic communities (see, for example, Modood et al., 1997; Goulbourne, 1998a).

Our third general preliminary conclusion was that family obligations and responsibilities were to a degree being met through the wider kinship network. Our data suggest that lone mothers in Britain may be no more 'alone' in many circumstances than are mothers in the Caribbean, because kin members are expected to, and often do, take on maternal, paternal and affinal responsibilities in circumstances which are not captured in the bald descriptions of formal structures of family life. Nevertheless, both established statistical data and our qualitative data suggest that women remain the central figure in Caribbean living arrangements and are responsible for the day to day household, and the maintenance of family and kinship contacts. In this regard, we also found that many men, particularly immigrants, run the risk of becoming marginal to, or subordinate in, the common enterprise of family life which involves privileges as well as duties and responsibilities. The apparent democratic or egalitarian principles which are sometimes presumed to underpin gender relations in Caribbean domestic relations may not be as strong as a cursory public gaze might suggest.

Fourth, the living arrangements of Caribbean people in Britain suggest sophisticated and strong multi-dimensional and transnational family and communal affinities. The sense of kinship solidity across generations and the Atlantic link families, and this is an important theme in the majority of individual narratives of family members. Caribbean families in Britain must be seen as an important element in the transnational relations and unified Atlantic world which transcend national boundaries. In general, it can therefore be said that the transnationalism of Caribbean families is well illustrated by the high incidence of return migrants to the Caribbean and the migration of their offspring and affinal relations to the region; the opportunities available to returnees to the region; the continuing closeness between family members in the region and Britain, irrespective of class and ethnicity and the length of settlement abroad; the interlinkages between social welfare and health provisions in Britain and the Caribbean; and the fact that Britain and the Caribbean are seen by many as resources in individual family profiles. These positive aspects of the return experience should not lead us to belittle the potential for conflict between returnees and those who had either traveled to the North America or remained behind. Some of these points of conflict are hinted at by Abenaty in Chapter 10 of this volume.

Fifth, consistent with Caribbean social and family patterns, living arrangements in Britain are strongly characterised by multi-ethnic features such as exogenous marriages, mixed parentage, step-siblings, mixed offspring and cultural diversity irrespective of class, gender, age and ethnic considerations. These characteristics constitute a strong pointer to the nature of the participation of Caribbean communities in what is deemed a multi-cultural Britain and their active participation in the dynamic growth of a legitimately diverse Atlantic community. Nonetheless, this pattern of Caribbean living arrangements is often a matter for debate in the UK, because some Caribbeans believe that in the long run the community risks losing its identity. This is a point taken up in the last chapter of this volume.

Sixth, a strong sense of neighbourhood expressed in familial terms in the Caribbean provided and continue to provide a model of community involvement in Britain. This is often articulated through loosely structured networks, social and religious groups. In parts of London we found families whose well-being depended on maintaining not only Trans-Atlantic networks but strong local networks for immediate and mutual support (Goulbourne, 1999a).

Seventh, a number of concerns and opportunities in Britain and the Caribbean arise from these considerations, and are often consistent with the research findings and social policy debates being conducted by others in Britain as evidenced by the contributions to this volume. These include the perceptions of men as being marginalised as well as the actual marginalisation of some elderly men; the disproportionately heavy burden placed on female members of families and households as mothers and often as breadwinners and carers; the problems faced by 'returnees' in health provisions and re-settlement (such as customs facilities, land and home purchasing, and differential cultural traits as a result of outward migration and change at the points of return); and, finally, the opportunities provided by a dynamic Atlantic world, such as cultural diversity, continuity and change, employment and career development, and family well-being in a vast world which enjoys relatively easy movement, communication and wide cultural assumptions and certainties (see Goulbourne, 1999b).

Conclusion

Several of these broad suggestions from our research are borne out by other research findings, some of which are reported in the contributions to this volume. Of course, as noted, not all the themes that we would have liked to include are represented here. However, the volume offers a sufficiently wide collection to provide the basis for empirically informed and theoretically sophisticated discussion. We are therefore confident that the collection will achieve its objective of stimulating empirically relevant academic and policy research into the Trans-Atlantic world of Caribbean communities with respect to societies such as France and The Netherlands, and Britain, as the Cheltenham Conference strove to achieve.

Part 1

The Atlantic Context

2 | The socio-political context of Caribbean families in the Atlantic world

Harry Goulbourne

Introduction

This chapter is a general description of the overall context of the transnationality of Caribbean communities and families in the Trans-Atlantic world. In particular, the discussion focuses upon three related aspects of this general context: first, the construction of Caribbean communities in Britain; second, the formal structures of relations between the UK and Caribbean countries, which conditions the transnationality implied in the close cross Atlantic links between families; and third, an illustration of how the fates of Caribbean families are intertwined with public events. In general the discussion suggests that Caribbean family affairs must be situated within the broader socio-political contexts of the Atlantic world.

The construction of Caribbean communities in Britain

There are at least three broad aspects of the Caribbean presence in Britain which demonstrates the consolidation of communities. These include, first, their size and distribution (geographical, age and gender); second, their variation and plurality; and finally, the fact of cultural proximity between these and the majority, indigenous, communities. Whilst a description of all three aspects is necessary for an understanding of the growth and consolidation of Caribbean communities in Britain, the demographic patterns of Caribbean communities need not be discussed in this chapter, because in Chapter 5 David Owen offers an authoritative account of these. It is important, however, to explain the plurality of the Caribbean population in Britain as a reflection of their backgrounds in the Caribbean and their proximity to – though not common identity with – the indigenous population.

Like other new minority and indeed the indigenous majority ethnic groups in Britain, people of Caribbean backgrounds do not constitute a homogenous entity. The diversity of the Caribbean derived communities is often hidden or subsumed under the common banner of blackness, being Caribbean or being Jamaican. But these communities are comprised of people from a wide range of islands and territories stretching well over a thousand miles along the Atlantic, and separated by the other (in the main, Spanish-speaking and French-speaking) Caribbeans, and extends both north and south beyond the geographical Caribbean into the wider Atlantic and the South American continent. The Commonwealth Caribbean includes Antigua, Anguilla, the Bahamas and Barbados (both in the Atlantic proper), Belize (in Central America), the British Virgin Islands, the Caymans, Dominica, Grenada, Guyana (on the South American continent), Jamaica, Montserrat, St Kitts & Nevis, St Lucia, St Vincent & the Grenadines, and Trinidad & Tobago. Moreover, both the land mass and population of this sub-region are comparatively small: Jamaica, the largest single island[1] (4,244 sq miles) also has the single largest population with about 2.5 million people; Guyana, the largest country (83,000 sq miles) has a far smaller population than Trinidad & Tobago with around 1.5 million people and under 2,000 sq miles in size. Some of the islands, such as Anguilla, are even smaller than Barbados with her 166 sq miles. In total, the population of the Commonwealth Caribbean is only about 6 million and, as Mary Chamberlain shows in the next chapter, migration to Britain and North America during the second half of this century marked a significant shift of population for the main sending countries.

The Caribbean derived communities in other European countries demonstrates still further the variation in these communities in Europe. Although there are fewer French-speaking islands in the Caribbean, taken together their populations are greater than those of English speakers. Haiti alone has roughly the same population as the Commonwealth Caribbean combined; Martinique and Guadeloupe are departements d'outre-mer (DOMs), as is French Guiana on the South American mainland. Migration from the DOMs to Metropolitan France is not, technically, migration from one jurisdiction to another, but movement within the same country. Nonetheless, the Caribbean DOMs are several thousand miles removed from France, and the presence in European France of people from these parts of the world is not very dissimilar to the presence of people from the Commonwealth Caribbean in Britain. In both cases people moved to Europe with citizenship rights, although the British colonies became independent states while the French colonies became part of France.

The Caribbean presence in Europe also includes Dutch-speaking people from Surinam (on the South American mainland) and may also include people from the Dutch dependencies of Aruba, Bonaire, Curaçao, Saba, St Eustatius and St Maarten. There is also a sprinkling of Caribbean people in Denmark and Sweden, either as a result of longstanding Danish interests in the Caribbean or, as in the Swedish case, secondary migration from Britain. Thus, whilst the concentration of Caribbean communities in Europe are to be found mainly in Britain, France and the Netherlands, there is a thin spread of Caribbean people in the wider membership of the European Union. It is, however, the Caribbean presence in Britain that has set the tone and pace for all communities from that background in Europe, partly because of its size, earlier entry and settlement and a paradoxical tradition of what I have described as Commonwealth Caribbean radical conservatism (see Goulbourne, 1991a).

The significance of this plurality of geographical backgrounds in the Caribbean is the social diversity that it lends itself to in Europe, contrary to what is often perceived as a homogeneous whole, largely due to the remarkable political unity achieved by these groups in their responses to problems faced in Britain (see, Goulbourne, 1991b; Phillips & Phillips, 1998). At the broad social level, however, groups of Barbadians, Antiguans, Jamaicans and others retain much of their distinctiveness within British cities, even where they live cheek by jowl with others from the majority ethnic as well as other new (such as South Asians) and old minority ethnic communities (such as the Irish). In terms of cuisine, music, language and other features, groups from Caribbean countries retain important aspects of their distinct national features, but they also change as a result of their proximity to others, or, as Malinowski (1961) might have argued, as a result of culture-contact.

In the first place, they change in relation to each other as Caribbean groups, because in the main they meet for the first time in Britain, not in the Caribbean where a Jamaican was not likely to meet a Guyanese or a Barbadian person outside the privileged and charmed circles of literature, cricket, the regional University of the West Indies and within the confluence of union and party political leadership. Second, as far as other groups and the majority indigenous populations in Britain are concerned, all Caribbean groups are Blacks or Jamaicans who constitutes a simple majority of the overall population of people of Caribbean backgrounds in Britain.

It has been, therefore, in Britain that people from the Caribbean islands have discovered much of their commonalities, and have therefore created and developed ethnic bonds which do not exist in the same way in the region itself. This fact is reflected in several peculiarly British practices which have come to define the Caribbean presence in Britain: the participation of Jamaicans in the (originally Trinidadian) Notting Hill Carnival (see, for example, Pryce, 1990) the popularity of reggae and Rastafarian life style beyond their narrow following in Jamaican communities, and the use of terms such as 'Afro-Caribbean' or 'African Caribbean' that have little or no meaning within the region itself. This creation of new ethnic identity, or identities, in Britain has been consolidated by such factors as cross-island marriage or partnership and households (Goulbourne, 1999a) leading to offspring who feel that they have common links with more than one country in the Caribbean and are migrating to the region in a reversed process to that followed by their parents in the 1950s and 1960s (see Chapter 10 in this volume; and Goulbourne, 1999b).

Paradoxically, therefore, perhaps apart from the regional University of the West Indies, migration to the UK has been the single most powerful factor in the promotion of Commonwealth Caribbean social integration, including the Caribbean Common Market (CARICOM), which is about to embrace the non-English speaking states in the region such as the Dominican Republic. Whilst in Britain it has been important for Caribbean people to seek to develop a distinct identity as part of their ethnic solidity, in the region itself this has not been as necessary where people of African backgrounds constitute a clear demographic majority or a strong cultural dominance (see, for example, Nettleford, 1972). Indeed, whilst people of African and Caribbean backgrounds in Britain were forging new ethnic bonds and icons, in the Caribbean it was more the people with historic backgrounds in the Indian sub-continent who were asserting their cultural distinctiveness against a dominant Creole ethno-cultural hegemony. This was particularly relevant in Guyana where South Asians constituted a simple majority, but African Creoles dominated the public spheres of politics, administration and public culture. The situation was similar in Trinidad, where South Asians made up the single largest ethnic group, but also felt that they were subordinated in the public representation (cultural, political) of the country. In Britain, however, the vast majority of people of Caribbean backgrounds, who also embrace a longer historical African background but had long been more aware of their British connections than of their African heritage, were forced to forge a new identity because their reception experience was in the main negative (Goulbourne, 1991b). Whilst enjoying formal citizenship rights (the franchise, nationality status), they increasingly felt excluded from the emotional sense of belonging to the nation and excluded from active and equal participation in the primary institutions of the British nation. The result has been that it is in Britain that Caribbean derived communities have come to define a common awareness of the Caribbean and to take on board the long neglected African heritage structurally undermined by slavery and settler/plantation colonialism within the Caribbean itself..

A final aspect of this sketchy background to Caribbean transnationality in Britain is the general cultural proximity between the indigenous European and Caribbean-derived cultural artefacts. It is hardly necessary to detail the obvious cultural presence of Caribbean people in Britain, but it is important to note that this presence continues to have a significant impact in various areas of British national life, including phrases in the popular use of language and music, style in every day life and sports. Popular phrases (to have 'street cred', or to be 'cool'), youth dress style (the turned-around basketball cap, ever larger unlaced trainers and big soft-looking boots, hanging T-shirts), D-Js and loud music in clubs and remodelled cars are examples of the visibility and audibility of the powerless. These features of black cultures in the African Diaspora cannot be easily marked off according to national boundaries because they are in constant interplay in a nomad-like fashion across juridical and political borders, particularly across the Atlantic. Thus, in each of these areas membership of a cross Atlantic African Diaspora, importantly embracing the USA and, of course, the Caribbean region, strengthens the presence and the impact of Caribbeans in Britain. What is observed of popular music, everyday use of language, and dress styles may also be observed with respect to the active participation in sports, entertainment and a presence in the advertisement of consumer goods.

No doubt, the proximity of Commonwealth Caribbean culture (language and literature, sports and entertainment, values and religion) to the dominant majority culture must be a factor in the visible and audible presence of Caribbeans in these areas in Britain. However, the differential social incorporation that occurs in advanced industrial societies that the late M G Smith (1974, 1988) spoke about, based on racial or phenotypic traits rather than ethnic differences, has also powerfully restricted the choice of social and economic participation in British life by people of African Caribbean backgrounds (see Goulbourne, 1998, Ch. 1). This helps to explain the fact that despite high levels of participation in the creative spheres of cultural life Caribbean people have little or no participation in the control or ownership of cultural production. For example, at the time of writing only Ruud Gullit,[2] from the Netherlands, has been manager of a prominent football club, and there are few if any trainers at national level in athletics or football. Except for Linford Christie, there is a conspicuous absence of Caribbean people owning football and athletics clubs or music companies, where their presence as creative performers is glaringly obvious.

These features of the background of the Caribbean presence give credibility to the notion that migration to Britain has not significantly changed the place of Black Caribbeans in the social structures that obtain in the Anglo-Caribbean world which straddles the Atlantic. The Caribbean that migrants left behind between the late 1940s and the early 1960s was a region in which the economy was dominated and owned by the small pockets of Europeans who remained after African Emancipation from slavery in 1838 and as the dominance of the West India interest in British society and politics gave way to those of the nabobs of the East India interest in London following the Corn Laws of the 1840s. Although political independence was won in the 1960s by most of these countries, economic control failed to materialise and the vast majority of Black Caribbeans remained outside the sphere of significant ownership as detailed by a generation of Caribbean scholarship (see, for example, Stone & Brown, 1977). But this is hardly the place to explain the patterns of ownership and control in the region; suffice it therefore to suggest that the incorporation of African Caribbeans into European or European British society has not been significantly different from the form of their historical differential incorporation within the Caribbean itself. Of course, within the Caribbean, the situation has been significantly changed during the last four or so decades: Black Caribbeans now have a stake in the economies of the countries they have won from buccaneer and settler Europeans, and a more complex class system has changed the racial differentiation that obtained under the colonial order. The commanding heights of these economies remain, however, in the hands of European-Caribbean families and other minorities, as well as transnational companies in agriculture, manufactures, mining (oil and bauxite) and tourism.

These general remarks provide a backdrop against which Caribbean families conduct their lives and their affairs. Another dimension, however, of this general context within which Caribbean families across the Atlantic are situated is the more formal structure of relations between European, particularly in this instance British, and Caribbean states.

The structure of formal and diasporic relations across the Atlantic

For convenience, the formal relations between the UK and the Commonwealth Caribbean may be separated into those that are of a bilateral nature and those that are established through regional or multilateral mechanisms. The former involve the exchange of High Commissioners (ambassadors) along with the usual officials and services that an embassy would provide for their nationals living, working or travelling abroad. Sometimes – but not always and not uniformly – these missions will have legal and trade attachés with specific tasks allocated. Antigua, Barbados, the Republic of Guyana, Grenada, Jamaica and the Republic of Trinidad & Tobago have High Commissioners in London, some with officials who pay regular visits to the provincial regions of the UK to service nationals and keep them informed about developments 'back home'. The Eastern Caribbean states of the Commonwealth of Dominica, St Kitts, St Lucia and St Vincent have shared representation in London, but it was expected that from around 1998 (later postponed) each of these states would have their own High Commissions. As expected, these High Commissions act as focal points for nationals and their families living and working in the UK and who need information or help about affairs 'back home' and, during the period of migration and settlement, some affairs in the UK. Similarly, there are UK High Commissioners in Bahamas, Barbados, Belize, Jamaica, Guyana and Trinidad; there are British representatives in Antigua and St Lucia but below High Commissioner level and, like the other East Caribbean states, come under the High Commissioner to Barbados. Montserrat, the Caymans, Turks and Caicos, and the British Virgin Islands enjoy internal autonomy with Britain providing overall security and exercising responsibility within the international community; the governors of these territories therefore exercise some executive power and a degree of control over the chief ministers who head the governments.

A second aspect of bilateral relations is the fact that the UK and nearly all Commonwealth Caribbean states share the serving British monarch as head of state. Additionally, the legal, administrative and political norms of the Commonwealth Caribbean are derived, as are North American norms, from the Common Law English system. These norms constitutes a powerful, unstated or taken for granted, set of ties within the region and between the region and Britain in ways that are often difficult to either explain to indigenous Britishers who have little knowledge of their own imperial past or to inquiring individuals whose ideological and intellectual bearings derive from other socio-political orders. Furthermore, there are close bilateral relations linking key EU states with the Caribbean. In particular, the Lomé Conventions link the region with the Union through a number of agreements between the African Caribbean and Pacific group of former colonies who wanted to secure their access to Europe's vast market when Britain joined the then EEC in 1971 (see, for example, Talburt, forthcoming). Another example is, of course, the membership and high level of participation in the Commonwealth of independent nation-states which grew out of the empire over the last half century.

Finally, nationality status is undoubtedly the most immediately important aspect of bilateral relations between Caribbean states and Britain which underpins the transnationality of Caribbean people across the Atlantic. This is most clearly expressed by the acceptance of dual nationality by both Britain and Commonwealth Caribbean states. It is possible, therefore, for an individual to be legally a Barbadian or Jamaican citizen as well as being a British citizen. Such a person may carry the passport of either country or both, own property,[3] vote and stand for office provided the usual residential qualifications under respective electoral laws are met.[4] The country's laws which apply to such an individual are those of the country in which they are, at a given time, resident or present. In the Commonwealth Caribbean citizenship is principally through birth but also can be acquired by descent, registration or naturalisation and, where migrants to Britain and their offspring are concerned, the issue of nationality does not appear to have been a political issue in any of these states. Two factors may explain this. First, most of these countries are points of departure in the migration process (as shown in Chapter 3 in this volume) and returnees are officially welcomed (as shown in Chapter 10 in this volume). Second, increasingly governments in the region have come to see communities abroad as a resource upon which to draw, in terms of investment and during times of natural disasters such as volcanoes and hurricanes.

Prior to the British Nationality Act 1981 (which came into effect in 1983) British nationality was also transmitted principally through birth, irrespective of the national status of an individual's parents. Under the 1981 Act British nationality is secured mainly by descent, but individuals may also attain citizenship by registration and naturalisation. The Act abolished the rule of *jus soli* whereby individuals acquired nationality simply by the fact or accident of birth on British soil, or within the space under British jurisdiction such as a ship or an aeroplane. In other words, the Act adopted the more common Continental European tradition of citizenship by descent as enshrined in the *jus sanguinis* principle. The Act also set out four new forms of British nationality: British citizenship, British Dependent Territories Citizens (BDTC), British Overseas Citizens (BOC), and British subject, but it has been pointed out that the 'question of who belongs to the four categories of citizenships ... cannot be determined simply by looking at that Act' (Supperstone & O'Dempsey, 1996: 6). Earlier laws, such as the British Nationality Act 1948, the Commonwealth Immigration Act

1962, the Immigration Act 1968, and the British Immigration Act 1971 may have to be consulted to determine an individual's citizenship. This has led to what Cohen correctly perceives as the 'fuzziness' of post-imperial British national identity (Cohen, 1994: Ch. 1). But this fuzziness is not entirely absent from the definition of national identities in Commonwealth Caribbean states which share with Britain, but perhaps particularly England, a kind of ambivalence not present in, for instance, African Commonwealth states, about 'the national' entity.

As Britain's colonies in the Caribbean gained their independence from 1962 onwards, Jamaicans, Barbadians and others – who had migrated to the UK from 1948 as colonials within imperial boundaries – found that they had lost their status as citizens of the UK and colonies (usually referred to by immigration lawyers as the CUKC category). Depending on period of residence and other factors, individuals in the Caribbean community could acquire UK nationality if they so wished. In any event, their legal, political or social rights in the UK were not affected, but if they left the country and stayed beyond a certain period they were deemed to have lost their right to return. The Immigration Act 1971 required that former CUKCs whose country of birth had become independent from Britain should become UK citizens through a process of registration. This volume of laws governing immigration and defining nationality, taken together with anti-racist discrimination laws – namely, the Race Relations Acts of 1965, 1968 and 1976 – provide many lawyers in Britain with a good living. The Labour government of Tony Blair is concerned nonetheless that, even with the salutary work of non- governmental organisations such as the Joint Council for the Welfare of Immigrants and the state's own unit on immigration matters, there is a need for better trained legal functionaries to work in this area (see, Lord Chancellor's Advisory Committee on Legal Education and Conduct, 1997).

Whereas people with British Overseas Citizens (BOC) status may be found in such places as Hong Kong, other parts of Asia and in Africa, in the Caribbean British Dependent Territories Citizens (BDTC) are more likely because there are still a number of British dependent territories in the region. With the return of Hong Kong to China in July 1997, Britain has 13 remaining dependencies across the globe. In the Caribbean, Montserrat has been much in the news because of the Soufriere Hills volcano's eruption in 1997–8 and Claire Short's unfortunate gaffe about aid to the islanders; Bermuda with the largest population (60,000[5]) of any remaining dependency is, of course, in the Atlantic, but because there is an African majority population the dependency is sometimes thought of as being a Caribbean territory.

The term 'dependency' is, of course, something of a misnomer, because whilst they all depend on Britain for defence and representation abroad, apart from piracy and drug barons there does not appear to be much that they require to be defended from. Some, such as Montserrat and St Helena (not a Caribbean island) may from time to time also require material help from Britain, but in the case of Bermuda the dependency has a higher per capita income than Britain herself; the Caymans are importers of labour and successful off-shore banking economies which have benefited from the return of Hong Kong to China as some transnational corporations relocated themselves. Hintjens (1997) has suggested that it would be desirable for the rights of persons with BDTC status to be changed, bringing them more into line with similar cases in the Dutch or the French DOMs. This would mean that BDTCs would have rights in the UK, such as right of entry, residence and the vote as citizens in the French dependencies in the region have in France and the right of entry as citizens in the Dutch Antilles have with respect to The Netherlands. Following a Foreign Office meeting addressing the problems of the British dependencies in London in early February 1998, *The Guardian* newspaper (1998) strongly supported this position and urged the Foreign Secretary, Robin Cook, and the Home Secretary, Jack Straw, to extend such rights to the dependencies, particularly since it is thought that people in these territories would not wish to settle in Britain. Indeed, there appears to be more of a concern on the part of some spokespersons in these territories that the real problem would be people from Britain relocating to the dependencies if there were to be a situation of reciprocity.

The process of migration from the Caribbean to Britain and the return migration that has been developing since the late 1960s (see, Peach, 1991; Goulbourne, 1999b; also, Chapter 10 of this volume) involved relatively little active state intervention. However, there has been at least one instance when Caribbean leaders felt compelled to intervene in British affairs pertaining to Caribbean communities and families. This was occasioned by the riots in Notting Hill, London in 1957 (see Pilkington, 1988), when young white men attacked black immigrants and the St Vincencian Kelso Cochrane was killed, triggering similar events in other British cities such as Nottingham in the East Midlands, and set the backdrop for the 1962 Commonwealth Immigration Act which drastically limited black and brown immigration. These events are properly described and analysed elsewhere (see, for example, Foot, 1969, Layton-Henry, 1992)) and need not detain us here. Suffice it to say that the events led to Norman Manley, Premier of Jamaica (acting on the behalf of the short-lived West Indian Federation) visiting London and seeing for himself the reaction to

West Indian entry. After holding discussions with relevant authorities about the conditions West Indian immigrants faced, a number of people on the liberal wing of British society collaborated with concerned West Indians to found the West Indian Standing Conference (WISC) whose main aims included representation of West Indian problems to the relevant authorities and promoting 'good race relations' between natives and newcomers. From the period of political independence, however, from 1962 to the 1990s Caribbean governments tended not to involve themselves closely with the lives of their nationals in Britain, and this may be because in general Caribbeans in the UK enjoy citizenship rights and their family welfare are not, therefore, always the direct and exclusive responsibility of governments in the Caribbean.

Nonetheless, these states have not been entirely silent about the fate of nationals and their families in the UK. There is evidence to suggest that governments, irrespective of which party was in office in the main islands, kept themselves aware of developments as these affected Caribbeans in the UK. There is also much that is not known about these states' responses to some of these major events in Britain. The responses of Caribbean governments to a wide range of problems faced by Caribbean people in Britain need to be further researched: the dramatic negative effects of the late J Enoch Powell's 1968 'rivers of blood' speech in Birmingham, the various immigration and nationality laws, the high incidence of brutal policing in Black communities, disproportionately high unemployment and prison rates, poor schooling, increasingly poor mental and physical health are some of these problems. In recent years a number of other problems have, however, concerned Commonwealth Caribbean governments with respect to British authorities. These include the frequent stopping at ports of entry of legitimate tourists, relatives visiting family members in the UK, and the British customs and Home Office's concern about the mobility or entry of drug traffickers associated with Jamaican 'yardies' and other transnational criminal fraternities. As Castells (1996) noted, the growth of the network society not only facilitates ease of communication across the globe, it also promotes more rapid criminal networking.

On the other hand, moments of crises in the Caribbean have from time to time elicited noticeable concern amongst the Caribbean population in Britain. Again, these need to be specifically researched, but a number of instances can be pointed to: the conflict symbolised by the African dominated People's National Congress (PNC) and the East Indian dominated People's Progressive Party (PPP) in Guyana led, respectively, by the late Forbes Burnham and the late Cheddi Jagan in Guyana; Maurice Bishop's 1979 New Jewel Revolution in Grenada against 'uncle' Eric Gairy's uncharacteristically repressive Commonwealth Caribbean government; invasion of Grenada (incidentally, a Commonwealth state) in 1983 by Ronald Reagan. In the same period of the early 1970s that the Tory government of Edward Heath was introducing a draconian industrial relations bill in the British Parliament, Michael Manley's radical and reforming government in Jamaica was also introducing a similar measure, and the veteran Jamaican trade unionist and politician, Richard Hart,[6] led the Caribbean Labour Solidarity group in London in opposition not only to Heath but also in opposition to his old comrade Manley. The impact of the US Black Power Movement in Britain and the Caribbean also involved Caribbean people in Britain. Not only did that movement stimulate political awareness and growth in Britain, but UK based Caribbeans also responded to the impact in the Caribbean. The two main incidents include the Rodney riots (see, for example, Payne, 1994; Rodney, 1969) in Kingston in 1968 (part of the world wide student-cum-academic revolt of that year), and the Black Power revolt in Trinidad in 1970. There are important connections between these events and the growth of political and national consciousness across the North Atlantic, and future research will no doubt elaborate and explain these connections.

Within Britain, as I have shown elsewhere (Goulbourne, 1990), Caribbean communities were quick to establish welfare/cultural activities to meet felt family and communal needs. These involved collective welfare needs and support. In the main, the basis for collective action and organisation is the fact of shared common affinities, which themselves have become the basis of exclusion and discrimination, whether wittingly or unwittingly, as Sir William McPherson (1999) defined 'institutional racism' in his report on the Lawrence Case in February 1999. The variety of West Indian or Caribbean social centres providing for the needs of the young, women or the elderly; the promotion of alternative education classes, training groups and so forth are examples of this kind of activity (see, Hinds, 1992; also, Hylton, 1999). So too are the many black-led churches which sprang up throughout British cities from the 1960s (see, for example, Edwards, 1992; Gerloff, 1992; Calley, 1965). In general, however, just as it might be said that Caribbean families are not best organised as units for rapid economic accumulation, so too Caribbean groups are not best able to exploit ethnic solidarity as a resource in the competition for scarce resources (Goulbourne, 1991a).

A second type of organised group in Caribbean communities are the brokers whose activities involve groups or individuals seeking to mediate between official organs (of the local or national state, statutory bodies, employers and providers of services), and the community. As the word suggests, brokers stand at a point from which they can mediate between actual or potentially conflicting interests. Increasingly, brokers are private individuals or small groups providing services for needy clients, groups or individuals, sometimes with conflicting interests. In all communities, however, there have long been large umbrella-like organisations which have functioned as brokers between state bodies and communities. The best known of these has been the West Indian Standing Conference (WISC) mentioned earlier. Whilst WISC continue to be consulted by officials,[7] the organisation is no longer the force it was in the 1960s when it was at the forefront of several struggles in the black community, particularly in North London where leaders such as Jeff Crawford and John LaRose were active over issues such as the bussing of children across London education authorities and police brutality against young Black men. This is largely because with the integration of Caribbean people into British society, not only have they variously participated in established organisations, but they have also initiated a large number of organisations in London, Birmingham and other cities (see, Hinds, 1992) where they have settled and negotiated their own relationships with the various high commissions in London and relevant local and national authorities. Moreover, these organisations have followed the broad patterns of those in the indigenous populations, representing youths, women, the elderly, people with particular ailments such as sickle-cell anaemia or mental illness.

There have also been various national or island associations of Barbadians, Jamaicans and so forth. Similarly to the village associations organised by Greek Cypriots in London, several Caribbean communities have established village, educational (old schools, universities) and health support groups. At one time it was thought that these bodies would fade with the passing of the migrant generation, but they appear to be continuing amongst younger people who wish to retain close links with the lands of their parents' birth. These organisations sometimes participate or even organise demonstrations around key issues, but in the main they have served as brokers with their respective High Commissions in London, and organised social events, thereby overlapping with welfare/cultural groups. They have also sometimes helped individuals to return 'home' after a period of settlement in Britain; some of them are now being linked with groups of returnees to continue giving mutual assistance on both sides of the Atlantic (Goulbourne, 1999b).

The private, the public and pluralism

As Caribbean colonies became independent states in the 1960s the ideology of oneness emerged in the region,[8] while in Britain, by the late years of the decade, the ideology of multi-culturalism came to replace the public philosophy of assimilation. Multi-culturalism legitimised differences and has sought to unite Black, Brown and White segments in an endeavour to build a more equal society in Britain. In the late 1970s Home Secretary Roy (now Lord) Jenkins gave official sanction to the view that 'the flattening process of uniformity' should give way to the nurturing of 'cultural diversity and mutual tolerance' of all cultures in British society (Jenkins, 1967), and this theme was later elaborated by the *1985 Swann Committee Report* into schooling in a multi-cultural Britain (Swann, 1985, p 5). Swann saw British society as being 'both socially cohesive and culturally diverse', and a society in which cultural differences are not barriers to the sharing of 'common aims, attributes and values' (ibid.). I have stated elsewhere my concerns about the contradictions in the notion of multi-culturalism or the new pluralism (Goulbourne, 1991a, 1991b), and they do not need to be repeated here. But it is worth noting that even if this public declaration were to fail to achieve the lofty ideals of its adherents, it must be recognised that multi-culturalism, as ideology and/or policy, has had the salutary effect of politically unifying groups over what appeared to be a common end, namely greater toleration of a range of legitimate differences.[8]

As hinted therefore in the last chapter, outside the region, Caribbean family life, kinship systems and living arrangements have rarely been the specific focus of either academic or policy discussions. This is somewhat surprising, because discussions about problems faced by Caribbean communities – particularly in Britain – are nearly always informed by one or other general assumption about their family and kinship patterns. Debates about the Caribbean community and education, employment, housing, the police and so forth have generally incorporated notions about family life, customs and traditions, but in recent decades there has been a noticeable absence of a specific focus on the family.

However, this lack of specific focus does not denote a situation of absence of comments about Caribbean families in Britain. Indeed, the types of family and general living arrangements that are associated with Caribbean communities are relevant to several broad aspects of British life, such as the assertion of individual autonomy as a feature of what some would see as post-modern Britain, and debates about the changing composition of the family and the implications for social policy. Whilst it is worthwhile commenting on these observations, it may be more useful first to say something about how Caribbean families have featured in studies on British society.

More than any other group, Caribbean families and communities have been closely linked to dramatic public events which result in intimations of change in the public sphere of British life. Perhaps the most dramatic of these was the Brixton disturbances[9] during the weekend of 10–12 April 1981. From the 1950s and 1960s Brixton was regarded as a prime destination of Caribbean migrants, and streets such as Somerlayton, Railton, Mayall, Shakespeare and other roads had become familiar to many Caribbean people, particularly Jamaicans (see, for example, Patterson, 1965) who may have started life in Britain in the area or in nearby Clapham or shopped at the famous Brixton market with its colourful stalls run by Jews who had earlier migrated from the East End. Brixton also became the central site of excessive policing in London and young Black men the focus of such police attention (see Scarman, 1982; also, Humphry & John, 1971). The disturbances of that fateful April weekend are chronicled by Scarman and have been variously commented upon (see, for example, Keith, 1993). The events are usually seen as the entry of the Black youth into British public life (see, for example, Solomos, 1988; also see, Hall, et al., 1978), and they triggered similar events in other major British cities such as Liverpool, Manchester, Birmingham and Bristol. The importance of this kind of entry into the political system was not only that the events highlighted the problems of excessive policing and lack of police accountability but also the problems of high unemployment, poor housing and the general marginalisation of Black people in British society. Like the commissions into urban disturbances in the great American cities in the 1960s, the Brixton events forced the British political elite and social establishment to bring onto the national political agenda the question of the place of new minorities in a post- imperial society which claimed to be multi-cultural, fair and democratic.

Caribbean families feature as a passive factor in the general literature on race relations in Britain. Indeed, early research on the new communities that were being established in the 1960s had much to say about the family forms that the new settlers were introducing to Britain. For example, in one of the few detailed empirical works conducted outside London on new minorities in Britain, Rex and Moore (1967) found that kinship network played a vitally important part in the determination of location of settlement. They stressed that:

> West Indians did not mention kinfolk very often, but the data from our sample show that in Sparkbrook they are more important than for the Irish, in the sense that they are seen

and 'used' more often, and in so far as they actually provide an obvious basis for a local community in which one can live, or at least feel one lives (Rex & Moore, 1967, p 107).

The point that newcomers would seek to locate themselves in places where they had kinfolk, or friends, is well borne out by other observers of the process of entry and settlement in post-War Britain, and is well documented in the general literature on migration. A notable example is Sheila Patterson's work on Brixton in the early 1960s. Patterson made several insightful points about West Indian entry and settlement in the area, and with the passing of time it can now be seen that her observation that families worked hard to maintain close links with the Caribbean has continued well into the 1990s and is likely to continue well into the next century. Patterson noted, for example, that '. . . the close trans-Atlantic consanguineous links between migrants and their kin at home' (Patterson, 1965, p 261) was of immediate relevance to the newcomers.

The experience of Caribbean families in key areas of national life is pertinent here, and two examples may be drawn upon to illustrate the general point. The *Rampton Committee Report* of 1981 and the *Swann Committee Report* of 1985 referred to earlier are two clear examples of the impact of Caribbean family concerns on public behaviour. These committees conducted enquiries into the state of education in a society that had changed from predominantly being a homogenous society to a transparently culturally diverse society as expressed in the ideology of multi-culturalism. The title of *Swann* was particularly revealing in this regard – *Education for All*. The report addressed the complex question of what kind of education children should be receiving in a multi-cultural society, but its sometimes contentious recommendations were largely ignored at national level whilst local authorities up and down the country sought as best they could to respond in an intelligent and reasonable manner to some of the recommendations that could be operationalised. The document celebrated diversity and posed its challenges and opportunities as matters that the country as a whole needed to grasp. For our purpose the content and fate of *Swann* are not of the moment; what is of relevance is the fact that the whole process commenced from an expressed need of Caribbean parents about the inadequate education their children were receiving in English schools. From the late 1960s Caribbean communities had been concerned about this (see Coard, 1971; Tomlinson, 1983; Goulbourne, 1998), but it was the articulation of their frustrations to the House of Commons' Select Committee on Race Relations and Immigration in 1977 that brought the matter to a head, leading to the establishment of both *Rampton* and *Swann*.

The second aspect of these enquiries that is of relevance to Caribbean families in Britain is the way in which the structure of these families featured in the ensuing analyses of the roots of problems. Thus, for example, the *(Interim) Rampton Report* sought to explain the underachievement of children of Caribbean backgrounds in English schools in terms of racism as the principal culprit, but since Asian children were presumed to be subjected to much the same racism, this was taken to be an inadequate explanation. Of course, it is always assumed that racism has only negative effects on all groups, and other variables were explored as possible contributing factors. For example, it was considered whether Caribbean Creoles interfered with language development and ruled out. Other presumed cultural factors such as corporal punishment of children in Caribbean homes, the absence of toys, and the low participation of the child's household members in the life of the school were pointed to as possible explanations of less than adequate performance in the class room. Despite the furore that was triggered by *Rampton*, it should be noted that both reports deliberately used language carefully so as not to state unequivocally that the household and family of the child of Caribbean background was the main reason for failure in the school system. Nonetheless, the attention paid to the hard lives that fathers and mothers led were portrayed in negative rather than positive terms, and this conveyed the distinct impression that the failures of these children were not to be laid at the door of the class room but were determined by some failure or deficit in the home.

The *Scarman Report* has already been mentioned, but it is important to stress its relevance to Caribbean families. In addition to analysing housing condition, educational performance, employment opportunities, and crucially the relations between the police and the Black communities in the Brixton area, Scarman repeated many of the shibboleths about the Caribbean family. Indeed, in describing what the *Report* calls 'the black community of Brixton', the sub-head of 'family' leads the cast of education, unemployment, discrimination and 'the young people of Brixton: a people of the street', and the section makes repeated references to the institution of the Caribbean family. It is not surprising that this should be so. After all, the institution of the family is still regarded as the key institution of the social order. Any dispassionate reading of *Scarman* or indeed *Rampton* and *Swann*, will suggest that members of these committees were, according to their lights, sensitive towards feelings about the typology of Caribbean families.

It is tempting to quote *Scarman verbatim* in its disposition on the Caribbean family, but this is hardly necessary, because anyone familiar with broad statements by colonial officials or a number of politicians in Britain in the 1960s and 1970s will recognise the summary which so easily states the problems of these families. It is worthwhile, however, mentioning a few of the broad conclusions drawn about Caribbean families. These include some acute observations such as the uncontested fact that from the 1940s to the 1960s (and beyond) families had to bring up their children without the help of the extended family members who would have been available in the Caribbean and the recognition of mothers, grandmothers and aunts as the mainstay of the extended family. In the context of Britain, however, not only were members of the extended family network absent, but mothers 'became in many cases wage earners who were absent from the family home' (ibid.: 9). Scarman does not blame the disturbances or 'scenes of violence and disorder in their capital city, the like of which had not previously been seen in this century in Britain' (p 1), but the description of the plight of family life forms part of the general social structure within which these events took place. There is, therefore, an implied correlation between family structure and disturbance within the British body social. For example, Scarman went on to point out the statistical evidence of 'the destructive changes wrought in their family lives by their new circumstances' in Britain (p 9); the higher than expected proportion of children of Caribbean parents in care and single-parent families in the borough, particularly in those wards in which there was a high concentration of Caribbean families and households.

Interestingly enough, if the Brixton disturbances were the most significant mass protest to influence the development of the multi-cultural society in Britain, in the last decade of the century the single most profound event to catch the public imagination and question the extent of the realisation of a fairer and more just society in post-imperial Britain has been the case of the Stephen Lawrence family. One of the hypotheses set out in the Caribbean family research project described in Chapter 1 was that Caribbean communities have been able to sustain themselves in less than favourable conditions because of the support provided by family, kinship and friendship networks. The Stephen Lawrence case is, sadly, a perfect illustration of this. Unprovoked, Stephen was brutally attacked, stabbed and killed in April 1993 in Eltham, South London. This was bad enough, but in the ensuing years until 1999, one problem after another piled on top of each other to compound the overall problems of race relations as they affect the police and Black families. Not only did the police fail to take prompt action against those suspected of the youth's murder, but the Crown Prosecution Service decided that there was insufficient evidence to have the suspected White youths tried in a court. It took pressure from

Doreen and Neville Lawrence, Stephen's parents, and their supporters across both minority and majority ethnic communities to force the authorities to hold a public inquest. On 13 February 1997 the Coroner, Sir Montague Levine, presented his report and nearly all national and several local newspapers carried articles and leaders on the case as a significant statement about the state of race relations in the country. It still took further pressure from the Lawrence family to reopen the whole case of the murder of their son and the failure of the police properly to investigate whilst his suspected murderers freely walked the streets. When in February 1999 the committee of inquiry led by a senior judge, Lord McPherson, issued their report the media was again dominated by the injustice Caribbean and Asian families experience in the supposedly liberal, just and multi-cultural society that has emerged in the post-imperial Britain of the second half of the century. The case is of profound importance in itself. But as a *cause celebre* in the last decade of the century, it has a particular significance for the overall context in which members of Caribbean communities bring up the young. British society as a whole owes much to the dogged tenacity of the Lawrence family in pushing the frontiers of realisable justice so that all major institutions are forced to question the extent to which they harbour 'institutional racism' in their practice, if not intentionally. For Caribbean communities, the Lawrence's experience has been perceived to reinforce the continuing relevance of family in upholding and sustaining the worth of the individual.

Conclusion

These observations of the long established links between the Caribbean and Britain are general, but they are intended to serve a limited purpose, namely, show that families of Caribbean backgrounds in Britain live in a cross Atlantic world that is relatively unified through shared heritages and common assumptions about a range of factors. This does not mean that the established communities and family forms in the range of societies across the vast Atlantic conform to a common model. They do, however, have much in common, and it is unlikely that family members living at different points of this community will as easily lose contacts in the near future. It is therefore now appropriate to turn attention to the patterns of migration and family narratives which give substance to the cross Atlantic links suggested in this chapter.

Notes

1   Of course, the Bahamas is larger than Jamaica, but it is made up of some 700 islands and the population is less than that of Jamaica.

2   It is interesting that at the very point of drafting this paper in the first two weeks of February 1998, Gullitt is involved in a deep dispute with the Chelsea Football management who sacked him during negotiations over a new contract. He subsequently became manager of Newcastle United, but by late 1999 he had resigned and seemed set to return to the Netherlands. The former Liverpool player, John Barnes Caribbean-born, also became a manager in 1999 of top Scotland team Rangers.

3   Indeed, presently a number of these states are actively taking advantage of what is being called 'economic citizenship', that is, generously endowing citizenship to rich individuals insuring against potential or actual insecurity in their own country. The price of such 'economic citizenship' varies, but is generally from US$50k, as in Dominica (and I believe Canada and the UK). In 1988, the popularity of St Kitts with people from Hong Kong, Taiwan and Russia pushed up the price to US$120k, which, it was hoped, would reduce demand. In the main, 'economic citizens' do not relocate, but hold their second citizenship as an insurance against future risks for themselves and their families.

4   In both Britain and Commonwealth Caribbean states such as Jamaica residential and age qualifications by a citizen of another Commonwealth country are enough to enjoy the franchise.

5   There are apparently only 160,000 remaining persons with this form of British status, and for a variety of reasons, including security and assistance in times of natural disasters (see, Hintjens, 1997) this relationship is more than likely to continue into the foreseeable future.

6   Hart occupies a unique position in modern Commonwealth Caribbean Trans-Atlantic politics. An eye witness to the events on the streets of Kingston, Jamaica, in the momentous events of 1938 which led to the Moyne Commission of 1938 and constitutional decolonisation in the region, Hart, a solicitor and historian of European-Caribbean background, became a major figure in Caribbean politics on both sides of the waters, returning to Jamaica in the early 1990s, but finally settling in London by the middle of the 1990s.

7   For example, in the preparation of the appropriate phrasing of questions about the ethnicity of individuals in the 1991 national census the Office of Population Censuses & Surveys consulted some of these organisations.

8   For example, the national motto of Jamaica became 'out of many, one people', and the national mottoes of the other states are variations on this theme.

9   There were, of course, earlier protests on London streets, such as those in Notting Hill over the Mangrove 9 and in Peckham over police activity in the early 1970s. These were well covered by the local and sometimes the national press, but they did not have the same impact as the Brixton events, perhaps because less property was destroyed in the earlier events.

3 | Migration, the Caribbean and the family

Mary Chamberlain

Introduction

The history of the Caribbean is a history of migration. At every level of society, imagined or actual horizons extended back to a past, forward to a future. The social structures and institutions, the forms and expressions, the values and beliefs, which constitute the culture of the Caribbean evolved and continue to evolve through the absorption and adaptation of global influences, of those who came, of those who left, of those who returned. The Caribbean had become an exemplar of globalisation, and its peoples part of a transnational community, long before it was fashionable to think in such terms. This migratory history and culture forms an important part of the context of discussion of the Caribbean family in what has been termed the Caribbean Diaspora (Cohen 1997; Goulbourne 1991). This chapter argues that the evolution of Caribbean families in Britain has been shaped as much by the cultural forces of the Caribbean as the structural changes generated by migration to Britain.

Historical background

Prior to the ending of the slave trade in 1807, the major migratory movement was into the region and involuntary, as enslaved Africans were brought in to labour (primarily) on the sugar plantations of the West Indies. Voluntary migration, including re-migration and return migration, was the prerogative of the European colonisers, although their migrations were determined by wealth and health. After Emancipation (1834) and the ending of Apprenticeship (1838) the social and racial composition, and the motives, of Caribbean migration to, from and within the region assumed a different complexion.

The hopes and expectations of the newly emancipated slaves incorporated from the earliest elements of mobility. Social mobility could not be separated from geographic mobility, either off the plantations, or off the island altogether. One of the major preoccupations of the planters in the post-emancipation period was to retain and secure their workforce in the face of what they perceived as an actual, or potential, exodus from the plantations. This exodus was fuelled by the promise of higher wages elsewhere, and by the symbolic promise, of affirming the spirit, as well as the letter, of the freedom implied by Emancipation. This movement away from the plantations and, particularly, abroad was noted as soon as Apprenticeship ended. It was most noticeable from Barbados and the Leeward Islands, with migrations to (primarily) Trinidad and British Guiana, prompting the Barbadian government to pass in 1838 the first of a series of legislative measures to restrict out-migration. By 1850 Jamaicans had also joined the movement abroad primarily to Panama, prompting legislation in 1852 which attempted to restrict out-migration (Newton 1984). Despite the restrictions on out-migration and the activities of recruitment agents, British West Indians continued to emigrate throughout the nineteenth century. Most of the destinations were within the Caribbean basin. In Barbados, for instance, The *Rules and Regulations framed and passed by the Governor in Council under the Authority of the Emigration Act of 1873*[1] listed as existing migrant destinations for Barbadians, Antigua, Demerera, Dominica, Grenada, Nevis, Nickerie, St Kitts, St Lucia, St Vincent, Surinam, Tobago and Trinidad. Jamaicans migrated to Nicaragua, Mexico, Honduras and Costa Rica, Windward islanders to Venezuela and Cayenne, Leeward islanders to Santo Domingo, Costa Rica and St Thomas (Richardson 1983; Newton 1984). Although data on the numbers migrating is difficult to come by, the scale of inter-island migration can be seen in the 1891 the census of Trinidad which recorded that in a population of 208,030, 33,071 were immigrants from the British West Indies (and a further 1,259 from 'foreign West Indies').[2]

While the majority of out-migration in the nineteenth century was by former slaves, or their descendants, there was also a significant migration into the region. Indentured labourers, primarily from the Indian sub-continent, were brought in at the behest of West Indian planters to work in the sugar plantations, to replace, or replenish, the existing workforce (Look Lai 1993; Laurence, 1994). Between 1834 and 1918, a total of 536,310 arrived in the West Indies, the majority absorbed by British Guiana, Trinidad and Jamaica, although significant numbers were also engaged in Surinam and the French West Indian colonies. Although repatriation was built into the indentureship contracts of those who arrived in this period, the majority remained in the region. By the late nineteenth century, however, many of these time-expired labourers had also absorbed a migratory ethos, either away from their employing plantations, and in some cases away from the colonies altogether. Thus in Jamaica, for instance, despite attempts to restrict the out-migration of Indian labourers, many preferred to re-migrate (to destinations in the Caribbean and central America) than re-indenture, repatriate, or move to urban areas (Shepherd 1998).

The difficulties and vagaries of nineteenth-century sea travel meant that even locations in the Caribbean would have been as distant to many of the nineteenth- and early twentieth-century migrants, as the mainland and metropolitan centres were to those later in the twentieth century. In 1873 (before the advent of steam ships) according to the *Rules and Regulations framed and passed by the Governor in Council under the authority of the Emigration Act 1873*,[3] it took, for instance, two and a half weeks in windy months, five weeks in calm months, to travel from Barbados to Trinidad, and five weeks in windy months, ten weeks in calm months to travel from Barbados to Demerara. The symbolic, and material rewards of migration may well have been spiced by an element of adventure, if not heroism.

A qualitative change in the nature of migration occurred with the opening of the Panama Canal project. Initially begun in the 1880s under French direction, and attracting considerable numbers of Jamaican, Barbadian and St Lucian workers, the project was abandoned, to be resumed by the Americans in 1904. Between 1904 and 1914, approximately 60,000 Barbadians, and between 1891 and 1914 90,000 Jamaicans migrated to Panama (Newton 1984), as well as migrants from other British West Indian territories. Although many of those returned, many also re-migrated after completion of the canal to Cuba and, in particular, to the United States. By 1890, there were already 19,979 foreign born black people in the United States, by far the majority of whom were West Indians, a figure which had risen to 73,803 by 1920 and 98,620 by 1930 (Kasinitz 1992). Yet between 1932 and 1937, more West Indians returned to the Caribbean than migrated to the United States (Kasinitz 1992:24).

In many ways, the migrations to Panama marked a watershed in the migratory history of the British Caribbean. The scale of the migration was significantly larger than any previous migration; at the same time, the destination, and the time frame, was focussed and not dispersed or protracted as in previous migrations. The governments, particularly of Barbados and Jamaica, had been forced to relax their restrictions on out-migration and began actively to promote it as a perceived solution to the domestic problems of poverty; and the horizon of migrant destinations was significantly expanded as South America, (notably Brazil, Venezuela, and Peru) were subsequently added to the list of central and North American territories. Migration continued – albeit on a smaller scale – throughout the interwar period, within the Caribbean and to south, central and North America.

Migration to Britain

The West Indians who came to Britain after World War II arrived therefore with a cultural, and often a family, history and tradition of migration. For many individuals, the experience of migration was not new. Many had already been migrants themselves – within the Caribbean, (to Curaçao or Aruba, for example) or to North America, primarily under the Farm Workers Programme 'H-2' (which was first instituted in 1942). Many had parents or grandparents who had migrated. Most had some family member or close family friend who had migrated. Migration, in other words, was a familiar (and often a familial) rather than an atypical experience. What prompted the large-scale migration to Britain was in part the response to labour shortages in Britain in consequence of the post-war programme of reconstruction (Peach 1968), and under- or un-employment in the Caribbean (Tidrick 1966). The majority of migrants, however, arrived after the McCarran-Walter Act of 1952 in the United States halted Caribbean migration there and directed an existing and potential flow to Britain – economic and political circumstances which, arguably, have always played a part in determining migrant destinations (Marshall 1979).

By 1951, there were 17,218 West Indians in Britain (Peach 1991), the majority of whom were Jamaican born. By 1961, the figure had risen to 173,659 (Peach 1991). Although the Jamaicans remained the largest migrant group, migration from Barbados had begun in the mid-1950s, prompted by the combined effects of Hurricane Janet in 1953, the sponsorship programme launched by the Barbadian government in 1955, a general recruitment effort (both formal and informal) and by the McCarran-Walter Act of 1952. Migration from both the Leeward and Windward islands and Trinidad appeared to have been equally well established by the mid-1950s, although that from Guyana did not get underway until the 1960s. In Britain, the 1962 and 1966 Immigration Acts effectively halted migration from the West Indies, although prior to both Acts there was a marked increase in the numbers arriving. By 1971, the Caribbean-born population of Britain stood at 304,070, and Peach (1991) estimates that the total Caribbean population in that year stood at 545,744. The Caribbean-born population at the beginning of the 1990s stood at 264,591, of which 224,126 are Black Caribbean (Peach 1991). These figures indicate a significant decline in the

Caribbean-born population, some of which is the result of death, but mostly the result of re- and return migration. In many ways, the scale of the migration to Britain, the relatively short time-frame in which it occurred, the distance involved, and the specific response to labour demands, show remarkable parallels to the migration to Panama in the early years of the twentieth century.

Explanation of migration

Some identifiable features in the nineteenth- and early twentieth-century migrations can be discerned which have a bearing on the contemporary practice. First, although it was individuals who migrated it was with, and for, the support of the wider family in the Caribbean. It was, in this sense, a family endeavour; contact between the migrant and the family in the Caribbean was usually maintained and, importantly, remittances were returned (Roberts 1955; Richardson 1983; 1985). Second, many of the migrants (who included independent women as well as men) returned home to the Caribbean (Roberts 1955; Richardson 1985; Kasinitz 1992). Indeed, these features were commented on by the 1895 *Barbados Emigration Commission Report*[4] which noted that the emigration pattern hitherto discerned was one of 'temporary migration ... for individual betterment'. Third, those who remained in their host societies, built new communities while retaining many of their cultural attributes (Johnson 1988; Kasinitz 1992) and family contact with the Caribbean. At the same time, contact between Caribbean migrant groups abroad helped foster a broader political identity, of which Padmore's Pan Africanism or Garvey's UNIA (United Negro Improvement Association) were early examples. By the early decades of the twentieth century, out-migration had become an integral feature of the Caribbean, and an increasingly important component of the domestic and national economy (Richardson 1983; Segal 1987; Cohen 1997). As such, many families became increasingly to rely on the migration of its members for returning remittances, in cash or kind, and promoted or supported the migration of its members. Out-migration had become, in other words, an active ingredient in the culture of the region, each migration reinforcing its 'image' as a positive activity (Thomas-Hope 1992), while family strategies evolved, and family structures accommodated, to encourage it.

Yet most of the early explanations of Caribbean migration were based on economic and structural models. It was assumed that migrants were motivated by economic necessity, pushed by high levels on un- or under-employment at home, pulled by the promise of employment and high wages abroad. That most migrants to the developed world, after the Second World War, appeared to come from under-developed nations both illustrated and validated the thesis (Todaro 1976; Wallerstein 1979). This notion held equal sway in British-based studies of Caribbean immigration to Britain. It lies at the basis of work by Davison (1962), Glass (1961) and Peach (1968). In this view, the post-war migration from the Caribbean was 'powered by market forces' (Peach 1991; 1968). West Indians arrived in Britain at a time of labour scarcity, and was 'highly and significantly inversely related to unemployment rates in Britain' (Peach 1991:7). At the same time, studies based in the Caribbean such as that by Maunder (1955) or Tidrick (1966), which highlighted the employment profile of the migrants at the point of departure and revealed significant levels of unemployment and a low-skill base, lent support to the argument.

Other theorists have pointed to the cyclical demands and dimensions of international capital, seeing labour migration as a rational (and beneficial) response to the vagaries of global capital, or as further evidence of its exploitative potential and neo-colonial perspective (Rubenstein 1983; Watson 1982; Petras 1988, 1980), or have explored the role of state at both the sending and receiving end of the migration process (Marshall 1979) and in the processes of settlement and incorporation (Grosfoguel 1998; Goulbourne, 1991a). While there is a clear correlation between employment opportunities abroad and periodic waves of migration from the Caribbean, recent years have, however, seen a revision of these premises, pointing out that economic and structuralist explanations fail to account adequately for the links between the environment and culture and migration (Richardson 1983) and arguing that models which assume migration to be solely 'the movement of labour' ignore 'interpretation (of migrant behaviour) at the level of societal meaning and personal consciousness' (Thomas-Hope 1992).

Anthropologists such as Fog Olwig (1993; 1998) and geographers such as Thomas-Hope (1992) point to explanation of migration not simply as a response to push/pull factors, but as individual choices informed by cultural values and social pressures, including gender (Byron 1998) in which the historical context of migration has played a formative role, and an informative function. Thus, for instance, some of the features identified in early migrations (such as the high rates of return, or the implementation of family strategy) make sense of contemporary elements such as that described by Thomas-Hope (1992) as the 'homeward orientation' of Caribbean migrants, or others (Palmer 1990; Conway 1988; Gmelch 1992) have identified as its 'circularity'.

The longevity of Caribbean migration traditions, and increasingly the longevity of Caribbean communities abroad has prompted further insights into Caribbean migration. Fog Olwig (1998), for instance, has highlighted the internationalisation of families through the extension of the domestic unit abroad, and pointed to ways in which family and neighbourhood structures in the Caribbean were well adapted to enable and support the process of migration, less likely to be fractured by its effects (Kerns 1984, Barrow 1986, Richardson 1983; Thomas-Hope 1992; Chamberlain 1997), and more likely to replicate or reproduce comparable structures, or comparable values, for survival in the host community (Byron 1998; Lutz 1998; Sutton & Chaney 1994; Basch et al. 1994). Such adaptations may be interpreted as a continuation of the process of 'creolisation' or indigenisation, already noted among the Caribbean community in the United States (Kasinitz 1992; Sutton & Chaney 1994), a process which necessarily contains transnationalism as its central agent (Basch et al. 1996), but is less remarked upon in the British context (Craig-James 1992). Indeed, the proximity of the Caribbean to North America and regular, easy and relatively cheap communications has resulted in a strengthening of the social, cultural and domestic links between West Indians in North America and the Caribbean to the point, as Nancy Foner has observed, that returning 'home' now is ceasing to hold such a powerful spatial meaning on the imaginations of West Indian migrants, while its imaginative and the material hold is retained and reinforced by regular contact.

Such empirical research into migration is beginning to explore its impact on families in the Diaspora, to see the family and family models as an explanatory factor in migration, and to highlight the importance of family networks in facilitating the passage of migration and settlement abroad. My own work, (Chamberlain 1995, 1997), which engaged with life-story interviews across three generations of Barbadian families, placed the family as central to understanding the process of migration, the settlement of migrants, the patterns of return and the impact of migration on the family and argued strongly for the importance of a family 'ethos' or dynamic in motivating migration.

Most recently, emphasis has turned on the nature of 'Diaspora' itself (Cohen 1997), recognising that the process of globalisation has not been confined to capital, but has been an integral component of a complex process of transnationalism 'from below' (Portes 1998), in which family links – among others – are central, and where Caribbean peoples may be seen as exemplars.

In some ways this relates to the approach taken by scholars such as Paul Gilroy (1993) who have argued for the existence of both a diasporic culture and its continuing and symbiotic impact on the cultural life and subject-identities of diasporic (particularly Black) peoples and their 'host' societies.

Thus while the migration to Britain coincided with labour short-ages there, it would be erroneous to view it solely as a response to economic drivers. Given the importance of migration within the culture of the Caribbean, given its circular and temporary nature, and given that many of those who migrated were not, it seems, as poor and as unskilled as earlier studies suggested, many of those West Indians who arrived in Britain regarded migration there as little different from other and earlier migrations. In this sense, Britain was one stop in a contin-uum of migrant destinations (Chamberlain 1997). Most who arrived intended their stay to be of short duration and anticipated an early return. Although families were subsequently sent for, or were created in Britain, most of those early migrants came alone. Remittances were returned and for the most part families separated by migration remained nevertheless in close contact. Far from a migrant being 'lost' to the family in the act of leaving, they retained close emotional and financial links and, following the experience of West Indians in the United States and elsewhere, evolved a form of family which tran-scended national boundaries, aptly termed by Rosina Brodber-Wiltshire (1988) as the 'transnational' family. As noted earlier, there is now a significant and growing movement of return to the Caribbean, particularly where family linkages have remained and retained their pull (Byron 1994). What appears to be emerging in the British context is evidence of the resilience of Caribbean culture to nurture, adapt and develop. In this the family, as one of the prime movers in socialisation, not only plays a key role but is itself evidence of, and a statement about, a Caribbean migratory culture.

The British Caribbean cannot, however, lay exclusive claim to a Caribbean migratory culture. The French, Dutch and Hispanic Caribbean have equally long traditions of migration. Migration from the Caribbean to the Netherlands is as old as colonisation itself (Oostindie 1998). Although in 1960 the Surinamese and Antillean origin population in the Netherlands was only 12,700, by 1970, it had risen to 42,615, by 1975 it stood at 125,375, and more than doubled between then and 1988 when it stood at 308,000 (Peach 1991), the vast majority of whom were from Surinam, whose migration was largely prompted by the military coup of 1980 and the 'December-murders' of 1982 (Kopijn 1998). In the case of France, the Caribbean population was 15,620 in 1954. By 1962 it had more than doubled and by 1975 had reached 115,465 increasing to 180,448 by 1982 (Peach 1991), the majority arriving under government sponsorship. Migration from the Hispanic Caribbean (Cuba, Puerto Rico, the Dominican Republic) and

Haiti has been almost entirely to the United States. Kasinitz (1992) suggests that in 1930 approximately 26,482 Haitians and Hispanic Caribbeans were present in the United States. The quasi-federal status of Puerto Rico vis-a-vis the United States undoubtedly explains its focus as a destination, and the large Hispanic-speaking population of the United States, and its proximity, has meant that circular migration to and from the Hispanic Caribbean has continued to the present.

Some theoretical perspectives

The focus on labour as the central explanatory force in migration has obscured the complexity of migration and its continuing dynamic within families. At the same time, it identified West Indian migrants in a one-dimensional form, as a particular kind of migrant – a labour migrant – free of ambivalence, agenda, or identity. Of course, West Indians arrived in Britain at a time when Britain itself was undertaking its post-war programme of reconstruction, not only of the health and welfare structures of Britain, but also its own identity of Britishness or Englishness in a rapidly changing – and de-colonising – world. It was assumed that, over time, West Indians would, could, and indeed desired, 'to become like us' (Huxley 1964), as the pecularities of Caribbean migration were subsumed under first an assimilationist, and then a multi-culturalist, agenda. Yet the difficulties of, and the resistance to, such easy incorporation were simultaneously acknowledged in the legislation and official reports which highlighted racial intolerance, prejudice and disturbance.

Furthermore, the focus on labour migration enabled understanding of its processes to be located within an alternative historic precedent. It has been assumed that the rural-urban migrations which accompanied the industrialisation of Britain (and Europe) and the engagement with modern modes of production led to the breakdown of traditional family forms. Migration necessarily disrupts the domestic process and traditional living arrangements, emphasising the new individual, rather than traditional communitarian, characteristics of modernity. In the case of the Caribbean family in Britain, it has been mooted that migration, by breaking the generational links, severed or at least disrupted patterns of socialisation and stability, leaving the Caribbean family disorientated and directionless (see Scarman 1982; Davison 1962; Patterson 1965). The 1991 census data highlighted what appeared to be deviation by the Caribbean community from the 'British' norm, revealing in particular high levels of single-parent mother-headed households. What is taken as a lack, or even breakdown, of the nuclear unit among the Caribbean population in Britain has been assumed to be the result of migration and a breakdown in the transmission of family values and authority between the generations, aggravated (in one view) by undue influences from the more libertarian sectors of the White community towards single parenthood and state dependency (Dench 1992; 1996). Far from West Indians becoming 'like us', Caribbean peoples in Britain appear to display a refusal to conform to the categories set by politicians or academicians, a refusal which itself has dogged debate about the Caribbean for generations (Trouillaut 1992).

Yet one alternative interpretation of UK census data could suggest, for instance, that rather than arguing for family breakdown, it revealed the persistence of Caribbean patterns of living arrangements. Indeed, patterns of Caribbean living arrangements and family structure in the UK may owe more to continuing cultural influences from the Caribbean than to distortions created by the disruption and dislocation of migration. Certainly, as our research (Owen 1998) has argued, 'The marital condition of UK born Caribbean people appears most similar to that of people resident in Jamaica and Barbados, perhaps suggesting that they have adopted partnership forms typical of the Caribbean, in preference to those espoused by their parents' generation'.

As Patterson (1965) first identified, there were close family links between the pioneer migrant in Britain and his/her family in the Caribbean. These links were both emotional and material. While it could be expected that family links over time would weaken, as distance, aging and death, reduced the emotional ties and the material obligations, our research (Chamberlain and Goulbourne, forthcoming; also, see Preface) indicates that on the contrary those direct family links have continued through the generations, and have been strengthened by return migration and by easier and cheaper communications. Indeed, the 'revolution' in communications has changed the shape of migration itself. As Foner (1998; see also Boyce-Davis 1994; Basch et al. 1994) has indicated for the USA, cheap flights have obviated the need to 'return' permanently and have made possible a pattern of migratory 'commuting', particularly for elderly Caribbeans. A comparable pattern is emerging with British-based West Indians (Plaza 1996), who either return to the Caribbean for protracted periods, or play host to Caribbean family members for up to six months (the legal maximum). Many of our informants indicated a desire on retirement to alternate periods spent in Britain and the Caribbean. This has important implications for families, enabling them to keep in close touch, and to replenish cultural contacts. Even without protracted visits, cheap communications allow both close and distant kin, in the Caribbean and in North America, to meet and keep in touch. Easy communications, and the possibility of dual nationality, also means that migrants are prepared to spend longer in their country of destination.

As a result of migration, Caribbean families have always been international and outward looking. Our informants (from Jamaica, Barbados and Trinidad and Tobago) referred frequently to family members in the Caribbean, and in North America (USA and Canada) who continue to play a central and supportive role (Goulbourne, 1999b). Geographical distance is no barrier to being a 'close' family and informants stressed the importance of those links, the 'tightness' of the emotional bonds, and the levels of 'trust' expected of and experienced between family members. Such bonds contribute to the replenishment of Caribbean cultural influences and to a sense of identity based on family as much as location, or ethnicity. Indeed, the importance of family and the emergence of a 'Caribbean' form of family in Britain may be an important indicator of that identity.

Nevertheless, however persuasive the argument of cultural retentions, the process of transmission, cultural, or trans-generational, is never uni-lineal. It is part of a dialogue, a dialectical process involving reception, perception, selection and absorption. Without that process, there would be no social change, no generational difference. But there is always a feed-back loop so that attitudes and behaviour, at both ends of the transmission process, are modified. Continuity and change, transmission and transformation, have a complicated history.

A second but related reading would locate the peculiarities of the Caribbean Diaspora within the processes of modernity. Migration and modernity went hand in hand, but whereas the latter was seen as a progressive and stabilising force, the former was regarded as potentially destabilising, unless and until the migrant could be fixed in time and space. The powerful narratives of migration which have shaped perceptions of the modern world assumed both permanency and purpose. The narrative of America, as much as the narrative of Empire, converted migrants into citizens through the claims of permanence and homogeneity. Desirable migrants could become citizens, possessing land and purpose. The Lockean principles which underpinned such notions necessarily excluded those without a stake – the natives who wandered the land, the enslaved labourers brought in to work it (Chamberlain 1998). It is no coincidence that the British who migrated to the dominions of Empire in the nineteenth century were from the start welcomed as settlers, while the Indians migrating into the West Indies were perceived as transients, for the narratives of migration were also racialised. Migration and modernity was a one-way traffic, of Europeans to Empire. African and Asians with their new-world origins in slavery or indentureship were thus excluded. But, as Gilroy (1993) has argued, the narratives of Western modernity, and the philosophies which underpinned them, could only be at the expense of the Black experience. This, in turn, has given rise to a 'double-consciousness' among Blacks of the Atlantic, Black and American, Black and European, 'who stand between (at least) two great cultural assemblages, both of which have mutated through the course of the modern world that formed them and assumed new configurations' (Gilroy 1993:1). This double consciousness, as Schwarz (1996:189) argues, is, in its formation, diasporic, hybrid and impure, dissolving all pretensions of a culture which creates for itself imperious myths of ethnic absolutism: it *works* by mixing and miscegenation'(original emphasis).

This may seem abstract, but it has some real implications. It returns us to the limitations of looking at migration as simply the movement of labour, the rational response of an economic underclass, the new vagrants of the post-colonial world. The assumption that migration is linked with economic disadvantage has led to a related and contemporary view that success be measured by economic indicators. Thus the study by Modood et al. *Ethnic Minorities in Britain: Diversity and Disadvantage* (1996) confirmed the link between ethnicity and mobility, but refined it by demonstrating the differential or divergent impact of ethnicity on mobility and within that, implicitly, on family form. In many ways these measurements were a variant on the more classic studies on social mobility (Goldthorpe 1987) which dominated British sociology in the 1980s, with race and ethnicity appended as an additional variable to class. Implicit in this, however, was an assumption that the low mobility performance by the Caribbean community in general which indicated marked gender differences with Caribbean women significantly outstripping their male counterparts in education and employment (Modood et al. 1997) was in some way related to family structures. Asian families, by contrast, stood up well to the markers of social mobility and did not display the variants in terms of gender noted for their Caribbean heritage counterparts.

This link between mobility and family accorded well with the British empirical tradition and British social policy. Indeed, much of Western European thought since the nineteenth century has linked family structure to economic indicators. The 'nuclear' family rests on the premise of a sole male breadwinner and family policy measures, in the twentieth century, including the post-war welfare reforms, were designed to bolster and support the nuclear family through economic and related measures (Lewis 1984). Indeed, there is an ironic parallel between nineteenth- century colonial debates on family form, social stability and citizenship and contemporary metropolitan debates on social exclusion. And, perhaps more ironically, as Webster (1998) points out, the post-war emphasis on domesticity was denied to West Indian migrants, *immigrants*, whose men were feared as a threat to White female sexuality, whose women were regarded as both primitive and dirty, and both together and separately produced too many – often dysgenic – children. Yet it was their presence in the labour force in Britain which enabled the post-war enterprise of domesticity.

Which returns us to the Caribbean, working by mixing and miscegenation, literally and metaphorically, at home and abroad. Continuing contact with the Caribbean and with family members elsewhere has, as suggested earlier, ensured a replenishment of cultural contacts and family ties. At the same time, the process of indigenisation continues, as new cultural forms emerge from the contact between the Caribbean and Europe, only this time on the latter's home ground. Music, style, dress, culture, as Goulbourne points out in this volume, have become one visible and influential form of this process. More importantly, as he indicates, they are also examples of the visibility and audibility of the powerless. But equally inter-racial unions are also examples of this process, as were (and are) the political, religious and social forms of solidarity which have been created in this period. To paraphrase Craig (1992), they have indigenised, where there were no original indigenes.

Given the peculiarities of this process to the Caribbean, given the peculiarities of Caribbean migration itself, and its relationship with family, that the form and structure of Caribbean families in Britain should be isolated as a singular and aberrant development, both the cause and effect of marginal mobility and maximal visibility, seems perverse. Rather, the focus of research on the family should perhaps be re-orientated to explore its Caribbean components and the ways in which these have become indigenised in the British context. Transnational connections have always been important to family life, contributing material and emotional support, and retaining vital cultural links and transactions. These Trans-Atlantic connections are an important part of the *gestalt* of the family, and of its identity, on both sides of the ocean. They have contributed to the sense of well being and identity of Caribbeans both in the Caribbean and in the Diaspora, and to the continuing cultural links within the Caribbean and without. Caribbean families are characterised by patterns of kinship support which cross the oceans and the generations (Goulbourne, 1999). Indeed, it is the strength and resilience of Caribbean families which have enabled them to survive the disruptions of migration. Caribbean families in the Diaspora have re-configured over time, and increasingly assume many of the characteristics, in values and structure, which have been identified of their counterparts in the Caribbean. At the same time, families in the Caribbean have also changed as material conditions, including a continuing process of migration and return, have altered the social and economic environment.

The enduring presence of transnational families may confirm the importance of a migration culture or tradition and hence help explain the increasing rate of return migration to the Caribbean. This, in turn, strengthens and renews family linkages and acts as an important conduit for the transmission and transference of values. It also provides important opportunities for members to utilise family networks to further their own employment or career profile, to broaden their experience base, and to strengthen family resources. Indeed, the spreading or dispersal of material and emotional resouces throughout the diasporic trajectory of each family provides diversity and security and incorporates within it many of the strengths and opportunities which have been identified as advantages of a globalisation 'from below' (Portes 1998), although in some cases it may militate against the concentration of material wealth.

Moving the emphasis on family structure as a fixed entity with immutable spatial and temporal boundaries, to one which looks at the family as a fluid and permeable state, transversing geography and generations, enables a more effective exploration of how the family functions in the transmission of values and the care of its members and how, through the life-cycle of the family and its members, the roles and positions within the family vary. From this perspective, the family structure is plastic and malleable. It would be mistaken, therefore, to view the family (any family) through a time-warp.

While there may be political mileage to be gained from evoking 'traditional' family values, there is little historical substance for such a notion, as Raymond Smith argues in this volume. The issue is further complicated by the diversity of family form throughout the Caribbean so that even if a 'traditional' family structure could be identified, it would be difficult to point to any one form as evidence of such tradition. Moreover, varieties of family structures can be found even within one family. It seems therefore inappropriate to direct research to identifying family structure, drawing up typologies, or to apply functionalist explanations for how one family type may have evolved within some families at particular moments in time.

Thus, for instance, although the strength of matrifocality has been noted for Caribbean families (MG Smith 1962; Clarke 1957), the explanatory emphasis was one which prefigured male absence (through disruption to slave families or migration) and concluded that female power within the family emerged 'by default' (Sutton 1994). Yet equally plausible is an explanation which prefigures the importance of lineage. Lineage and blood ties (consanguineal) may be a stronger organising principle than conjugal and affinal links. Within this perspective, women, particularly mothers and grandmothers, become special as actual or potential bearers of lineage (Kerns 1984). This may help account not only for the respect which accrues to mothers and grandmothers, and by extension to other female kin, but to their specific roles and obligations within the family, which varies over time. The high incidence of children born to women who are not married and often in non-cohabiting relationships, in Afro-Caribbean communities in both the Caribbean and its Diaspora, may relate less to deviance and dysfunctionality and more to the desire to continue lineage 'as if we're carrying on a tradition we're not even aware of'. Within this, the willingness of kin, particularly maternal female kin, to participate in, and sometimes assume, the role of parenting is not merely practical but broadens the protective function of kin, strengthens the kinship links and reinforces lineage as an organising principle. Conversely, the much-vaunted male 'marginality' becomes less of an issue (but also less noted) in a kinship structure organised around lineage, where men play active roles in the support of their female blood relatives and their children (Barrow 1998).

This could be pursued further. The emphasis on consanguineal links works both vertically, across the generations, and horizontally, within them. Within the life-cycle of the family, the vertical links constantly reconfigure through birth and death, while the horizontal links between siblings and cousins remain broadly constant. Within the life-cycle of the individual, therefore, while their position within the vertical hierarchy will vary, their relationship to their generation peers is likely not only to be a formative influence on their lives but to becoming the enduring relationship, surviving both absence and distance. At the same time, neighbourhood networks are often described in the metaphors of lateral kin and express a strong sense of communal responsibility, reinforcing the importance of family and providing a model of community organisation (Chamberlain 1998). This model can transcend the migration process and reconfigure in formal and informal support structures in the destination domiciles particularly in the Black churches which provide not only leadership and support, but also the belief in the regenerative capacity of the human soul (Austin-Broos 1998).

Conclusion

Perhaps the central ingredient of globalisation, whether from above or from below, is the disregard of national borders. This is a theme repeated in much of the literature of the Caribbean, whether in the novels of Chamoiseau (1997) or the critical works of Linda Basch et al. (1996), who titled their work *Nations Unbound*. Fluidity, not fixity, characterises Caribbean migration, a concept which can be seen to lie at the heart also of the Caribbean family, whose boundaries are rarely fixed, and often mixed, through trans-oceanic and transgenerational links (Chamberlain 1999, forthcoming), and through the varieties of, and inconsistencies in, family form. The borders of the Caribbean are, in the words of Susan Craig (1992), emotional rather than geographic. The same may be also said of the Caribbean family.

Notes

1　Barbados, Department of Archives. Pam A45.
2　Colonial Office Records, Public Record Office, London. CO298/47.
3　Barbados, Department of Archives. Pam A45. 23 September 1873.
4　Barbados, Department of Archives. Pam C676.

4 | Caribbean families: questions for research and implications for policy

Raymond T Smith

Introduction

Almost thirty years ago a young Jamaican spent four years in Bristol gathering information for a doctoral dissertation on the life-styles of West Indian immigrants and their children.[1] The book based on this research is useful as a record of the experiences of the first wave of post-war immigrants to Britain, and their children, but it is marred by false assumptions about 'the Caribbean family' and the part it is supposed to play in the generation of social pathologies. After discussing homeless, unemployed young men who either are – or potentially are – delinquent, Pryce attributes their condition to the 'peculiarities of family life in the West Indies' which he describes as follows:

> In the early stage of adult life, instead of a man and a woman getting married and setting up their own separate household for procreation and domestic purposes, the partners live apart with their separate kin and the man visits his mate. These 'visiting relations' may or may not be converted into legal marriage. If the man and woman finally decide to live together in a separate household, they more often than not live in consensual cohabitation. When this union breaks up the children generally remain with their unmarried mother, who then goes to live with her mother. Because of this, in Jamaica, as in other parts of the West Indies, there is a matriarchal situation, with a high proportion of husbandless households consisting of women, their children, and their grandchildren. If a common-law union endures long enough to take the form of 'faithful concubinage', the partners will marry each other, but they marry not during their child-bearing years but later in middle age. These practices stem directly from slavery, which was responsible for the total

48

destruction of conventional family life among the slaves. And today economic constraints are so persistent in the life of the rural and urban poor that they cannot break out of the patterns laid down under slavery (Pryce 1979:15–16).

There is just enough truth in this description to render the whole plausible and encourage misinterpretation. These assumptions about family life are by no means peculiar to Ken Pryce. Practically all discussions of *the* 'Caribbean family' (the assumed uniformity is spurious) begin by assuming that certain features – such as high rates of out-of-wedlock birth, unstable conjugal unions, and complex household structures – are the result of slavery or African ancestry, with the added implication that either the cruelties of slavery or the backwardness of Africa forced a deviation from a 'normal' human condition. However, there is no normal human condition.

This supposedly normal family is itself a product of numerous false assumptions that are repeatedly presented as though they were immutable truths. For example, the idea that the nuclear family of man, wife and their children is a universal human institution is wrong.[2] Human families can assume many forms and children can be nurtured and raised under a wide range of conditions. This is not to say that familial relations cannot be dysfunctional or undesirable, nor does it mean that a society should not develop laws and standards defining acceptable patterns of behaviour in this as in other aspects of life, but an objective analysis must take into account the whole range of social relations within which kinship operates. In the case of the family life of African Americans a demeaning ideology of profound difference has been developed, and perpetuated, in which that life came to be defined as 'problematic' and 'disorganised'. This ideology grew most strongly in the post-emancipation Caribbean and was reinforced in both the Caribbean and the United States, when – from about 1930 onwards – the social sciences began to formulate 'scientific' explanations of poverty and backwardness.[3]

In the beginning: slavery and the origin of the dual marriage system

Although there is no such thing as *the* Caribbean family, the societies of the Caribbean have peculiar features that have made kinship a salient concern. Those features have their beginning in the very formation of these societies – societies that were created for the generation of wealth for states, companies and individuals in Europe.

During the slavery period prior to the development of an emancipation movement, there was little concern about the moral qualities of the family life of slaves. The laws of the colony of Antigua in the seventeenth and eighteenth centuries paid careful attention to marriage, family life and procreation, but they concerned white persons rather than slaves (see Lazarus-Black 1994:60–61). Different rules governed the three major classes – free persons, indentured servants and slaves – and those classes constituted a hierarchical order defined in terms of status as a worker rather than colour or race. As Lazarus-Black shows, the laws enacted by the Antigua legislature in 1716 were most restrictive in respect of unions among white indentured servants and between an indentured servant and a free white person, to the extent that it could cost a free person his or her very freedom for a period of years if marriage to an indentured servant was contemplated. These workers were hired as *individuals* and treated as such. The consequence was the development of a system of marrying status equals and entering into non-legal unions with women of lower status, a system that I have elsewhere referred to as the dual marriage system (see RT Smith 1987b). No wonder then that in 1753 in St John's, Antigua, 34 per cent of the households of *free persons* (who were almost all white) were female headed (Lazarus-Black 1994: 29). Similar proportions were reported for Barbados in 1715. Female-headed households were as common among eighteenth century free settlers in St Johns, Antigua, as they are today among West Indians generally; roughly 32 per cent of all households (Lazarus-Black 1994:37–38). And, of course, slaves participated in what Lazarus-Black calls the 'common order' of Antiguan society.

By the latter part of the eighteenth century in Jamaica a similar system was so firmly established, this time based on non-legal unions among white men and slave or free coloured women, that even an avowed racist such as Edward Long was forced to recognise its existence and shape his view of the future of the society to accommodate it.[4]

Missionaries, marriage and motherhood

West Indian law makers quickly defined African slaves and Indians as 'heathens' with whom Christians were forbidden to engage in 'Carnall Coppulation', a futile prohibition that soon enough fell into desuetude. After the abolition of slavery and the mass conversion of slaves to Christianity an ideology emerged that focused exclusively upon the black, ex-slave, population, ignoring the history of inter-racial unions and attributing their particular patterns of kinship and conjugal unions to a combination of African heathen practice and the degradation of slavery. This appears quite early in the writings of missionaries who lament the difficulty of stamping out informal unions and contrast the supposedly idyllic family life of their converts with the disorganised way of life of the less devout. It was to become a constant refrain in West Indian affairs, reaching a climax in the late nineteenth century when illegitimacy came to be redefined as an exclusively black lower class problem.

In Jamaica by the 1880s illegitimacy rates were already at the level – between 60 and 70 per cent of live births – that they were to maintain for the next 100 or more years, but now this 'problem' became the rallying cry of the new post-emancipation middle class. The Governor of Jamaica was bombarded with petitions demanding legislation to address the problem by making mandatory the registration of fathers of illegitimate children. He declined to take action on the grounds that such measures were impossible to carry out. What he did not say was that large numbers of those fathers were prominent members of the middle and upper classes. The most vocal critics of vice and immorality, and staunch defenders of the sanctity of marriage, became middle-class coloured women who were themselves the privileged descendants of non-legal unions, but now needed to distinguish themselves from lower class women. Legal marriage was now associated with middle-class status and the lower classes were stigmatised as having unstable marriage, high illegitimacy rates and all those pathological characteristics that supposedly kept them in their depressed condition.

When the British Government set up a Colonial Development and Welfare organisation in the wake of massive West Indian labour unrest in the late 1930s, the notion that the economic problems of the West Indies are due to family disorganisation got a new lease on life. The most fascinating document from this period is TS Simey's book, *Welfare and planning in the West Indies*. Published in 1946 it became the primary text book for the Social Welfare Training Courses held in Jamaica, and the received wisdom of social planners. Briefly stated, Simey's position was that the poverty of the working classes in the West Indies leads to a family system incapable of carrying out its proper functions of producing personalities adequate to the task of transforming society in the direction of 'normal' middle class values and culture (see RT Smith 1982 for a fuller discussion of Simey and his influence). This kind of psychological analysis was pushed much further by Madeline Kerr, a social psychologist and a close associate of TS Simey, in a remarkable book, *Personality and Conflict in Jamaica* (1952). It reads very oddly today: culture conflict, she says, leads to lack of personality integration that shows itself in regression to primitive and hysterical forms of behaviour – the main ones being religious conversion and 'getting the spirit'. Although Madeline Kerr had a lot to say about the frustrations arising from being coloured in a society that values whiteness, it is interesting that when she subsequently carried out a similar study in a Liverpool slum inhabited mainly by people of recent Irish Catholic descent, her findings were curiously similar; the people of Ship Street, as she called them, also suffered from culture conflict leading to role-deprivation, immaturity and lack of personality integration (Kerr 1958). Perhaps even more interesting is her statement that:

> The most salient feature which all Ship Street people have, whether male or female, is this incredibly strong tie to their mothers ... Mum is the central figure and ... the household revolves around her. One of the psychological results of this tie is to be seen in the immaturity of adult relationships (Kerr 1958:166).

After a disclaimer that she does not want to advise or alter people or pass judgement on them she nonetheless concludes that the strength of the tie to the mother has all kinds of deleterious effects including insecurity, loss of ego strength, an attitude of reliance and inability to accept responsibility, inability to plan, immaturity leading to violence, and a matrifocal mother dominated culture (Kerr 1958:166–7).

Kerr's work is astonishing in its unreflective class prejudice, but also echoes much of the then prevailing wisdom about the abnormality of lower class family life; whether it was in Liverpool or the West Indies does not seem to have mattered. She has no references to the work of Elizabeth Bott (1957), or Young and Willmott (1957), whose books had appeared in the year before hers and which took a very different view of class differences in family life.

The North American experience

In the North American colonies, as in the West Indies, little attention was paid to the family life of slaves. Even after slavery ended, so long as the majority of African Americans remained in the Southern States, tied to the land through share-cropping arrangements that left them little better off than they had been under the slave regime, their social life excited little interest.[5]

The few descriptions of family life in the American South after the Civil War shows that kinship practices were remarkably similar to those in the West Indies. For example, WEB Du Bois writing about rural Georgia at the end of the nineteenth century referred to '. . . easy marriage and easy separation. This is no sudden development, nor the fruit of Emancipation. It is the plain heritage from slavery. In those days Sam, with his master's consent, "took up" with Mary. No ceremony was necessary, and in the busy life of the great plantations of the Black Belt it was usually dispensed with' (Du Bois 1961 [1903]: 108).

In the early 1930s Hortense Powdermaker carried out field research in the town of Indianola, Mississippi, and its rural hinterland. In spite of the various shortcomings of her theoretical and methodological approaches, and the bias introduced by her almost exclusive access to female informants, she stresses (and no doubt exaggerates) the 'matriarchal' nature of lower-class African American kinship, the fluidity of household membership, the fragility of marriage and common-law unions, and the strength of consanguineal ties (Powdermaker 1993 [1939]).[6] She is particularly interesting on what she calls infidelity, citing one woman informant as saying that 'she didn't leave her husband because he ran around with other women. All men do that, and she doesn't believe in following a man around and hunting him down. If women left men just for going around with other women, they'd be leaving them all the time' (Powdermaker 1993:156). She left him because he did not contribute to household expenses while she had to work so hard. Powdermaker also has extensive discussions on inter-racial unions, stressing the ubiquity of sexual relations 'between white men and Negro women' (Powdermaker 1993:181).

In the now classic study by Davis, Gardner and Gardner, *Deep South: a Social Anthropological Study of Caste and Class* (1941), the descriptions of family life break through the conventions of household counting and convey a more accurate image of the nature of kinship ties. They note that the immediate family ties between a man, his wife and children are important for the maintenance of the system of share-cropping agriculture in the cotton growing areas of Mississippi, and indeed that system encouraged the emergence of 'the patriarchal family' which included sons and their wives and children. However, over 14 per cent of the tenant cotton farmers in their area of study were women presiding over 'matriarchal families'. Even more important is their discussion of 'miscegenation', an offensive term that is, regrettably, still in use:

> Many colored informants stated that, even as late as fifteen years ago, several white planters rode with their white and colored families in the same carriage, the colored sitting on the coachman's seat, and the white family on the master's seat (Davis & Gardner 1941:406).

The massive normalcy of non-legal unions between white men and black women in the United States has been obscured by the need to explain the harshness of race relations that continued after the abolition of slavery, and was indeed exacerbated by the reaction to Reconstruction. Historians dealing with the aftermath of Emancipation and the Civil War are rightly impressed by the evidence showing the determined attempts by the newly-emancipated slaves in the American South to reconstitute their families, including efforts to find members who had been sold and moved considerable distances from their original homes (see Foner 1988; and some of the essays in McGlynn and Drescher [eds.] 1992, for example). And it was doubtless much more difficult for unions to be established across the deepening racial divide. However, it would be surprising if those unions disappeared entirely and evidence such as that presented in Powdermaker's *After Freedom and Deep South* indicates that they did not. More importantly, the simple proportions of different types of household composition tell us nothing about the dynamics of household formation, development and dissolution (see RT Smith 1996, Ch. 4, for a discussion of the developmental cycle of domestic groups).

When, in the latter half of the twentieth century, patterns of statistical distribution of female-headed households, teenage pregnancy and illegitimacy similar to those found in the West Indies appeared in the cities of the United States, it occasioned an even more alarmist reaction than the concerns expressed in the Caribbean, especially when those statistics were combined with data showing an increase in the number of persons on the rolls of the public welfare agencies.

Newspapers, radio and television, often drawing on the work of academics, have become experts at fabricating images of African American disorder, delinquency, violence and backwardness. These negative images contain references to 'broken families', welfare mothers, teenage pregnancy and female-headed households, frequently held to be responsible, in part if not entirely, for the problems of poverty, unemployment and crime. Although these images are more explicitly formed and expertly presented in the United States, Caribbean societies have their own interpretations of family disorder, and terms such as 'underclass' and 'ghetto' are gaining currency there as urban problems approximate, or surpass, those of the United States. Even in Britain similar ideas are circulated, as the earlier reference to Pryce's work shows. In the prosperous 1990s of 'New Labour New Britain', it is tempting to believe that 'intractable family pathologies' no longer have the salience that they had when Daniel Patrick Moynihan was writing his report on poverty in the United States entitled, oddly enough, *The Negro Family: the Case for National Action*, or Lord Justice Scarman (1981) was writing his report on *The Brixton Disorders*, in which he found it necessary to refer to the 'matriarchy' of Black families in Britain.

The supposed 'facts' out of which these images are constructed are not wholly imaginary of course; in the United States unemployment, poverty, poor living conditions and high rates of crime are found in the inner cities. Statistics show that African Americans bear high proportions of babies out of wedlock, that some of the mothers of those babies are teenagers (though the proportion of teenage mothers has actually been falling since the 1960s), that they live in households with a disproportionately high number of female heads, and that in the United States at least a high proportion of those women receive government assistance. In 1987 just over half of all African American women with children under 18 years of age were not living with a husband, as opposed to 16.5 per cent of white women (Jencks 1992:195).

In Jamaica the illegitimacy rate has varied between 60 and 70 per cent of live births ever since reliable records were first kept in the 1870s. In the United States the picture is rather different; the illegitimacy rate among African Americans was only 17% in 1950, rose to 48% in 1980, and reached 62.6% in 1986 (as opposed to 14.5% for whites). However, the proportions were much higher in both groups among women with little education, being as high as 82.9 per cent among Black women with 9 to 11 years of schooling as opposed to 38.2 per cent for White women with the same amount of schooling (Jencks 1992, p 195).[7] The proportion of low income households in the United States recorded as being headed by women has increased dramatically over the past 30 years, but among poor Blacks the proportion has increased even more rapidly.

Aggregate data and family images

The images of disorder and disorganisation disseminated by the media seem to be validated by these statistics, but the appearance is deceptive. Interpretations and explanations of Caribbean and African American family life based upon aggregate statistics and economic explanations are, at best, inadequate and at worst, grossly misleading.

The idea that facts are facts, and statistics do not lie, is only marginally true. Facts are constructed in terms of what we assume the world is like, in terms of what we are looking for, as well as in terms of what actually exists, and as for figures – statistics – they depend entirely on the assumptions and definitions used to collect the data on which they are based.

For more than 900 years census takers have followed the example of the Domesday Census of AD 1086 in using the 'household' as their unit of record. In 1086 and for a long time afterwards this made sense, since everybody had to belong to a household, each was headed by a male master to whom women, children, servants and apprentices were subservient. But that is hardly the case in Britain or the United States of the 1990s, and it was never the case in the Caribbean where family members often live in several different households. However, some social scientists – not to mention politicians and sundry members of the general public – continue to believe that everyone *should* live in households with, if not a male head, then at least a married couple and their children. This is a perfectly reasonable value position, but it cannot be buttressed with claims about what is 'natural'. Nearly all the generalisations about 'family disorder' are based on surveys and censuses that assume that households are the same thing as families, much as was the case in 1086.

In the rural areas of both the Caribbean and the Southern States of the United States complex patterns of kinship rooted in wide-spreading ties of reciprocity and mutual aid were developed in conjunction with all the supposed 'pathological' features of female-headed households, unstable and non-legal unions, and teen-age pregnancy. Numerous anthropological studies have shown the viability of these kinship systems, not to mention their functional appropriateness under conditions of irregular and unstable economic resources (see RT Smith 1956; Stack 1974; Aschenbrenner 1975). Certainly in close-knit rural communities where people lived near to subsistence and with a minimum of consumption of manufactured goods, the reciprocal relations among a relatively wide-spreading network of kin was, functionally, far more important than stable conjugal unions. When African Americans migrated to urban areas in search of improved economic opportunities, they – like other migrants – often went through periods of dislocation and distress, exacerbated by racial discrimination. In spite of prejudice and social exclusion, black migrants to the urban areas of North America and Europe have been an invaluable source of cheap labour and many have managed to become upwardly mobile into middle-class occupations. However, in the United States, large reservoirs of unemployed persons have been left behind as the economic base which drew them in the first place disappeared in a burst of industrial transformation, or as the industries that once employed them have moved to other geographic areas. In the Caribbean, the cities have never been able to absorb all the migrants from rural areas into reasonable employment so that they either moved on to other countries or remained in urban slums making a living by 'scuffling' or, increasingly, through criminal activities of one kind or another. In all these areas in the late 1990s consumption expectations are far higher than they were 40 or 50 years ago.

In the United States and Europe the availability of government welfare support has resulted in much higher levels of health and well-being than would have been imagined in the middle of the twentieth century. It is, however, ironic that just as higher levels of living have become more widespread in modern societies, those societies continue to be administered in terms of 'nuclear family households' while divorce, unstable unions and female headed households reach ever higher proportions among all income groups.

Survey research merely reports deviations from a presumed norm of family and household formation and then seeks variables that might explain these deviations. It is imperative that means be found to understand the actual way in which kinship and family relations are generated.

The ethnographic approach

Many survey researchers have realised that crucial information is often written in the margins of questionnaires by frustrated interviewers who try to modify the rigidities of standard answers to survey questions. However, they are rarely able to use that information because their 'tabulation programme' is already determined according to the categories built into the survey instrument.

Ethnographic study, by its very nature, is intensive and restricted, either to a limited geographic area or to a small number of cases subjected to prolonged and thorough study. Its critics argue that it is 'unrepresentative' and 'impressionistic' and therefore of limited value for understanding the general condition of a large population group. Such criticism conceals a deeper difference of theoretical approach. Whereas the survey researcher generally assumes that the aggregation of individual characteristics or 'attitudes' provides a definitive picture of the state of social reality, the anthropologist/ethnographer is more likely to assume that social behaviour is a complex resultant of cultural principles and assumptions interacting with the conditions of action in a particular social environment. Such cultural principles and assumptions are widely shared among the members of particular groups but are not easily observed or elicited. Perhaps the best description was given a long time ago by Max Weber when he said that:

> In the great majority of cases actual action goes on in a state
> of inarticulate half-consciousness or actual unconsciousness

of its subjective meaning. The actor is more likely to 'be aware' of it in a vague sense than he is to 'know' what he is doing or be explicitly self-conscious about it. [However, this does not] prevent the sociologist from systematizing his concepts by the classification of possible types of subjective meaning. That is, he may reason as if action actually proceeded on the basis of clearly self-conscious meaning (Weber 1968: Vol. 1, 21–22).

But, he continues, it is then necessary to bear in mind the difference between this and reality when it comes to the investigation of concrete cases. The construction of these types of subjective meaning is the anthropologist's most difficult task and can only be accomplished through the analysis of voluminous bodies of text collected in as non-directive manner as possible from informants. Some anthropologists counter the 'representativeness' argument by pointing out that it is perfectly possible to study a language by analysing the structure embedded in the utterances of just one competent speaker. Similarly, they argue, one properly socialised adult will bring to the tasks of everyday life an embodied array of cultural principles and, like language, those principles will change as they are used in social interaction. Pierre Bourdieu, again following Max Weber, has called these embodied cultural principles the *habitus* (see Bourdieu 1990: Ch. 3).

Ideally, there is enormous scope for cooperation between ethnographers and survey specialists, but that cooperation should be phased in a particular way. In designing a research project – and here I am thinking of family studies but it can apply across a wide range of social issues – a long lead time is essential (though rarely allowed when quick answers are needed). Detailed ethnographic studies should precede the design of questionnaires and not be regarded as a supplementary source of anecdotes to support conclusions drawn from the survey. On the basis of long and detailed discussion of the ethnographic data, very narrow targeted surveys could be designed to answer very specific questions on issues for which wide general information is needed.

Even so it must be recognised that survey research has severe limitations in the field of family studies. With all the care in the world, with all the focus group testing of questions, and the consequent refinement of the wording, it is impossible to get at the complexities of kinship in most low income populations. Even something as apparently simple as a woman's child-bearing history is not readily forthcoming in a survey interview situation; certainly anyone who has carried out anthropological field research over an extended period of time knows that it takes several hours of patient interviewing before intimate details come pouring forth.

One of William J Wilson's central theses is that the populations of America's inner cities are socially isolated and lacking in adequate role models that would provide patterns for a proper participation in 'mainstream' social life (Wilson 1987). The painstaking collection of individual's genealogies in which every relative through any and every link is recorded and discussed, shows just how misguided is such a conclusion. The advantage of such a method of data collection is that it documents in detail both the knowledge of, and the experience of, kinship ties of all kinds. All this is well known to anthropologists who have worked in this kind of environment, but unfortunately it has had little impact on sociologists who work in the policy field. That is partly because they have a social organisation and a culture that is not easily changed. Surveys provide a spurious feeling of certainty and the data can be readily used by a wide range of scholars, who modify and build upon the results. Such a research culture is unlikely to undergo major changes in the near future.

Conclusion: implications for policy

Two major conclusions emerge from this discussion. Both have clear policy implications. The time has passed when familial and kinship relations can be force ordered into neat nuclear family households. This does not mean that 'the family' is disintegrating or that kinship no longer plays an important part in modern social life. Nor does it mean that absolutely any kind of behaviour is socially acceptable. Virtually all accounts of the family, and social policies based on them, contain unexamined, taken-for-granted conceptions of what the family is, and what the family should be. Those conceptions are the orthodox images of the nineteenth- and early twentieth-century bourgeois, nuclear family. In spite of a huge increase in female participation in the labour force, and rapidly changing patterns of gender relations – of what men and women are and should do – old ideas about 'sex roles' continue to shape thinking about the family. It is particularly ironic that these bourgeois standards should have been invoked in judgments about the Caribbean working class family, since female participation in the labour force has always been high, just as it has in the case of the African American family in the United States. Combined with the fact that available work has generally been casual, seasonal, temporary and poorly paid for both men and women, work experience has not in itself reinforced stable and long-term marital relationships. However, it would be a mistake to make a facile causal association between unstable employment and unstable marriage, as so much survey research has been inclined to do. The societies of the Caribbean and the southern United States have long traditions of exploitative gender relations and status-linked forms of conjugal union. These traditions have placed heavy burdens on women especially when they have been isolated from wider bodies of supportive consanguineal kin, as when they have migrated to urban areas or foreign countries. If men frequently have been irresponsible in relation to the mothers of their children, they have, nonetheless, generally been supportive of their mothers and sisters who have, in turn, redistributed resources to needy relatives. Instability of marital and other forms of conjugal union is a reality that must be faced in the framing of policy. In the case of people of Caribbean and African American descent, powerful historical forces have shaped the institution of marriage; those forces are more complex than is suggested by the word slavery.

The second conclusion is that it is totally unjustified to attribute all the problems of poverty and social exclusion found among low income people of colour to deficiencies in their family structure, whether those supposed deficiencies are seen to be due to either 'loose' or 'overly rigid' organisation. As we saw from the discussion of the work of Madeline Kerr, the family life of the poor in modern societies has frequently been at the centre of attempts to explain the persistence of class differences, while conveniently ignoring the realities of class itself and the gender aspects of hierarchical structures.

In Europe and the United States alike family policy does not confront problems that are uniquely Caribbean, African American, immigrant or minority; the problems of poverty, unstable marriage, female-headed households, and welfare dependency affect every part of society. Where minority groups are disproportionately represented in the lower class they will be particularly affected, but their often more supportive patterns of familial solidarity have a mitigating effect on certain kinds of problem. For example, among African Americans in the United States, aged and infirm relatives are almost always cared for in the homes of children or grandchildren, rather than being placed in institutions, frequently at enormous personal cost in time and emotional energy, but with a commensurate decrease in public costs. On the other hand, a long tradition of transient conjugal unions converging with a falling age at menarche, freer attitudes toward sex, and a shrinkage in the size of supportive kinship networks has served to make the burdens placed upon women who fail to make a satisfactory marriage much more onerous than in the past. It is doubtful that public policy, in itself, can bring about demographic changes. In the light of a continuing growth of single-parent households (*not* 'families' as most policy documents have it), there is a pressing need for arrangements that will ensure that the 'missing' parent both contributes to, and participates in, the life of children. Where either of those things is not possible, the state has a responsibility to take up the burden. This has long been recognised in the case of widows and orphans and is no less necessary in the case of abandoned family fragments. Only an exaggerated sense of moral condemnation makes it seem otherwise.

What kind of questions can be addressed by research in the future? I have indicated that a particular pattern of gender roles has been integral to the formation and development of the Caribbean family, reaching its most vivid expression in a quotation from one of our Jamaican informants who said:

> Jamaicans love a whole lot of woman, you know. Lot of woman, not just one. They don't stick to one, they must have girls outside, that's just the way…They love sport [laugh]. Married men, unmarried men, it don't matter (DeVeer 1979: p 150, cited in RT Smith 1982, p 133).

As I have said elsewhere, it is not possible to attribute beliefs such as this to poverty or adaptation or any of the other popular causes. Changes in economic circumstances do not seem to make a great deal of difference to patterns of mating in the Caribbean even though legal marriage is clearly associated with higher status. Rather than seeing living arrangements as an adaptation to difficult economic circumstances, or even to the truncated extended family networks consequent on migration, I would be inclined to try to understand the way in which individuals make sense of their situation in terms of their embodied beliefs and assumptions about the nature of the social world in which they find themselves. Only in that way can we discover what is truly different about Caribbean peoples and what is changing as they become part of their new surroundings.

Notes

1   The doctoral dissertation in sociology presented by Kenneth Pryce to the University of Bristol is entitled, *The Life-styles of West Indians in Bristol: Study of a Black Toiling Class in an English City*.
2   For example, the Congress of the United States passed a law in 1996 entitled the *Personal Responsibility and Work Opportunity Reconciliation Act*, better known as the Welfare Reform Act. In its collective wisdom the The Congress declared the following:
   (1)   Marriage is the foundation of a successful society.
   (2)   Marriage is an essential institution of a successful society which promotes the interests of children.

(3)   Promotion of responsible fatherhood and motherhood is integral to successful child rearing and the well-being of children.

It then went on to examine the increasing rates of divorce, separations, out-of-wedlock births, and teen-age pregnancy before declaring 'Therefore, in light of this demonstration of the crisis in our Nation, it is the sense of the Congress that prevention of out-of-wedlock pregnancy and reduction in out-of-wedlock birth are very important Government interests . . .' However, on reading the document it soon becomes evident that the primary interest is in reducing the extent of 'welfare dependency' which is (erroneously) believed to depend upon the incidence of teen-age pregnancy and out-of-wedlock births.

3   Michel Foucault (1978) and Jacques Donzelot (1979) have shown that all modern states have, at certain stages of their development, been preoccupied with the supposed pathologies of the personal and family life of poor people.

4   (See Long 1774 for detailed discussions of the system of conjugal unions, and RT Smith, forthcoming, for a discussion of Long's view of eighteenth-century family life in Jamaica).

5   In the United States slavery ended only after the Civil War of 1861 to 1865.

6   In their introductory essay to the 1993 reprinted edition, 'Hortense Powdermaker in the Deep South', Brackette F Williams and Drexel G Woodson provide a sympathetic critique of these theoretical and methodological issues.

7   Consideration of these figures requires a good deal of caution. For example, one factor leading to an increase in the proportion of children born out of wedlock was the absolute decline in the number of children born to married women, a trend that is continuing. According to a recent report from the National Center for Health Statistics the number of unmarried women bearing children has been falling substantially over the past 20 years, but because the number of children born to married women has been declining even faster, the *proportion* of out-of-wedlock births remains high.

Part 2

Demographic and Trans-Atlantic
Characteristics of Caribbean Families

5 | A profile of Caribbean households and families in Great Britain

David Owen

Introduction

The Caribbean population of Great Britain is one of the longest-established of the new population groups which have emerged since the end of the Second World War. The mass migration of Caribbean people to the United Kingdom both began and ended relatively early (the bulk of immigrants arrived during the second half of the 1950s and early 1960s) and consequently, the 1991 Census of Population revealed both that older people were more common within the Caribbean population than for other minority ethnic groups and that nearly half of the Caribbean population had been born in the UK. Despite their relatively long period of settlement, Caribbean people in Britain have remained disadvantaged in social and economic terms. Caribbean families and households are also distinctive from those of White people and other minority ethnic groups in terms of their organisation and material circumstances.

This chapter begins by outlining the structure and evolution of the Caribbean population in Great Britain, and then goes on to bring together Census of Population and survey data to paint a picture of the key characteristics of Caribbean families and households in the early 1990s.

Definitions

The Caribbean population is defined here as comprising the Black-Caribbean and Black-Other ethnic groups from the 1991 Census ethnic group classification. This definition is adopted because many of the children of Black-Caribbean parents were recorded as 'Black British' on the Census form or were the children of 'mixed' partnerships, both of which were classified as 'Black-Other' in the published output from the Census (Owen, 1996). The Black-Caribbean ethnic group on its own contained relatively few children, while the Black-Other ethnic group was extremely youthful. Thus, it is probably valid to combine the two, in order to capture the UK-born children of people originating in the West Indies and hence produce a population group which does not separate parents from children. Using this definition, the Caribbean population of Great Britain was 678,365 in 1991 (499,964 of whom were classified as Black-Caribbean), representing 1.2 per cent of the total population.

However, the Black-Other category also covers a range of Black people with non-Caribbean and non-African origins, notably Black American servicemen. It would probably be more accurate to only add the 'British' and 'Mixed' components of the Black-Other ethnic group to the Black-Caribbean total, yielding a total for the Caribbean population of Great Britain of 633,425 in 1991. Combining the Black-Caribbean and Black-Other ethnic groups therefore certainly overestimates the magnitude of the Caribbean population, but this cannot be avoided, since neither Census nor other survey data is tabulated for the individual components of the Black-Other ethnic group (the composition of the Black-Other ethnic group is analysed in detail in Owen, 1996). Where data from other sources is used, the term 'Afro-Caribbean' or 'Caribbean' is used to represent the Caribbean population.

Unfortunately, though a substantial percentage of the population of Caribbean countries such as Trinidad & Tobago are of South or East Asian ethnic origin, 'Indo-Caribbean' people are not readily identifiable in the Census of Population or in the major survey data sets. They tend to be split across the Black, South Asian and 'Other' categories, and their numbers are too small for surveys to have identified large enough numbers to analyse. Consequently, their characteristics are only addressed incidentally in this chapter.

Population structure

The origins of the Caribbean population of Great Britain lie in the relatively large numbers of migrants from the West Indies during the 1950s and early 1960s (Figure 5.1). The passing of the Commonwealth Immigration Act of 1962 is regarded as having effectively ended mass migration to the UK, but it also encouraged a sudden surge of Caribbean migrants just before it came into force. The rapid growth of the (relatively youthful) Caribbean population during the 1950s and 1960s was also fuelled by high birth rates among the

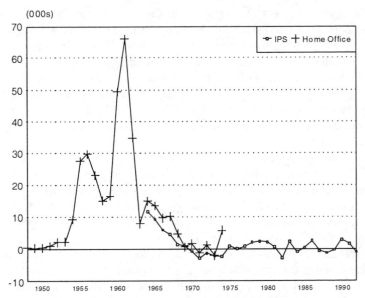

Figure 5.1   Net migration to the UK from the Caribbean
(*Source*: International Passenger Survey [IPS] and Home Office data).

migrant population (Figure 5.2); by the time of 1971 Census, there were estimated to be 244,000 British-born Caribbean people.

The bulk of Caribbean-born people came from Jamaica. This island accounted for 57 per cent of all Caribbean-born people in 1961, 56.5 per cent in 1971, 55.6 per cent in 1981 and 64.2 per cent in 1991. Jamaicans arrived in the UK earlier than people from other islands, with the growth in the number of Barbados and Guyana-born being faster in the 1960s. The number of Guyana- and Trinidad & Tobago-born has remained more stable over time than the number of Jamaica and Barbados-born people, the decline in whose numbers started earlier than for the other Caribbean countries.

There is considerable uncertainty over trends in the Caribbean population over time, resulting from the absence of a consistent measure of the Caribbean population (Peach, 1996). What is certain is that the number of people actually born in the Caribbean and living in Great Britain reached a peak in the mid- 1960s, and has been declining ever since. Indeed, Census data reveals that the number of Caribbean-born people fell by 30,600 (from 295,179 to 264,591) between 1981 and 1991, while the number of people living in households with Caribbean-born heads declined by 20.5 per cent over the same period. However, in the absence of an explicit question on the ethnic composition of the population in Censuses before 1991, measurement of the

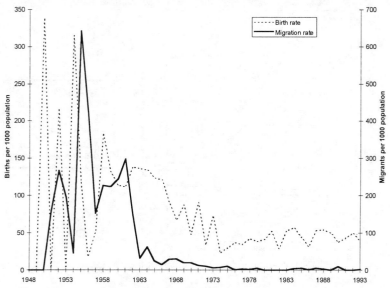

Figure 5.2   Migration and birth rates for Black-Caribbean people
Source: Family and Working Lives Survey, 1994/5.

entire Caribbean population (those born in the Caribbean and their descendants) has been much more uncertain. It was estimated to be 548,000 in 1971, 528,000 in 1981 and around 495,000 in 1986-8 (the latter being estimates of the West Indian and Guyanese ethnic groups from the Labour Force Survey), indicating rapid early growth followed by stability and decline. While there was some return migration to the Caribbean, and a growing (but still relatively small) number of deaths over this period, this degree of contraction in a relatively youthful population is not plausible. Indeed, the population of the 'mixed' ethnic group in the LFS ethnic classification, which would contain many of the children of unions between Caribbean people and other ethnic groups, increased by 42 per cent during the 1980s, which implied that the British- born component of the Caribbean population was continuing to increase.

Figure 5.3 presents a set of estimates of birth, death and migration rates for the West Indian ethnic group for the 1980s, formed by combining demographic data by country of birth with Labour Force Survey data on the ethnic composition of persons by country of birth. The estimated West Indian (the term used by the Labour Force Survey) birth rate was relatively low during the 1980s (quite close to that for White women) and was declining by the end of the decade, while the death rate was increasing as the population aged. Emigration exceeded

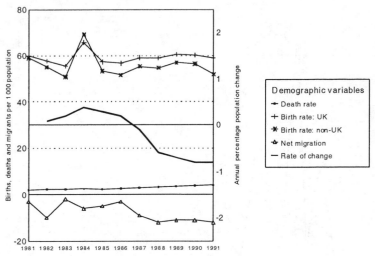

Figure 5.3   Demographic influences on West Indian population change, 1981–91

immigration for this ethnic group, and was probably mainly responsible for the estimated decline in the West Indian population after the mid-1980s.

The structure of the Caribbean population in 1991 is summarised in the population pyramid presented in Figure 5.4. This reveals three 'generations': the original post-war immigrants, who had reached later middle age in 1991; their children, born in the 1960s; and their grandchildren, born to UK-born parents. The second generation was the largest, with the largest single age cohort being people aged 25 to 29 in 1991. The pyramid reveals a relatively small number of people of retirement age and over, but a much larger number of people in middle age, who would retire by the end of the 1990s or in the early 21st century. There was a relative deficit of people aged 35 to 49, with the great mass aged from 20 to 34. There was again a deficit of people aged 10 to 19 (reflecting the smaller number of potential parents in their 30s and 40s), but the number of children of primary school and pre-school age was much larger, mainly the children of the 'second generation', aged 20 to 34. This pattern indicates that the number of Caribbean births rose during the 1980s, as a result of the increasing number of people in the second generation reaching the child-bearing ages. However, the number of children was less than the number of adults in this age group, indicating declining fertility. The shape of this population pyramid indicates that the number of Caribbean entrants to the labour market will rise markedly around the turn of the century,

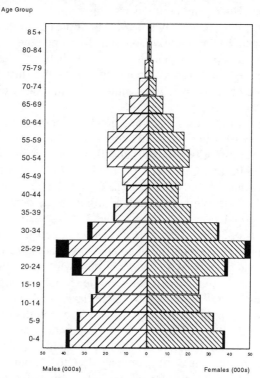

Figure 5.4   Population of each age group by gender, 1991

and that the number of Caribbean secondary schoolchildren will increase substantially in the late 1990s, but will thereafter probably decline sharply. 'Ageing' the 1991 population by age, ethnic group and sex forward to 1995, constrained to match total British population change across all ethnic groups, yields an estimated increase of 5.9 per cent in the Caribbean population (within which the Black-Other component was growing at twice the rate of the Black-Caribbean population) over the period 1991 to 1995.

The 1991 Census is thought to have only covered around 98 per cent of the population, resulting in an underestimate of around 1.2 million people. The degree of underestimation was greatest for young people (especially men aged 20 to 29) and hence the impact on minority ethnic groups was greater than for White people. The actual Caribbean population is thought to have been nearly 4 per cent larger than the Census figure in 1991. The differential impact of under-enumeration by ethnic group and gender is depicted by the black shading at the end of each bar in Figure 5.4, clearly being greatest for young men. Under-enumeration was also most severe in inner city areas where there were many houses in multiple occupancy. This factor would have had a particularly large influence upon the enumeration of the Caribbean population, and it is therefore believed that the Census underestimated the Caribbean population by more than 6 per cent in Inner London and by over 7 per cent in the other large cities, such as Birmingham.

Table 5.1 outlines the age and gender structure of the Caribbean population in 1991 in more detail, comparing it with the White population and other minority ethnic groups. Females were in the majority of both the White and Caribbean populations, but males outnumbered females in other minority groups. The Caribbean population was more youthful than the White population, although the percentages of the Caribbean population aged 16 to 24 and 25 to 44 were similar to those for White people and there was a relative deficit of Caribbean men aged 25 to 44. The percentage of compulsory school age was greater in the Caribbean than the White ethnic group, while pre-school age children were nearly twice as common in the Caribbean population. The percentages of pre-school age were similar in the Caribbean and the other minority populations, but school age population were more common in the latter. Males were more common among Caribbean people aged under 16 than in the White population, while women were more common than men for people aged 16 to 44, but the percentage aged 25 to 44 was greater for all minority groups than for Caribbean people. People aged from 45 to retirement age were more common in the Caribbean population than for other minority ethnic groups. In all

Table 5.1　**Age and sex structure of the Caribbean population compared with other ethnic groups**

Age group	White		Caribbean		Other minority ethnic groups	
	Male	**Female**	**Male**	**Female**	**Male**	**Female**
Population (000s)	25,066.4	26,807.4	327.0	351.4	1,181.6	1,155.1
Males per 1000 females	935		931		1023	
% aged 0–4	6.7	6.0	11.4	10.4	11.2	11.1
% aged 5–15	13.8	12.2	19.5	17.6	23.2	22.6
% aged 16–24	13.0	12.1	15.6	16.3	15.8	16.4
% aged 25–44	29.8	28.2	27.9	32.9	31.9	34.2
% aged 45–59/64	22.8	16.6	20.6	15.3	14.9	10.9
% of pensionable age	13.9	24.8	5.1	7.4	2.9	4.7

Source: 1991 Census of Population (Crown Copyright).

three sections of the population, men formed the majority of people aged from 45 to retirement age, but there were more women than men among people of pensionable age.

Geographical distribution

Nearly two-thirds of all Caribbean people lived in South-East England in 1991, compared with just over half of all people from minority ethnic groups (Table 5.2). There was a very marked urban bias in their location, with over half of the Caribbean population living in Greater London, and a further eighth (13 per cent) in the West Midlands metropolitan county. There were smaller concentrations of Caribbean people in the Greater Manchester and West Yorkshire (former) metropolitan counties. Only in Greater London and in the West Midlands metropolitan county was the Caribbean share of the local population greater than the average for Great Britain (1.2 per cent), reaching a maximum of 5.6 per cent of the population of Greater London.

The concentration of Caribbean people within Greater London is emphasised by Table 5.3. The local authority districts in which the Caribbean share of the population was greatest were all located in south, east and west London, with three central southern London Boroughs having more than 10 per cent of their population from Caribbean ethnic groups. The largest concentration of Caribbean people outside London occurred in Birmingham, which contained 53,600 (a larger number than in any one London Borough), accounting for 5.6 per cent of its population and 7.9 per cent of all Caribbean people in Great Britain in 1991. The next largest shares of Caribbean people in the resident population were found in Wolverhampton, Luton, Nottingham, Manchester, Reading and Slough. Two-thirds of the Caribbean population of Great Britain lived in the 31 districts listed in Table 5.3.

Household characteristics

The 1991 Census revealed that households with Caribbean heads were similar in size to White-headed households in 1991, but were about two-thirds the average size of households in other minority ethnic groups (Table 5.4). The difference in size was partly due to the smaller average number of dependent children per household in White and Caribbean households. Dependent children formed a much smaller percentage of the Caribbean population than in other minority ethnic

Table 5.2 Regional distribution of Caribbean people within Great Britain, 1991

Region, county and metropolitan county	Total population	Minority ethnic groups (000s)	Percent of regional population	Share of G.B. total (%)	Caribbean population (000s)	Percent of regional population	Share of G.B. total (%)
South East	17,208.3	1,695.4	9.9	56.2	432.4	2.5	63.7
Greater London	*6,679.7*	*1,346.1*	*20.2*	*44.6*	*371.6*	*5.6*	*54.8*
East Anglia	2,027.0	43.4	2.1	1.4	12.1	0.6	1.8
South West	4,609.4	62.6	1.4	2.1	19.0	0.4	2.8
West Midlands	5,150.2	424.4	8.2	14.1	96.9	1.9	14.3
West Midlands MC	*2,551.7*	*373.5*	*14.6*	*12.4*	*87.9*	*3.4*	*13.0*
East Midlands	3,953.4	188.0	4.8	6.2	35.1	0.9	5.2
Yorks & Humberside	4,836.5	214.0	4.4	7.1	31.7	0.7	4.7
South Yorkshire	*1,262.6*	*36.2*	*2.9*	*1.2*	*8.6*	*0.7*	*1.3*
West Yorkshire	*2,013.7*	*164.1*	*8.2*	*5.4*	*21.3*	*1.1*	*3.1*
North West	6,243.7	244.6	3.9	8.1	37.7	0.6	5.6
Greater Manchester	*2,499.4*	*148.2*	*5.9*	*4.9*	*26.3*	*1.1*	*3.9*
Merseyside	*1,403.6*	*25.9*	*1.8*	*0.9*	*6.4*	*0.5*	*0.9*
North	3,026.7	38.5	1.3	1.3	3.0	0.1	0.4
Tyne & Wear	*1,095.2*	*19.9*	*1.8*	*0.7*	*1.3*	*0.1*	*0.2*
Wales	2,835.1	41.6	1.5	1.4	6.8	0.2	1.0
Scotland	4,998.6	62.6	1.3	2.1	3.6	0.1	0.5
Great Britain	**54,888.8**	**3,015.1**	**5.5**	**100**	**678.4**	**1.2**	**100.0**

Source: 1991 Census of Population Local Base Statistics (Crown Copyright).

Table 5.3 Largest local Caribbean populations in 1991

Local authority district	Caribbean people (thousands)	Percent of local population	Percent of all Caribbeans in Great Britain
Lambeth	37.4	15.3	5.5
Hackney	27.6	15.2	4.1
Lewisham	29.0	12.5	4.3
Brent	30.2	12.4	4.4
Haringey	23.5	11.6	3.5
Southwark	23.1	10.6	3.4
Newham	18.6	8.8	2.7
Waltham Forest	18.0	8.5	2.6
Wandsworth	19.5	7.7	2.9
Hammersmith and Fulham	11.4	7.7	1.7
Islington	11.4	6.9	1.7
Croydon	18.7	6.0	2.8
Birmingham	53.6	5.6	7.9
Ealing	15.1	5.5	2.2
Wolverhampton	12.1	5.0	1.8
Westminster,City of	8.5	4.9	1.3
Tower Hamlets	7.6	4.7	1.1
Enfield	11.8	4.6	1.7
Luton	7.7	4.5	1.1
Nottingham	11.6	4.4	1.7
Manchester	15.4	3.8	2.3
Merton	6.3	3.8	0.9
Kensington and Chelsea	5.0	3.6	0.7
Greenwich	7.2	3.5	1.1
Reading	4.4	3.4	0.7
Slough	3.4	3.4	0.5
Sandwell	9.4	3.2	1.4
Redbridge	7.1	3.1	1.0
Forest Heath	1.7	3.0	0.2
Harrow	5.8	2.9	0.8
Camden	4.8	2.8	0.7
Sum of above	466.9	–	68.8
Caribbean total	**678.4**	**1.2**	**100.0**

Source: 1991 Census of Population Local Base Statistics (Crown Copyright).

groups, but were slightly younger on average (since the percentage of pre-school age was higher). The percentage of households containing dependent children was twice as high for the Caribbean than the White ethnic group, and was slightly higher than the average for other minority ethnic groups. The relative youth of minority populations in comparison with White people was reflected in the much smaller percentage of households containing pensioners. However, the percentage of pensioners was much higher in the Caribbean population than for other minority ethnic groups, reflecting the substantial number of adult migrants who arrived in the 1950s. As the population aged, the number of pensioner households was likely to increase quite rapidly during the 1990s, which though only small numbers were involved, were significant in representing a new type of client group for health and social services (especially significant outside the main geographical concentrations of Caribbean people).

Table 5.4   *Households and housing conditions by ethnic group of household heads, 1991*

	White	Other minority ethnic groups	Caribbean
All households	21,026,565	616,016	254,741
Persons in households	51,150,591	2,264,216	640,886
Mean number of persons per household	2.4	3.7	2.5
Dependent children aged 0–18	10,908,270	852,292	182,551
Mean number of dependent children per household	1.8	2.3	1.8
Dependent children as percentage of population	21.3	37.6	28.5
Percent of dependent children aged 0–4	30.4	29.4	33.3
Percent of dependent children aged 5–15	61.1	61.2	59.0
Percentage of households			
Containing dependent children	15.4	27.2	29.8
Containing pensioners	25.7	3.2	6.6
Households with 1 adult	31.1	20.0	45.6
Households with 2 adults	52.2	50.1	37.0
Households with 3 or more adults	16.7	28.8	17.3
Owner-occupied	66.6	65.0	46.4
Private rented	7.0	12.5	6.8
Renting from a Housing Association	3.0	4.2	9.9
Renting from the public sector	21.4	16.1	35.5
Not in self-contained accommodation	0.9	2.5	2.2
Living at a density greater than 1 person per room	1.8	16.5	4.9
Lacking or sharing a bath or WC	1.2	2.3	1.6
Lacking central heating	18.9	17.7	17.9
Without a car	33.0	35.2	54.4
Percent of population in households			
Living at a density greater than 1 person per room	3.7	28.0	9.3
Lacking or sharing a bath or WC	0.8	1.4	1.0
Lacking central heating	16.8	18.1	16.3
Without a car	24.6	30.1	47.9

Source: 1991 Census Local Base Statistics (Crown Copyright).

The Caribbean ethnic group was distinctive in having a high percentage of households containing only one adult; at approaching half of all households, the incidence of lone adult households was twice as great as for other minority ethnic groups. Conversely, large households (with three or more adults) were much less common than for other minority ethnic groups. Though Caribbean households were of similar size to White households, a much larger percentage of Caribbean people lived in overcrowded conditions. This indicates that Caribbean households were less able than White households to afford more spacious accommodation.

As a result, Caribbean people were also more dependent upon rented accommodation. Less than half of Caribbean households owned their accommodation, compared to two-thirds of households from other ethnic groups. Caribbean households were also far more likely than households from other ethnic groups to be renting from Housing Associations or the public sector (local authorities, Scottish Homes or New Towns). Probably because of this, the physical standard of housing occupied by Caribbean people was little worse than that occupied by White people, though other minority ethnic groups were more likely to lack basic amenities such as exclusive use of a WC or bathroom, or central heating. However, further evidence of the relatively low incomes of Caribbean people is provided by the much larger percentage of households in the Caribbean ethnic group than of those from other ethnic groups which did not own a car (though most Caribbean people lived in cities with good public transport).

The Policy Studies Institute's Fourth National Survey of Ethnic Minorities (conducted in 1994/5) contains some direct evidence on the incomes of Caribbean families (Table 5.5). Households headed by

Table 5.5   Weekly Caribbean household income before income tax (per cent of households)

Sex of household head	Age group	<£154	£155–£289	£290–£500	£501+
Male	16–29	37.3	15.7	29.5	17.5
	30–49	16.9	27.8	38.0	17.3
	50–74	47.3	25.5	19.6	7.7
	75+	100.0			
Female	16–29	57.1	20.3	17.8	4.8
	30–49	34.8	29.7	22.6	12.9
	50–74	60.9	20.4	13.2	5.4
	75+	100.0			

Source: Policy Studies Institute Fourth National Survey of Ethnic Minorities.

women, pensioners and young people experienced the lowest weekly incomes, with much higher percentages than for households headed by men or persons aged 30–49 falling into the lowest income category. All households with heads over 50 were likely to have low incomes, and around two-thirds received under £290 per week before tax. In contrast, nearly two-fifths of those with male heads aged 30–49 received a weekly household income of £290 to £500, with about a further sixth of this category and households with male heads aged under 30 receiving more than £500 per week. However, the relatively low incomes of the bulk of households is particularly problematic, because most Caribbean people live within local labour markets with relatively high wage rates (i.e. London and Birmingham) and hence higher paid jobs should be accessible to a relatively large percentage of the population.

Socio-economic background of households

Table 5.6 demonstrates that Caribbean household heads were much less likely than those from other ethnic groups to be from higher status social classes, with the largest deficits being in Social Classes I and II. Though Caribbean household heads were more likely than those from other ethnic groups to be skilled workers, they were also more likely to be semi-skilled or unskilled. A higher percentage of Caribbean heads were also employed in the Armed Forces, but the percentage with a Social Class 'not stated' was also high (most of whom would have never had a job).

Table 5.6　Percentage of household heads by social class, 1991

Social class	White	Other minority ethnic groups	Caribbean
I Professional	6.3	10.2	2.8
II Managerial and technical	29.9	26.2	20.3
III Skilled : non-manual	13.0	14.0	18.5
III Skilled : manual	29.0	23.6	24.8
IV Partly skilled	15.0	18.4	20.3
V Unskilled	4.8	4.4	9.0
Armed forces	0.9	0.4	1.4
Inadequately described	0.5	0.9	0.8
Not stated	0.5	2.0	2.3
Sample size	122,935	4,162	1,332

Source: 1991 Census of Population 1 per cent household Sample of Anonymised Records.

Table 5.7 Economic status of household heads

Economic class	White	Other minority ethnic groups	Caribbean
Employed	53.6	48.8	56.8
Self-employed	11.2	16.1	4.2
Unemployed or on scheme	5.5	14.7	11.7
Economically inactive	29.6	20.4	27.4
Unemployment rate	7.8	18.5	16.1

Source: 1991 Census of Population 1 per cent household Sample of Anonymised Records.

Caribbean household heads were more likely to be employees than those from other ethnic groups (Table 5.7), but less likely to be self-employed. Household heads from minority ethnic groups were more likely than White heads to be unemployed or on government schemes. White household heads were more likely to be economically inactive than those from minority ethnic groups other than Caribbean (as a result of their greater average age), but inactivity rates were also high for Caribbean heads, despite the much lower percentage of people above retirement age than in the White ethnic group. The unemployment rate for minority ethnic group household heads was over twice that for White heads, but slightly lower for Caribbean heads than for heads from other minority groups. This may be because of the higher percentage of female heads in the Caribbean ethnic group, and the lower unemployment rates experienced by women.

Caribbean families were more likely than those from other ethnic groups to be headed by a woman, with 45.5 per cent having female heads, compared with 18.1 per cent of White families and 16.4 per cent of families from other minority ethnic groups. The great majority (85.5 per cent) of female family heads were lone parents and nearly two-thirds (64.1 per cent) of all female family heads were lone parents with dependent children. Overall, 29.3 per cent of people in Caribbean-headed households lived in such families, compared with 8.4 per cent of people in households with heads from other minority ethnic groups and 6.7 per cent of those living in households with White heads.

Type of accommodation

Table 5.8 contrasts the type of accommodation in which White people, Caribbean people and people from other minority ethnic groups lived in 1991. There were clear differences between ethnic groups. Most White people lived in semi-detached or terraced houses, but a fifth

Table 5.8   Types of dwelling by ethnic group of household head, 1991

Dwelling category	White	Other minority ethnic groups	Caribbean
Detached	20.7	9.7	3.6
Semi-detached	30.2	20.5	13.7
Terraced	28.7	40.4	37.3
Flat	19.2	27.3	43.9
'Bedsit'	0.1	0.3	0.2
Rooms	0.5	1.7	1.3
Other non-permanent dwelling	0.4	0.1	0.1
No. of households	206,197	5,785	2,387

Source: 1991 Census of Population 1 per cent household Sample of Anonymised Records.

lived in detached houses, indicative of a higher average level of income. The share of households from minority ethnic groups in detached and semi-detached housing was much smaller. However, while two-fifths of people from other minority ethnic groups lived in terraced housing, 43.9 per cent of Caribbean households lived in flats and more than four-fifths were in either terraced houses or flats. This arises from the concentration of Caribbean people into the public rented sector (within which the type of housing reflects their household structure) and their inability to afford more spacious private sector accommodation. The relatively small percentages of Caribbean (and other minority ethnic group) households living in semi-detached and detached housing also reflects the relatively small percentages of these ethnic groups living in suburban and semi-urban areas.

Family composition of the Caribbean population

The family composition of the Caribbean population differed greatly from the rest of the population in a number of respects in 1991 (Table 5.9). It was more similar to the White population than other minority ethnic groups in that more than a quarter of all households consisted of only one person (though the high percentage for White people was partly a result of a relatively large percentage of pensioners living alone), while the average for other minority groups was only about half as high. Two person households were more common than for White people, but less so than for other minorities. Other minority ethnic groups were much more likely to live in households containing more than one family, and a larger percentage of households with heads from these ethnic groups consisted of families.

Table 5.9 *Family composition of Caribbean households, 1991 (10 per cent sample of all households)*

Family type	White		Other minority ethnic groups		Caribbean	
	Number	Percent	Number	Percent	Number	Percent
Total households	**2,061,033**	**100.0**	**59,160**	**100.0**	**23,935**	**100.0**
Households with no families	615,002	29.8	11,780	19.9	7,662	32.0
Households containing one person	549,060	26.6	8,655	14.6	6,594	27.5
Households containing two or more persons	65,942	3.2	3,125	5.3	1,068	4.5
Households containing one family	1,430,072	69.4	43,820	74.1	15,925	66.5
Households containing 2+ families	15,959	0.8	3,560	6.0	348	1.5
Total families	**1,462,155**	**100.0**	**51,355**	**100.0**	**16,641**	**100.0**
Married couple families	*1,158,145*	*79.2*	*42,699*	*83.1*	*7,762*	*46.6*
Married couple, with 0 dependent children	521,239	35.6	9,156	17.8	2,501	15.0
Married couple, with 1+ dependent children	454,428	31.1	29,774	58.0	3,551	21.3
Married couple, with non-dependent children	182,478	12.5	3,769	7.3	1,710	10.3
Cohabiting couple family	*112,198*	*7.7*	*1,451*	*2.8*	*1,856*	*11.2*
Cohabiting couple, with 0 dependent children	70,929	4.9	892	1.7	887	5.3
Cohabiting couple, with 1+ dependent children	36,642	2.5	523	1.0	886	5.3
Cohabiting couple, with non-dependent children	4,627	0.3	36	0.1	83	0.5
Lone parent family	*191,812*	*13.1*	*7,205*	*14.0*	*7,023*	*42.2*
Lone parent with 1+ dependent children	113,512	7.8	5,430	10.6	5,330	32.0
Lone parent with non-dependent children	78,300	5.4	1,775	3.5	1,693	10.2

Source: OPCS/GRO(Scotland) (1993) Country of Birth and Ethnic Group report.

While married couple families were more common among other minority groups than in the White population, less than half of all families in the Caribbean population contained married couples. Cohabiting couples were much more common than in other ethnic groups, accounting for nearly an eighth of all families. However, the most spectacular difference was for lone-parent families, which were almost as common as married couples in the Caribbean population (a rate four times higher than for other ethnic groups).

In the White ethnic group, less than a third of all families consisted of married couples with dependent children, compared to nearly three-fifths of those from other minority ethnic groups, but only a fifth of Caribbean families. Due to its greater average age, families from the White ethnic group were more likely than those from minority ethnic groups to contain children who were not economically dependent on their parents. Cohabiting families were more likely to have dependent children in the Caribbean than the White ethnic groups. Overall, nearly a third of Caribbean families consisted of a lone parent with dependent children, three times the average for other minority ethnic groups.

Most Caribbean households in which children were present contained between one and three dependent children (Table 5.10). Households with heads aged over 50 were least likely to contain dependent children, and those with dependent children usually only contained one, the main exceptions being for cohabiting (living with partner) and divorced household heads. Amongst people in the main childbearing age range for women (from 16 to 49), household heads in work tended to have fewer dependent children than the unemployed and economically inactive. Cohabiting household heads tended to have fewer children than married heads, as did those aged 16 to 29 with a regular partner who they did not live with. However, people in such 'visiting' relationships aged 30 to 49 had a similar number of children to married households heads of the same age. In the youngest age range, the largest median number of dependent children were in households were the head was separated and economically inactive, and this pattern was repeated for 30- to 49-year-old heads, also including widowed and divorced household heads. Amongst formerly married household heads, those in work had fewer dependent children than those who were not working.

The family 'life cycle'

The concept of the 'family life cycle' expresses the way in which the domestic organisation of individuals evolves over time, from the initial

Table 5.10 Median number of children (aged 0–15) in Caribbean households by status and age of household head

Age, economic status and marital status of household head	Married	Living with partner	Regular partner, not cohabiting	Single	Separated	Divorced	Widowed
Aged 16–29							
In work	2	1	1	1	–	–	–
Unemployed	–	2	2	1	–	–	–
Economically inactive	3	1	1	2	3	1	–
All	2	2	1	1	3	1	–
Aged 30–49							
In work	2	1	2	2	2	1	2
Unemployed	3	2	3	1	3	2	–
Economically inactive	2	2	2	2	2	3	7
All	2	2	2	2	2	1	2
Aged 50–74							
In work	1	3	–	–	–	2	–
Unemployed	1	1	–	–	–	–	–
Economically inactive	1	–	–	1	–	–	1
All	1	2	–	1	–	2	1

Source: Health Education Authority survey of the Health of Black and Minority Ethnic Groups in England, 1994.

Table 5.11 Family life-stages by ethnic group, 1991

Age of family head	Children and ages	Couple or not?	White		Other minority ethnic groups		Caribbean	
			% of type	% of age band	Number	% of age band	Number	% of age band
16–24	none	not	67.9	36.3	75.5	54.5	58.0	47.5
16–24	present	not	32.1	17.2	24.5	17.7	42.0	34.3
16–24	all	not	100.0	53.5	100.0	72.2	100.0	81.8
16–24	none	couple	64.2	29.9	62.9	17.5	63.9	11.6
16–24	present	couple	35.8	16.6	37.1	10.3	36.1	6.6
16–24	all	couple	100.0	46.5	100.0	27.8	100.0	18.2
All aged 16–24				*(4.5)*		*(6.5)*		*(8.3)*
25–34	none	not	63.9	23.3	58.1	28.2	49.3	31.8
25–34	0–4	not	20.4	7.4	29.0	14.1	25.4	16.4
25–34	5–10	not	13.5	4.9	11.4	5.5	20.7	13.3
25–34	10–15	not	2.3	0.9	1.6	0.8	4.6	2.9
25–34	all	not	100.0	36.5	100.0	48.5	100.0	64.5
25–34	none	couple	36.1	23.0	27.8	14.3	34.7	12.3
25–34	0–4	couple	49.3	31.3	60.5	31.1	47.7	16.9
25–34	5–10	couple	13.1	8.3	11.0	5.6	16.2	5.8
25–34	10–15	couple	1.5	0.9	0.7	0.4	1.4	0.5
25–34	all	couple	100.0	63.5	100.0	51.5	100.0	35.5

Table 5.11 Family life-stages by ethnic group, 1991 (continued)

Age of family head	Children and ages	Couple or not?	White		Other minority ethnic groups		Caribbean	
			% of type	% of age band	Number	% of age band	Number	% of age band
All aged 25-34				*(17.4)*		*(26.9)*		*(32.7)*
35-54	none	not	67.4	36.5	44.8	25.1	62.5	45.2
35-54	0-4	not	4.9	2.6	15.6	8.7	11.1	8.0
35-54	5-10	not	9.8	5.3	20.4	11.4	14.8	10.7
35-54	10-15	not	17.9	9.7	19.2	10.8	11.7	8.4
35-54	all	not	100.0	54.2	100.0	56.0	100.0	72.3
35-54	none	couple	40.1	18.4	16.4	7.2	39.5	10.9
35-54	0-4	couple	18.5	8.5	37.7	16.6	27.1	7.5
35-54	5-10	couple	26.4	12.1	34.2	15.0	21.4	5.9
35-54	10-15	couple	15.0	6.9	11.7	5.1	11.9	3.3
35-54	all	couple	100.0	45.8	100.0	44.0	100.0	27.7
All aged 35-54				*(34.6)*		*(48.0)*		*(31.8)*
Aged 55 to pensionable age				*(13.3)*		*(12.0)*		*(15.7)*
Pensionable age				*(30.2)*		*(6.5)*		*(11.5)*

Source: 1991 Census of Population 1 per cent household Sample of Anonymised Records.
Note: Figures in brackets are percentages of all households; other percentages are of the age group.

formation of households by young people after leaving the parental home through the raising of children by younger adults, the ageing of children in families and then the withdrawal of family heads from economic activity as they near retirement and their children leave home. Clearly, since minority ethnic groups are relatively youthful, a smaller percentage of their populations than of the White population will have progressed through all the stages of family formation. Table 5.11 presents the characteristics of families in the age range 16 to 55, the age range within which most families are formed and completed. Only 56.5 per cent of White family heads fell within this age range, compared with 72.8 per cent of Caribbean family heads and 81.4 per cent of those from other minority ethnic groups (of which nearly half were aged 35 to 54). The percentage of heads aged under 35 was higher in the Caribbean than in other ethnic groups, but family heads in later middle age were also more common in the Caribbean ethnic group than for other ethnic groups. Pensioner family heads were much less common in the minority ethnic groups than for White people, but 11.5 per cent of Caribbean family heads were above retirement age in 1991.

Throughout the age range, family heads from Caribbean ethnic groups were less likely than those from other ethnic groups to be in a 'couple'. The main exception to this rule was that a greater percentage of 16 to 24 year old family heads from other minority ethnic groups were single, without children. Amongst people not in couples, Caribbean family heads were also more likely to have children than people from other ethnic groups, regardless of age. Over a third of Caribbean family heads aged 16 to 24 were not in couples, but had dependent children, though only a third of those in couples had dependent children, a similar percentage to other ethnic groups. In the 25 to 34 age range, two-thirds of Caribbean family heads were not in couples, half of whom had dependent children. Among 35 to 54 year olds, nearly three-quarters of Caribbean family heads were not in couples, but like White people, most of these were childless.

White people in couples were more likely than other ethnic groups to be childless, across the age range. In the 25 to 34 age group, Caribbean people with children tended to have more older children living with them than was the case for other ethnic groups, indicating that many Caribbean people had children at a relatively early age. A higher percentage of 35- to 54-year-old family heads had young dependent children than White heads, indicating that family completion occurred later, but not as late as in other minority ethnic groups. In the 35 to 54 year age group, Caribbean people were more likely than people from other minority ethnic groups to be childless, and not in couples.

Partnerships

A highly distinctive feature of the Caribbean population is the high percentage of unmarried adults. Table 5.12 demonstrates that more than half of men and women in 1991 were single, a far larger share than in other ethnic groups. Moreover, a higher percentage of the population was divorced than in other ethnic groups.

The percentages married and single were similar for both men and women across all age groups, with the exception that nearly three-fifths of men aged 50 to 74 were married, compared with just over half of women (Table 5.13). After the age of 30, women were more likely than men to be divorced or widowed, while men were more likely to have remarried.

Given that older Caribbean people are predominantly migrants, while younger people were mainly born in the UK, differences in marital status by age might therefore reflect the influence of an upbringing in countries with contrasting social norms. In order to identify such systematic differences, the cross classification of marital status by age and sex was repeated for people born in and outside the Caribbean (the latter mainly UK-born). A clear tendency for Caribbean-born people to be more likely to be married than the non-Caribbean born is revealed for both men and women, across the age range. The largest differences occur in the youngest age group. Nearly a third of women and a quarter of men aged 16 to 29 born in the Caribbean were married, but only about a tenth of non-Caribbean born young people were married. Overall, two-thirds of Caribbean-born people were single, compared with seven-eighths of the non-Caribbean born in this age group. Caribbean-born people were more likely than those born elsewhere to be divorced, especially in the younger age range, but slightly less likely to have remarried. However, the identification of contrasts between the Caribbean-born and the non-Caribbean born is made more difficult by the small numbers of non-Caribbean-born older people and of Caribbean-born young people.

Table 5.12   Marital status of people aged 16 and over

	White		Caribbean		Other minorities	
	Male	**Female**	**Male**	**Female**	**Male**	**Female**
single	29.5	22.6	50.2	52.6	33.2	27.0
married	61.0	56.1	40.1	33.7	63.3	63.6
widowed	3.9	14.5	1.8	3.8	1.1	5.8
divorced	5.5	6.8	7.9	9.9	2.4	3.7

Source: 1991 Census of Population (Crown Copyright).

Table 5.13   Marital status of Caribbean people by age, sex and country of birth

	Men				Women			
	16–29	30–49	50–74	All	16–29	30–49	50–74	All
All Caribbean people								
Single	88.6	38.9	12.3	52.2	87.2	39.2	12.1	53.3
Married	9.7	47.4	58.9	34.8	11.3	42.2	50.4	31.0
Remarried	0.4	5.0	11.5	4.9	0.2	4.2	5.1	2.8
Divorced	1.2	8.0	13.1	6.6	1.3	12.8	22.9	10.2
Widowed	0.0	0.8	4.2	1.4	0.1	1.5	9.5	2.7
Born outside Caribbean								
Single	89.5	50.4	15.9	77.8	88.5	47.1	13.8	76.3
Married	9.1	37.5	51.3	17.1	10.1	37.3	46.8	17.6
Remarried	0.3	5.7	12.4	2.0	0.2	5.3	6.4	1.6
Divorced	1.0	6.1	15.9	2.8	1.2	9.7	20.2	3.8
Widowed	0.0	0.2	4.4	0.2	0.1	0.7	12.8	0.7
Born in Caribbean								
Single	66.2	31.0	11.9	21.1	65.0	35.1	11.9	26.2
Married	25.7	54.1	59.6	56.3	31.6	44.8	50.8	46.9
Remarried	1.4	4.6	11.4	8.5	0.9	3.7	5.0	4.1
Divorced	5.4	9.3	12.8	11.2	2.6	14.4	23.2	17.8
Widowed	0.0	1.2	4.2	2.9	0.0	1.9	9.2	5.1

Source: 1991 Census of Population, 1 per cent Sample of Anonymised Records (Crown Copyright).

Therefore, the overall averages for the two sections of the population simply emphasise the youth of the non-Caribbean-born and the relative age of the Caribbean-born.

The age contrast in partnership status is reinforced by Figure 5.5, which contrasts the partnerships of people in three broad age groups by social class (using data from the *Health Education Authority Survey of Black and Minority Ethnic Group Health for England*, 1994). The percentage of household heads married rose and the percentage single declined with increasing age, but there was also a tendency for marriage rates to be particularly low for people with semi- skilled and unskilled jobs. Moreover, cohabitation was most common among young people and in social classes associated with low status occupations. This diagram reveals that marriage rates did not increase in the oldest age group, in which the unmarried were more likely to be widowed or divorced than single.

The Family and Working Lives Survey provides a longitudinal perspective on a sample of people aged between 16 and 70 interviewed in 1994/5. This was used to produce Figure 5.6, which shows how the partnership composition of the British-born Caribbean population has changed over time. This population is predominantly youthful, and hence the percentage single remained high throughout the period 1974–1993. There was a gradual increase in the percentage married as the population aged, but the percentage cohabiting was almost as large, though declining slightly during the 1990s.

Inter-ethnic group partnerships

Caribbean people display a higher rate of inter-ethnic group partnership than people from other ethnic groups. This has been demonstrated by analyses of both Labour Force Survey (Berrington, 1994) and Census data (Berrington, 1996). The 1991 Census showed that Caribbean people were also less likely than people from other ethnic groups to live in a household headed by a person from the same ethnic group. While 99.1 per cent of White people and 86.8 per cent of people from other minority ethnic groups lived in households whose head was from the same ethnic group, only 70.5 per cent of Caribbean people lived in such households. More than a quarter of Caribbean people lived in households with White heads. Children from the Caribbean ethnic group were slightly more likely to live with Caribbean parents; 75.8 per cent lived in households with Caribbean heads, 19.3 per cent in households with White heads and 4.9 per cent in households with heads from other minority ethnic groups.

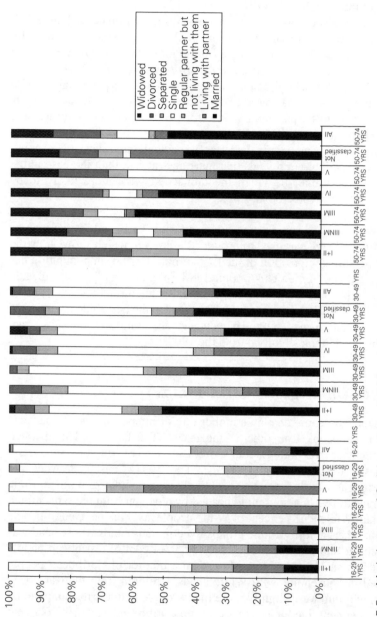

Figure 5.5 Marital status of Caribbean household heads by age and social class
Source: Health Education Authority, Survey of Black and Minority Ethnic Health (1994).

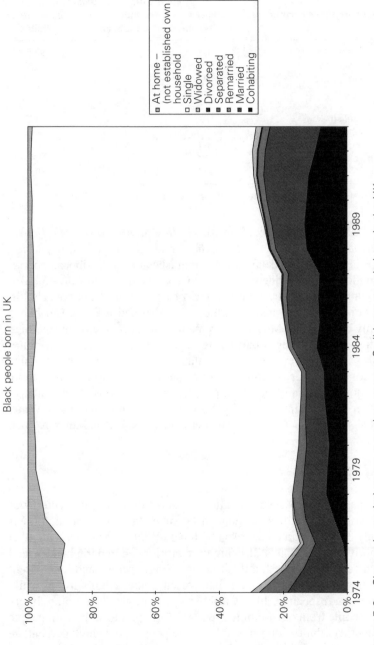

Black people born in UK

Figure 5.6   Change in marital status over time among Caribbean people born in the UK
Source: Family and Working Lives Survey (Unpublished).

Table 5.14   Partnerships of Caribbean people

| Family origins of partner | Family origins of person | | |
	Black Caribbean	Indian Caribbean	Mixed other eligible
Black Caribbean	74.5	7.6	32.5
Indian Caribbean	0.2	38.1	
Pakistani	0.5		
Indian	0.5	7.9	
Irish	1.1	2.9	
White British	19.6	34.1	54.5
Somewhere else	0.7	4.4	
Other European origins	0.8	4.9	6.3
Mixed other eligible	2.1		6.8
	100.0	100.0	100.0

Source: Policy Studies Institute Fourth National Survey of Ethnic Minorities.

Table 5.14 (derived from the *Policy Studies Institute's Fourth National Survey of Ethnic Minorities*) breaks down Caribbean partnerships in a little more detail, and distinguishes Indian-Caribbean people. It confirms earlier evidence from the Census and *Labour Force Survey*, showing that in about three-quarters of Black-Caribbean households, the household head had a partner who also had a Black-Caribbean family background. Most of the remainder had a White British partner, with small percentages partnering people of 'mixed' ethnic origin or Irish people. A very small percentage had a partner from an Asian ethnic group. Cross-ethnic group partnerships were even more common for Indian-Caribbean people, only two-fifths of whom had a partner with a similar family background, a third having a White British person as a partner. A smaller percentage had an Indian partner.

Conclusion

This paper has provided a summary of some of the key characteristics of Caribbean families resident in Great Britain. This population is highly distinctive in comparison both with White people and with other minority ethnic groups. It is highly concentrated geographically, and has a very distinctive family structure. Single people and lone parent families are more prominent than for any other ethnic group, while Caribbean (especially Indo-Caribbean people) people are more likely than people from other ethnic groups to form partnerships with people from other ethnic groups (mainly White people). The high percentage of single and cohabiting people is more typical of the British-born generation than the migrant generation, though non-traditional family forms are more significant for older Caribbean people than for people of around the same age from other ethnic groups. Caribbean families tend to be small, but a high percentage are headed by a lone parent, and many children live with a widowed or separated parent.

Caribbean people remain economically disadvantaged, suffering high unemployment rates despite having a strong degree of commitment to the labour market. Caribbean workers are more likely than other ethnic groups to be employed in lower status white-collar jobs, or semi- and un-skilled manual occupations. As a consequence, a relatively high percentage of Caribbean households have low incomes, which is a particular problem for people in later middle age and female family heads. Larger families and partnerships not involving marriage are more common among the more economically disadvantaged households.

6 Demographic characteristics of families and living arrangements in the Commonwealth Caribbean

Godfrey St Bernard

Introduction

In the Commonwealth Caribbean, the family is a social institution that assumes an elusive character. This is primarily due to individuals' myriad interpretations of structures and inherent social relations that characterise the family. To be more specific, the concept of the family is predicated upon individuals' conception of kinship, the bounds of which may vary when interpreted by different individuals. For the purposes of censuses and surveys that capture data relevant to the family, the household has often constituted a basic unit of analysis. As a consequence, many of the pronouncements about the family have been based upon assessments of consanguineal and affinal relationships within household contexts.

A household is defined in terms of the collective functions of individuals within dwelling units. While it is defined according to physical space and the collective functions of individuals, a family is primarily defined in terms of kinship status (consanguineal or affinal) which determines whether or not the individuals within a household constitute a family household or non-family household. In some cases, reference has been made to multi-family households in which two or more distinct family units coexist in a household setting. By collecting data at the level of the household, it is possible to capture structural arrangements deemed characteristic of the different typologies defining Caribbean families and households. As such, the data will have great utility in facilitating assessments of social conditions and social opportunities that might be associated with differences in living arrangements across household settings.

This chapter addresses these concerns from the standpoint of the Commonwealth Caribbean. It uses, as much as possible, data emanating from the most recent round of censuses in the 1990s. Where possible, evidence will also be drawn from a wide range of secondary sources including country specific monographs.[1] In essence, the chapter examines the demographic characteristics of living arrangements within households in Commonwealth Caribbean countries. In addition, it throws light upon implications for social policy formulation and prospective implementation, and examines variations in characteristics such as headship status, household size, age composition of households, socio-economic well being and living standards. The paper also enables one to discern whether regular patterns persist across the countries of the region.

The focus of past research into families in the Caribbean

Since the 1940s, the Caribbean family has been a social institution targeted for investigation by foreign scholars and administrators. The resultant inquiries were instrumental in stimulating scholarly research efforts that had not only refined thinking about social relations and the value systems of Caribbean families, but also paved the way for expanding knowledge of the dynamics associated with such processes, and raised additional questions for which answers had to be sought. In the context of the Commonwealth Caribbean, the literature reflects variations in living arrangements and social relations across social groups defined by socio-economic status and ethnic origin. In most instances, the target populations were primarily of African or East Indian origin, and subjected to investigative processes deemed to be biased in favour of middle-class ethnocentric principles regarding social standards that were manifest in the structures, relations, value systems within families and their implications for societal well being. As such, it was not surprising that lower class sub-populations were the primary targets of such efforts, many of which were perceived to be misrepresentations of life experiences among families in the lower social strata of Caribbean societies. Over the past four decades, however, there have been efforts by scholars attempting to redress this situation.

In order to foster a greater understanding of the family as an institution, the principal contributions focused primarily upon a few countries, namely Jamaica (Henriques, 1953; Clarke, 1957 and Smith, 1962), Guyana (RT Smith, 1956; RT Smith and Jayawardena, 1959 and Jayawardena, 1962), Trinidad and Tobago (Schwartz, 1964; Rodman, 1971; Agrosino, 1978; Nevadomsky, 1982; and Sharma, 1986) and

Grenada (Smith, 1962). For instance, Smith (1962) examined intersections between place of residence and social class and thus, the impact of their interaction upon variations in family structures and value systems among the working class of Grenada and Jamaica. Henriques (1953) dealt with the linkages between skin colour and different aspects of family structure and style of life across social class settings in Jamaica. He reinforced the notion of colour as a principal determinant of social class and thus, the 'white bias' as a yardstick for determining membership in the upper reaches of the social ladder.[2]

The populations of Caribbean countries are also differentiated on the basis of ethnic origin. Most of the Anglophone countries have had overwhelmingly large populations of African origin,[3] the exceptions being Guyana, Trinidad and Tobago which have had East Indian populations that have either been equal to or outnumbering populations of African origin, and thus substantially larger in number when compared to East Indian populations in other countries in the sub-region. In examining living arrangements in the Commonwealth Caribbean, ethnic origin has traditionally been a critical variable in scholars' attempt to explain structural arrangements, social relations and value systems. While Clarke (1957), Smith (1956), Smith (1962) and Rodman (1971) made pronouncements about living arrangements in predominantly Afro-Caribbean communities, the works of Niehoff (1959), Smith and Jayawardena (1959), Jayawardena (1962), Schwartz (1964), Agrosino (1976), Nevadomsky (1980 and 1982) and Sharma (1986) provided valuable insights pertaining to the salient characteristics of living arrangements in Indo-Caribbean communities, primarily in Guyana and Trinidad and Tobago. Collectively, these contributions reinforce the multi-ethnic character of the region's population.

The literature advances the view that there is a matrifocal character of lower class Afro-Caribbean families, even in cases where male household headship is evident. While male members are often present, father figures are absent in a number of instances and extra-residential unions are pivotal in order to facilitate the sustenance and well being of respective family members. Despite the predominance of legal marriage, the evidence suggests that in the case of Non-Indians (Africans in particular), the prevalence of common-law unions was indicative of orientations that were linked to socio-economic status. Among lower class women of African origin, the evidence is also indicative of other characteristic features such as a greater responsibility for children, marital shifting and child shifting. These features are consistent with their reliance upon adaptive processes as means toward sustaining their family units and could be functions of male marginality that is linked to poverty in such settings.

With respect to East Indian families, there is sufficient evidence supporting the retention of some elements of traditional structures and value systems, for example, marriage as a primary medium for initiating a first union and the prevalence of patriarchal systems of authority across sub-institutional settings. Whether in terms of marriage or their orientations toward marriage, recent studies support the persistence of racial endogamy among East Indians (St Bernard, 1994 and 1997a). Nevertheless, there is some recognition that changes have been taking place due to social forces akin to creolisation. Such changes include a greater orientation toward marriage based upon free choice as opposed to being arranged, the occurrence of marriage at older ages and an increasing proclivity to common-law and visiting unions. Among younger generations of East Indians, nuclear family units have been becoming increasingly prevalent, although there is another school of thought suggesting that this phenomenon is unfolding with the persistence of the 'domestic group'[4] which ensures the well being of the family. There has also been evidence suggesting that younger generations of East Indians have been having lower levels of fertility and been relying more frequently upon fertility control (Abdulah, 1991 and Nevadomsky, 1982).

From a socio-demographic standpoint, a number of relevant studies were undertaken during the 1960s, 1970s and 1980s. The researchers were primarily sociologists and demographers who drew their conclusions from survey and census data. Inasmuch as the characteristic features of living arrangements including family size are determined by fertility and social roles performed by various family members, historical patterns regarding women's conjugal status also constitute an important explanatory variable. Several studies have attempted to provide a better understanding of mating behaviour (conjugal patterns) in Caribbean countries. Most have focused upon Non-Indian populations and in particular, lower class African populations in different Caribbean countries (Roberts and Braithwaite, 1967; Ebanks, George and Nobbe, 1974b; Roberts and Sinclair, 1978; Lightbourne and Singh, 982; and Harewood, 1984).

With regard to African and Creole women, Roberts and Braithwaite (1967) show that considerable numbers would have commenced childbearing while in visiting unions. They also support the view that women may have lower fertility as a result of being in a first union that assumed the form of a visiting relationship or because they remained in visiting as opposed to other kinds of conjugal unions throughout their childbearing lives. They found lower levels of fertility among women who spent most of their childbearing lives in common-law unions as opposed to marrying subsequent to being in a common-law union. For women who commenced childbearing in a union, the highest levels of fertility had been evident among those who commenced in marriage and lowest among those who commenced in visiting unions. Despite the relatively long period of time found to elapse between entry into visiting unions and the onset of a first birth while still in such unions, women were generally found to commence childbearing at younger ages than their counterparts who commenced childbearing in common-law and married relationships. Roberts and Sinclair (1978) made reference to the social and biomedical characteristics associated with high fertility among women. These included low educational status and the commencement of childbearing in common-law or visiting unions. For mothers who were in visiting unions, Roberts and Sinclair claimed that economic forces were the primary factors influencing their resort to child shifting. The principal factors were identified as mothers' participation in work and a lack of financial support from children's fathers.

Ebanks et al. (1974) found that instability of partnerships and by extension, unions, increased rather than inhibited fertility and suggested that Caribbean countries could decrease levels of fertility by embracing practices that stabilise unions. They based their findings on some important facts about social behaviour within lower class Caribbean societies, namely, the prominence of visiting unions as a first union type among women exposed to the risk of early childbearing, the relatively higher likelihood of dissolution of visiting relationships due to a pregnancy and the prospect of partnership changes without any reductions in the period of exposure to the risk of pregnancy between partnerships. Lightbourne and Singh (1982) also support a positive association between the number of partnerships and fertility. However, they allude to the number of partnership dissolutions as a more appropriate indicator of instability of partnerships and conclude that a greater number of such dissolutions is associated with higher fertility levels, providing that exposure to the risk of pregnancy is held constant. Lightbourne and Singh also examined the association between current union status and fertility across time and suggested that by the 1970s, contraceptive behaviour was a real factor altering exposure to the risk of pregnancy and permitting women to limit childbearing to a desired number.

Harewood (1984) provides further support for the notion of a visiting union as a fertility depressant and a common-law union as a fertility stimulant. He also reveals some interesting departures from traditional processes that have characterised the formation of first unions among women of all ethnic groups. For instance, young women from other ethnic groups were found to have been initiating first unions earlier than their Indian counterparts. This was evident in Guyana and in Trinidad and Tobago and contrary to patterns that have been traditionally observed among older cohorts of women. Harewood also indicates that there have been increases in the incidence of initial unions assuming the form of visiting relationships. However, in cases where younger cohorts of Indian women have formed such unions, a very short period elapsed before the onset of legal marriage, and in most cases to the same partner.

Contemporary living arrangements in the Caribbean

Generally speaking, variations in the stock of households in different Caribbean countries are consistent with variations in their respective population sizes (see Table 6.1 and Table 6.2). For the period between 1980 and the 1990s, there have been increases in household stock in almost every Commonwealth Caribbean country (see Table 6.2). While, however, there have been general increases, changes have occurred at differential rates across the countries. For instance, an increase of 62.2% was registered in the British Virgin Islands (BVI). Several countries experienced changes between 20% and 40% – the Bahamas, Barbados, Belize, St Lucia and St Vincent and the Grenadines. For Trinidad and Tobago and Dominica, the changes were

Table 6.1   Census population by sex, 1990/1991 – selected countries

Country	Population	Male	Female
Antigua and Barbuda	60,840	29,638	31,202
Bahamas	255,049	124,958	130,091
Barbados	260,491	124,571	135,920
Belize[1]	189,392	96,325	93,067
BVI[1]	16,116	8,263	7,853
Dominica[1]	71,183	35,471	35,712
Grenada[1]	95,597	47,030	48,567
Guyana[1]	723,673	356,540	367,133
Jamaica[P]	2,366,067	...	...
Montserrat[1]	10,639	5,290	5,349
St Lucia[1]	135,685	65,988	69,697
St Kitts and Nevis[1]	40,618	19,933	20,685
St Vincent & the			
Grenadines[1]	106,499	53,165	53,244
Trinidad and Tobago	1,213,733	606,388	607,346

[1]Census conducted in 1991. In the Bahamas, Barbados and Trinidad and Tobago, the Census was conducted in 1990.
For Jamaica, the figures for 1990 are provisional.

Table 6.2   Stock of households – selected countries

Country	1980/81	1990/91	Percentage change
Antigua and Barbuda[4]	...	18,476	...
Bahamas[2]	48,233	66,962	38.8
Barbados[2]	67,138	82,204	22.4
Belize[3]	27,298	37,944	39.0
BVI[3]	3,287	5,332	62.2
Dominica[1]	17,310	19,371	11.9
Grenada[1]	21,017	21,974	4.6
Guyana[3]	149,734	150,575	0.0
Jamaica[5]	517,297	588,710	13.8
Montserrat[3]	3,708	3,855	4.0
St Lucia[3]	24,733	33,079	34.1
St Kitts and Nevis[3]	11,615	12,056	3.8
St Vincent & the Grenadines[3]	20,290	27,002	33.1
Trinidad and Tobago[2]	234,727	274,846	17.1

[1]Census conducted in 1981 and 1991.
[2]Census conducted in 1980 and 1990.
[3]Census conducted in 1980 and 1991.
[4]1980 Census round was not conducted. However, 1990/91 data relate to a census conducted in 1991.
[5]Census conducted in 1982 and data are provisional for 1990/91.

relatively lower, being 17.1% and 11.9% respectively. For Grenada, Montserrat and St Kitts and Nevis, the changes were less than 5% being 4.6%, 4% and 3.8% respectively. There was virtually no change in Guyana over the intercensal period. Over the same period, each of these countries had experienced a decline in mean household size (see Table 6.3).

Based on the data from the last round of censuses in the first part of the 1990s, there is support for the prominence of the nuclear family as the primary living arrangement among households in three Caribbean countries. In the context of Trinidad and Tobago, Hewitt (1996) permits one to surmise that as much as 58.7% of all households assumed the form of nuclear family units. In the case of the Bahamas, Gomez et al. (1996) show that nuclear family units accounted for almost half (49.6%) of that nation's households while in the British Virgin Islands, it can be deduced that about 46% of all households assumed the form of nuclear family units (Phillips, 1996). Given the traditional role associated with family networks in Caribbean societies, the prominence of nuclear families might be indicative of spouses and single parents preference for independent living within their families of procreation. This might also be a plausible explanation in cases where

Table 6.3   Average household size – selected countries

Country	1980/81	1990/1991
Bahamas[2]	4.3	3.8
Barbados[2]	3.6	3.3
Belize[3]	5.3	5.0
BVI[3]	3.3	3.0
Dominica[1]	4.2	3.6
Grenada[1]	4.2	3.9
Guyana[3]	5.1	4.7
Jamaica[5]	...	...
Montserrat[3]	3.1	2.8
St Lucia[3]	4.6	4.0
St Kitts and Nevis[3]	3.7	3.4
St Vincent & the Grenadines[3]	4.8	3.9
Trinidad and Tobago[2]	4.2	4.1

[1]Census conducted in 1981 and 1991.
[2]Census conducted in 1980 and 1990.
[3]Census conducted in 1980 and 1991.
[4]1980 Census round was not conducted. However, 1990/91 data relate to a census conducted in 1991.
[5]Census conducted in 1982 and data are provisional for 1990/91.

family heads preserve their physical space within households and dwelling units despite lacking the economic and social mechanisms to maintain a satisfactory livelihood. It is also possible that they may often rely upon other relatives and close acquaintances for assistance, whether financial or in kind. Across the countries of the Commonwealth Caribbean, differences in the structure of family units are likely to range from being subtle to substantial and could be predicated upon country specific differences in the distribution of social and demographic attributes such as ethnicity, socio-economic status and individuals' age.

Whether in the Bahamas, the BVI or Trinidad and Tobago, the available evidence suggest that about one quarter of all households contain extended family units. The extended family is often viewed as an adaptive mechanism that enables family heads and members to resist social and economic challenges that could jeopardise individual and group well being. It hinges upon the development of social bonds that, in many cases, imply reciprocity and a system of exchange between social favours and social sacrifices on one hand, and economic gain on the other. Based upon earlier discussions, the extended family is more likely to be a characteristic feature of lower middle class and lower class households than households belonging to higher social strata. This is also likely to be true for domestic groups in which members thrive in conditions of poverty or face the threat of a livelihood in such conditions. According to the World Bank (1996), estimates for the early 1990s showed that 21% of the population of Trinidad and Tobago lived below the poverty line as opposed to 5% in the Bahamas. While poverty and the threat of it might provide some explanation for the persistence of extended families in Trinidad and Tobago, the relatively low prevalence of poverty observed in the Bahamas is indicative of two possible scenarios. The first is that social forces unrelated to poverty could be largely responsible for the prevalence of the extended family in Bahamian households. The second is that extended family units might be instrumental in reducing the proportion of the population living below the poverty line and by extension, the prevalence of poverty in the Bahamas. If the prevalence of extended family structures among Barbadian households is comparable with that of the Bahamas, then the Barbadian situation could be interpreted in much the same manner since 8% of the Barbadian population had been estimated to be living below the poverty line.

At best, the census data permitted poor coverage of the characteristics of households with single parent families in the form of an adult and his/her dependent children. In the case of the BVIs, Phillips (1996) indicated that 10.2% of the households assumed the form of single parent families while Hewitt (1996) permitted one to deduce that the corresponding proportion was about 11.3% in Trinidad and Tobago. In the case of the Bahamas, Gomez et al. (1996) may have included this proportion within the category they referred to as nuclear family households. While it is believed that single mother families constitute the majority of single parent families, no further pronouncements about living arrangements in such families can be made since none of the studies differentiates between the sex of the parents. Nonetheless, an attempt will be made to address such concerns in the next section which focuses upon the findings of a sample survey conducted in Trinidad and Tobago during 1994.

The 1990/1991 Census data show substantial variation in the concentration of single person households across the countries of the Commonwealth Caribbean (See Table 6.4). In countries such as Antigua and Barbuda, Barbados, the BVI, Dominica, Grenada and St Vincent and the Grenadines, more than one fifth of all households consisted of persons living alone. Higher proportions were observed for Montserrat and St Kitts and Nevis (34.1% and 30.3% respectively). In St Lucia and the Bahamas, the respective proportions were 17.7% and 18.7% while the lowest proportions were observed in Belize, Trinidad and Tobago and Guyana (11%, 13.3% and 8% respectively).

Table 6.4 Concentration of single person households – selected countries

Country	1980/81	1990/91
Antigua and Barbuda[4]	...	28.6
Bahamas[2]	16.5	18.7
Barbados[2]	22.0	21.8
Belize[3]	13.7	11.0
BVI[3]	26.1	25.5
Dominica[1]	20.1	24.6
Grenada[1]	20.0	22.7
Guyana[3]	9.5	8.0
Jamaica[5]	...	...
Montserrat[3]	29.4	34.1
St Lucia[3]	16.6	17.7
St Kitts and Nevis[3]	27.6	30.3
St Vincent & the Grenadines[3]	15.6	22.0
Trinidad and Tobago[2]	12.7	13.3

[1]Census conducted in 1981 and 1991.
[2]Census conducted in 1980 and 1990.
[3]Census conducted in 1980 and 1991.
[4]1980 Census round was not conducted. However, 1990/91 data relate to a census conducted in 1991.
[5]Census conducted in 1982 and data are provisional for 1990/91.

Among the youth, the principal motivation for living alone could have been the need to obtain independence and freedom. Such a status is usually attained upon leaving their families of orientation or upon the dissolution of childless partnerships. In contrast, the 'empty nest syndrome' and/or the death of a spouse could have been primarily responsible for elderly persons living alone.

Among persons living alone, these two sub-populations are of significance since they have been among the most vulnerable to have relatively greater risks of exposure to poverty. In the case of the youth, an important consideration will not only be to determine the proportion that live alone and have jobs, but also the fraction of the latter who might be exposed to the following: minimal financial rewards, poor conditions of work, and definite prospects of termination within the short to medium term. While some elderly folk may have made provisions for financial security that should cover them comfortably for the remainder of their lives, it will be important to determine the extent to which the elderly who live alone depend upon fixed incomes, for example, pensions and transfers which, in many cases, place constraints upon their spending power in externally propelled Caribbean economies. Moreover, the elderly have higher risks of exposure to chronic degenerative diseases that are not only costly to treat but more important, may require them to cease living alone.

For the 1990/1991 period, Table 6.5 shows the concentration of single person households with youths living alone. In each country, a relatively greater number of these youths were male, this being especially apparent in St Vincent and the Grenadines where as much as 12.6% of the single person households were occupied by youths (males occupying 10.8% and females, the remaining 1.8%). Similar patterns were evident in Belize and Dominica where as much as 12.3% and 10.7% of single person households were occupied by youths. In Barbados, on the other hand, 2.9% of single person households consisted of youths living alone. This could be due to the fact that Barbados has relatively fewer youths in its population when compared to the other Commonwealth Caribbean countries. From the standpoint of youths living alone, these findings suggest that their living conditions should be monitored in relation to their educational and training credentials, their capacity to remain gainfully employed in the labour force, and changes in their conjugal status; this being especially important in countries such as St Vincent and the Grenadines, Belize, Dominica, Guyana and St Lucia. In difficult times, these youths may rely upon assistance from their parents, siblings or other relatives, thus placing additional burdens upon family

Table 6.5   Concentration of single person households with youths, 1990/1991 – selected countries

Country	Both sexes	Male	Female
Antigua and Barbuda[1]	7.1	5.3	1.8
Bahamas	8.3	5.9	2.4
Barbados	2.9	1.9	1.0
Belize[1]	12.3	9.9	2.4
BVI[1]	8.2	5.6	2.6
Dominica[1]	10.7	8.8	1.9
Grenada[1]	6.8	6.1	0.7
Guyana[1]	9.4	6.7	2.6
Jamaica[P]	...	...	...
Montserrat[1]	7.1	5.3	1.8
St Lucia[1]	9.6	7.4	2.1
St Kitts and Nevis[1]	8.3	6.85	1.6
St Vincent & the Grenadines[1]	12.6	10.8	1.8
Trinidad and Tobago	5.5	4.3	1.1

[1]Census conducted in 1991. In the Bahamas, Barbados and Trinidad and Tobago, the census was conducted in 1990.
For Jamaica, the figures for 1990 are provisional.

entities, which could already be strained given the prevalence of poverty[5] in these countries.

Greater proportions of single person households were occupied by an elderly person aged 65 and over than by a youth (See Table 6.6). With the exception of Belize, the BVI and St Kitts and Nevis, there was a relatively greater number of females among elderly persons who lived alone. Table 6.6 also shows that concentrations of elderly persons in single person households were greatest in Barbados (40.4%), Montserrat (36.8%), St Kitts and Nevis (32.7%), Trinidad and Tobago (31.1%) and Grenada (31%), and lowest in the Bahamas (18.5%) and in the BVI (15%). These proportions were consistent with the concentrations[6] of elderly persons in the respective populations. With regard to the elderly living alone, the aforementioned concerns, for example, social security and health care provisions, will be of paramount importance if these trends persist especially in Barbados, Montserrat and St Kitts and Nevis. In addition, they should be entertained in most of the other countries of the Commonwealth Caribbean since the relative sizes of their elderly populations are also likely to increase and spawn relative growth in the proportion of single person households consisting of elderly citizens.

The determination of household and family headship is a contentious issue in family sociology. In some quarters, there is a general

Table 6.6   ***Concentration of single person households with elderly persons, 1990/1991 – selected countries***

Country	Both Sexes	Male	Female
Antigua and Barbuda[1]	27.3	12.9	14.4
Bahamas	18.5	7.5	11.0
Barbados	40.4	16.9	23.5
Belize[1]	29.5	15.9	13.6
BVI[1]	15.0	9.1	5.9
Dominica[1]	27.9	13.3	14.6
Grenada[1]	31.0	14.1	16.9
Guyana[1]	24.9	11.9	13.0
Jamaica[p]	...	...	...
Montserrat[1]	36.8	16.1	20.6
St Lucia[1]	29.4	13.4	16.0
St Kitts and Nevis[1]	32.7	16.7	16.0
St Vincent & the Grenadines[1]	21.4	10.5	10.9
Trinidad and Tobago	31.1	14.8	16.3

[1]Census conducted in 1991. In the Bahamas, Barbados and Trinidad and Tobago, the census was conducted in 1990.
For Jamaica, the figures for 1990 are provisional.

feeling that the concept should be eschewed given its elusive character and susceptibility to a wide variety of interpretations. Conventionally, households have been characterised as either male headed or female headed with consistently higher proportions being found to have male heads. Given gender differentials in labour force characteristics and the fact that the majority of households assume nuclear family formats predicated upon husband-wife or common-law partner associations, a reliance upon the significance of members' economic contributions to a household would render the prominence of male headship as a plausible outcome. Nonetheless, Massiah (1991) recognised the importance of other criteria – the management of household affairs, primary decision making, differentials in the display of household power and authority, and members' contributions toward maintaining emotional stability within household units, considering them to be components in determining headship status. She also made reference to the idea of 'female supported' or 'female maintained' households, a concept which hinged upon the recognition of different sources of household support. For instance, she noted that household support can be seen not only in terms of ownership of a dwelling unit which becomes the family home but also in terms of members' earnings which contribute toward the well being of the household.

These conceptual issues are important insofar as they bring into focus the idea of a 'jointly headed' household. They reinforce the prevalence of more egalitarian arrangements that may in fact be more characteristic of contemporary Caribbean society. Nevertheless, traditional conceptions have been used to assess headship status among households in a wide cross-section of Caribbean countries. They have revealed that between one fifth and a half of all households were headed by females; a situation that has persisted from 1970 to as recent as the early 1990s (Table 6.7). The available evidence is also indicative of substantially higher levels of female headship in countries such as Antigua and Barbuda, the Bahamas, Barbados, Dominica, Grenada, Montserrat, St Kitts and Nevis, St Lucia and St Vincent and the Grenadines (in excess of 35%) when compared to other countries such as Belize, the BVI, Guyana and Trinidad and Tobago (between 20% and 30%). For the two groups of countries, these results could be indicative of noteworthy differences in the structure of living arrangements within households. In this regard, Massiah made reference to some interesting associations between headship status predicated upon gender and the structure of families within households.

Based upon data from the 1980 census, Table 6.8 shows that nuclear families were generally more prevalent than extended families irrespective of whether men or women were the heads of such house-

Table 6.7   Female headed households, 1970, 1980 and 1990/91

Country	% Female Headed Households		
	1970	1980/81	1990/91
Antigua and Barbuda[4]	...	41.5	
Bahamas[2]	...	...	35.8
Barbados[2]	42.9	43.9	48.3
Belize[3]	24.8	22.4	21.9
BVI[3]	24.3	25.4	28.7
Caymans	35.5	...	...
Dominica[1]	42.4	37.7	36.9
Grenada[1]	25.3	45.2	42.7
Guyana[3]	22.4	24.4	28.3
Jamaica[5]	33.8	38.1	...
Montserrat[3]	43.7	42.1	39.6
St Kitts and Nevis[3]	46.6	45.6	43.9
St Lucia[3]	40.9	38.8	40.3
St Vincent & the Grenadines[3]	45.4	42.4	39.3
Trinidad and Tobago[2]	27.0	25.3	28.1
Turks and Caicos Is.	40.3	32.4	...

Note
1970 and 1980 figures were extracted from Massiah (1991). The figures for 1990/1991 were calculated in accordance with data contained in 1990/1991 Census Monographs.
[1]Census conducted in 1981 and 1991.
[2]Census conducted in 1980 and 1990.
[3]Census conducted in 1980 and 1991.
[4]1980 Census round was not conducted. However, 1990/91 data relate to a census conducted in 1991.
[5]Census conducted in 1982 and data are provisional for 1990/91.

holds. While similar data from the 1990/1991 censuses were not readily available and precluded efforts to re-assess this situation, the importance of Massiah's observations comes to the fore when one examines variations in household structures according to gender differences in headship status. She observed that there was a greater prevalence of nuclear family units among male headed households than among female headed households, and in contrast, a greater prevalence of extended family units among female headed households than among male headed households. To provide further support for her observations, Massiah alluded to findings (see Table 6.9) based on data from the Women in the Caribbean Project (WICP).[7] Insofar as female headed households were more likely than male headed households to be extended vertically, Massiah suggested that they might also have higher dependency ratios. Other qualitative differences were also acknowledged on the basis of marital status and economic activity.

Table 6.8 *Percentage distribution of households by sex of head and type of household, 1980*

Country	Male Heads				Female heads			
	Nuclear	Extended	Composite	Total	Nuclear	Extended	Composite	Total
Barbados	72.5	21.5	5.9	37,600	55.6	37.0	7.4	29,500
BVI	73.2	17.6	9.3	2,400	63.5	27.5	9.0	800
Dominica	62.0	28.8	9.2	10,800	47.3	42.5	10.2	6,500
Grenada	64.9	27.8	7.3	11,500	48.0	44.4	7.6	9,500
Guyana	67.5	28.7	3.8	113,100	49.2	45.1	5.7	36,500
Montserrat	73.0	20.6	6.4	2,100	54.7	36.8	8.5	1,600
St Kitts/Nevis	68.8	25.2	6.0	6,300	51.1	42.1	6.7	5,300
St Lucia	66.4	26.6	6.9	15,100	53.1	38.6	8.3	9,600
St Vincent	62.3	29.2	8.5	11,700	43.6	46.9	9.4	8,600
Turks	62.1	28.1	9.7	1,100	46.8	44.5	8.6	500

Note
Nuclear = Head of Household, Spouse/Partner, Children of Head and or spouse/partner
Extended = Above plus other relatives of head or spouse/partner
Composite = Above plus boarders, domestic employees or others.
Source: Massiah, 1991.

Table 6.9 Household type by sex of head of household, WICP

Household type	Barbados			St Vincent			Antigua		
	1	2	3	1	2	3	1	2	3
Woman Alone	–	4.1	–	–	1.6	–	–	4.1	–
Simple Family:									
Woman and Partner and Children	27.2	4.1	3.1	28.5	4.0	2.6	25.3	5.8	2.5
Woman and Children	–	11.2	–	–	10.3	–	–	11.1	–
Multiple Family:									
Vertically Extended	8.1	14.7	0.8	8.2	11.5	1.7	8.8	11.5	0.6
Laterally Extended	1.5	2.8	0.2	4.1	6.0	–	3.3	3.9	0.6
Vertically and Laterally Extended	4.2	4.8	–	5.2	8.4	1.2	5.1	10.7	0.2
Other	5.3	7.9	–	2.5	4.2	–	3.1	3.3	0.2
Percentage Total	46.3	49.6	4.1	48.5	46.0	5.5	45.6	50.4	4.1
Total of Household Type	**100% = 581**			**100% = 439**			**100% = 486**		

Key
1 = Male Head; 2 = Female Head; 3 = Joint Headship
Source: White, 1986.

These included higher rates of unemployment and a greater likelihood of separation, divorce and widowhood among female heads.

The prevalence of female-headed households was lower in Guyana and in Trinidad and Tobago than in most of the other Caribbean countries. This could be indicative of the ethnic composition of the populations in those two countries which have relatively large concentrations of East Indians, who (as in the UK) have overwhelmingly upheld patriarchal traditions that predispose male family members to positions of authority within their respective domestic settings. Moreover, on average, marriage usually occurs relatively early and the large scale practice of marital monogamy in conjunction with their more stable union states reduce the prospect of union dissolution and the onset of family units that could be headed by women. In contrast, 'union shifting', serial partnerships, and higher rates of dissolution have been found to be more prevalent among all groups apart from people of South Asian backgrounds and, by extension, in countries with large African or European populations. As such, it should not be surprising that the prevalence of female-headed households was found to be higher in most of the other Commonwealth Caribbean countries when compared to Guyana and Trinidad and Tobago.

The case of Trinidad and Tobago

St Bernard (1997a) offers a preliminary analysis of the findings of a survey[8] summarising living arrangements in contemporary Trinidad and Tobago. It provides further support for earlier observations regarding the distribution of households according to structure. Specifically, 13.9% of the households were found to have persons living alone, 63.6% were estimated to be nuclear families and 21.4% were estimated to be extended families. Estimates also show that single parent families had accounted for 14.4% of all households (11.9% being single mother and 2.5%, single father). These estimates seem to be consistent with the pattern captured by Hewitt (1996) based upon her analysis of data from the 1990 Population and Housing Census.

Table 6.10 and Table 6.11 show interesting associations between household structure and geographic region in Trinidad and Tobago. These associations are important since they are likely to reflect the joint effects of the ethnic composition of the population in the different regions and well established associations between ethnicity and familial characteristics in countries such as Guyana and Trinidad and Tobago. In accordance with Table 6.10, for example, Western Caroni is the zone found to have the highest proportion of husband-wife families

Table 6.10 Percentage distribution of households by structure according to regional zones

Household structure	All zones	East West Corridor	Western Caroni	San Fernando Region	Secondary towns	Rest of Trinidad	Tobago
No. of Households	1,973	805	226	218	186	458	80
			PERCENTAGE DISTRIBUTION				
Living Alone	13.9	14.9	10.2	14.2	16.6	12.4	15.0
H/W No Children	6.3	7.1	4.4	8.7	7.5	5.0	2.5
H/W Children	34.0	25.7	47.3	39.9	39.8	38.6	22.5
CLP No Children	1.9	2.2	2.2	0.5	0.5	2.2	2.5
CLP Children	7.1	8.0	4.9	3.2	5.9	8.3	10.0
Single Mother	11.9	14.3	8.4	15.6	10.8	9.2	5.0
Single Father	2.5	1.7	3.1	0.9	2.2	3.3	6.3
Grandmother Extended	5.7	7.1	4.4	2.8	5.4	3.9	13.8
Other Extended	15.7	17.4	13.7	12.4	10.8	16.4	21.3
Adult Siblings	1.0	1.4	0.9	0.5	0.5	0.7	1.3
Non-Relatives	0.3	0.2	1.4	1.4	–	–	–

Source: St Bernard,1995.

Key:

H/W = Husband/wife

CLP = Common-Law Partnership

Table 6.11 *Percentage distribution of households by structure according to administrative area*

Household structure	All counties	St George (including P.O.S. and Arima)	Caroni	Eastern counties	Victoria (incl. San Fernando)	St Patrick (incl. Point Fortin)	Tobago
No. of households	1,973	826	272	160	405	229	81
		PERCENTAGE DISTRIBUTION					
Living Alone	13.9	14.6	11.8	14.4	13.1	14.4	14.8
H/W No Children	6.3	6.9	5.1	5.0	6.2	8.3	2.5
H/W Children	34.0	25.9	43.8	36.3	43.2	37.6	22.2
CLP No. Children	1.9	2.2	2.2	2.5	0.7	1.7	2.5
CLP Children	7.0	7.9	5.5	10.0	4.9	6.6	9.9
Single Mother	11.9	14.2	10.3	8.1	12.3	9.6	4.9
Single Father	2.4	1.9	2.9	6.3	1.5	0.9	6.2
Grandmother Extended	5.7	6.9	3.7	5.0	3.7	4.8	13.6
Other Extended	15.7	17.8	13.6	12.5	13.3	14.8	22.2
Adult Siblings	1.0	1.5	0.7	0.0	0.2	1.3	1.2
Non-Relatives	0.3	0.2	0.4	0.0	0.7	0.0	0.0

Source: St Bernard,1995.

Key:

H/W = Husband/wife

CLP = Common-Law Partnership

with or without children. Table 6.11 also shows Caroni and Victoria (including San Fernando) as the Counties with the highest proportions of households consisting of husband-wife families with or without children. Compared to the other Counties, the findings seem consistent with the view that the populations of Caroni and Victoria have the greatest concentrations of East Indians.

In contrast, Table 6.11 shows the Eastern Counties[9] and Tobago as the two zones having the highest proportion of common-law partnership families with or without children. This finding seems consistent with two important facts. First, the fact that concentrations of Africans in the populations of the Eastern counties and Tobago have been among the greatest in Trinidad and Tobago. Second, the fact that people of African origins have been found to be more likely to form common-law unions as a basis for initiating cohabitation or in response to partnership changes subsequent to the dissolution of an earlier union. Compared to other zones and regions, Table 6.10 and Table 6.11 show that Tobago has the highest prevalence of households containing extended family units. This is especially true in the case of extended units where there is a lone grandmother as a central figure. Table 6.10 also shows a relatively higher prevalence of households having extended units in the East West Corridor and in rural Trinidad in spite of evidence pointing toward the ubiquitous character of the extended family in Trinidad and Tobago.

St Bernard (1997a) paints a grim picture of the situation confronting households consisting of single mother families on one hand, and extended families with lone grandmother figures on the other. Respective proportions of 52.5% and 44.1% were estimated to have nobody working on a full time basis, although this might not always be the case depending upon the availability of extra-household support. It must be remembered that in these kinds of settings, partnerships built around visiting unions or perhaps, other domestic arrangements fit within the context of a 'domestic group' which survives because of financial and emotional support emanating from extra-household sources. Households consisting of extended families with lone grandmother figures were the most likely to have at least one pensioner/retired person and nobody working on a full time basis. A grim situation was also evident among single person households since it was estimated that as much as two thirds had an individual who was not working on a full time basis. This has implications for elderly persons, since the majority are likely to be out of the labour force and, perhaps, in receipt of pensions.

With respect to households having children younger than 15 years, the survey data were analysed to facilitate assessments of parent-child living arrangements. As many as 64% of all households were estimated to have both biological parents living with their off-spring, 22.3% had at least one child who lived without his/her biological father, 4% without his/her biological mother and almost 10% without any of his/her biological parents. The most interesting findings related to extended family units with lone grandmother figures, and were expressed as follows:

> ... the vast majority (41.3%) of such households consisted of at least one child who was not living with any of his/her biological parents while another 35.9 percent reported having at least one child who was living with his/her biological mother but not with his or her biological father. This suggests that more than three quarters of these households (77.2%) had at least one child who was not living with his /her biological father ... With respect to 'grand Ma' extended households, 15.2 percent of the families had children living with both biological parents (St Bernard, 1997a).

It has already been mentioned that 'child shifting' is a strategy that facilitates childcare arrangements and enhances the economic resources of domestic groups. These findings provide additional evidence to support claims that extended families with lone grandmother figures continue to be primary units for the nurture of children in the absence of both biological parents. In many instances, these children may have been the products of 'casual encounters' or unions that have since been dissolved. They may have lived for a period of time with their biological mother who might have died or left them in the care of relatives in order to pursue another relationship or become actively employed. The latter reinforces the practice of child shifting as a strategy to enhance economic well being within domestic units.

The case of Laventille: a working class Afro-Caribbean community

Laventille is an urban working class community on the eastern fringe of Port of Spain, the capital city of Trinidad and Tobago. Over four-fifths of its population are of African origin, 10% of Mixed origin and 3% of East Indian descent. For local government purposes, the community has been part of the 'San Juan/Laventille Region' which, according to the Ministry of Social Development (1996), is estimated to have the greatest proportion of the nation's poor (12.7%) and a rate of poverty in the vicinity of 37.4%. During the 1994–1995 period, Laventille was the focus of a study[10] commissioned by the Institute of Social and Economic Research, The University of the West Indies, St Augustine, Trinidad. St Bernard (1997b) examines different aspects of kinship and family dynamics in Laventille and provides a contemporary analysis that reflects features likely to be characteristic of working class Afro-Caribbean living arrangements.

According to this analysis, the extended family appears to be the most common form of family organisation characterizing households in Laventille (26.9% of all households). Among households at the national level, husband-wife families were observed to be the most common family format (40.3%) and found to be much more commonplace than common-law partnership families (8.9%). In Laventille, however, the reverse was found with common-law partnership families being a bit more commonplace than husband-wife families (19.4% as opposed to 17.9%). More specifically, the prevalence of common-law partnership families in Laventille was estimated to be much greater than at the national level (19.4% versus 8.9%). While husband-wife family units are clearly visible, a higher prevalence of common-law partnership and extended families may be characteristics of working class, Afro-Caribbean family households.

In the context of Laventille, children (less than 15 years) were mostly found to be in extended family households and to a lesser extent, households consisting of husband-wife and common-law partnership families. Interestingly, households containing common-law partnership families were just as likely as those containing husband-wife families to have children. At the national level, the pattern was different insofar as children were mostly found to be in households containing husband-wife families and to a much lesser extent, in households containing extended families. In Laventille, as at the national level, the extended family is a source for nurturing children who do not live with their biological parents. However, a slightly larger proportion of households from Laventille was estimated to have children who were not living with their biological father (80% as opposed to 77.2%).

Conclusion

In summary, there have been some interesting findings pertaining to gender, age, conjugal experiences and fertility behaviour in Laventille. Among women, there is a relatively high assumption of motherhood while in visiting unions. The findings also point to visiting as a principal medium through which younger men engage in sexual unions, perhaps with multiple partners simultaneously. Interestingly, the common-law union has been found to be a medium through which younger women could be seeking stability once they have given birth to their first child. Another set of findings reveal that substantial periods of time have been spent in marriage by notable proportions of older women, the majority of whom may no longer be in unions and currently living in extended or single mother households. Also evident, was a notion of marriage as a premium among older men aged 45 and over. These findings are note-worthy insofar as they might be deemed characteristic of working class Afro-Caribbean communities such as Laventille.

From a comparative standpoint, two interesting points were noted with respect to the fertility behaviour of young women from Laventille. For women less than 25 years, the prevalence of childlessness was esti-mated to be lower than that found nationwide even after taking ethnic origin into account. They also had their first births, on average, one to two years earlier. Given the nature of conjugal patterns observed in Laventille, the relatively earlier onset of first births could adversely affect the life chances of young women and their offspring. For example, pregnancy, childbirth and subsequent childcare may conflict with their efforts to acquire educational and training credentials deemed essential in their quest to attract equitable financial rewards, avail themselves of adequate resources, and sustain their respective primary groups. This is especially relevant in cases where fathers have been delinquent in meeting their financial commitments to their off-spring and where young women have been unable to seek work because of having no access to appropriate means to care for their chil-dren. It therefore should not be surprising that many of these young women may have had no alternative but to resort to practices such as child shifting and/or partnership shifting to make ends meet.

In each Commonwealth Caribbean country most studies of the family focused upon specific social groups predicated upon social status, ethnicity and place of residence. In most cases, lower class Africans, East Indians and other groups were central to the investiga-tions conducted. In contrast, middle and upper middle class groups were hardly found to be the subjects of inquiry, perhaps due to their adherence to North Atlantic family ideals deemed to be socially acceptable. A principal objective of this chapter has, therefore, been to determine whether living arrangements in the 1980s and 1990s could be different from those reflected in the research efforts of the 1950s, 1960s and 1970s.

Though limited in scope, the available data suggest that very little may have changed with regard to inherent structures within lower class living arrangements. The chapter also claimed that the aging of populations in countries such as Barbados, Montserrat and St Kitts and Nevis may result in growing proportions of single person households consisting of elderly persons who are more likely to be female. This trend is likely to persist in the near future and perhaps also in other countries of the region. In the main, Caribbean populations have embraced traditions and legislative mechanisms that are akin to modern western societies. These include a greater orientation toward free choice and the establishment of decrees that have increased the grounds for divorce. Such options are not only consistent with increases in the prevalence of union dissolution; they also spawn a greater preponderance of nuclear units assuming the form of single mother and common-law partnership families. Despite the greater prevalence of nuclear family arrangements, it is clear that the extended family will survive as an institutional arrangement. This may be due to a number of different social forces including the threat posed by the prospect of poverty.

The available data, though limited in content, point toward definite parallels and hence, some consistency pertaining to inherent structures, social relations and perhaps, value systems characterising household entities across Caribbean societies. However, there appears to be some divergence dependent upon the extent to which ethnic differences influence the heterogeneous character of these societies. This is especially relevant in the context of the majority of small Anglophone islands of the Eastern Caribbean when compared to the more ethnically diverse countries such as Belize, Guyana and Trinidad and Tobago.

Notes

1   These monographs were commissioned by the CARICOM Secretariat and sought to link population and human development issues in specific countries across the region. At the time of writing this chapter, the following country monographs were still outstanding: Jamaica, Grenada, Dominica, Guyana, Antigua and Barbuda and St Kitts and Nevis. However, the following country studies were available and used to generate and provide estimates based on the 1990/1991 census: Trinidad and Tobago (Hewitt, 1996), St Vincent and the Grenadines (Heath, 1996), Barbados (Forte, 1996), St Lucia (St Bernard, 1996), Belize (Roberts et al. 1996), the Bahamas (Gomez et al. 1996) and the British Virgin Islands (Phillips, 1996).

2   Given the relatively strong correlation between social class and family structure, Henriques made reference to differences in family structure that were linked to skin colour so that the 'coloureds' and 'whites'; those in the middle and upper strata of the society, were found to have embraced family ideals that approximated English family traditions.

3   Based on the Censuses of Population, the respective figures relate to populations of specific countries within the Anglophone Caribbean. They represent the proportions of persons of African origin in the respective populations. They are as

follows: Antigua and Barbuda (1991) – 91.3%, Barbados (1991) – 92.6%, British Virgin Islands (1991) – 83.4%, Jamaica (1982) – 74.2%, St Lucia (1991) – 86.5%, St. Vincent and the Grenadines (1991) – 77.1% and Trinidad and Tobago (1990) – 39.5%.

4   In the context of lower class family groupings, Henriques (1953) assigned the label 'domestic group' which, in addition to capturing the family as a nuclear unit consisting of a father, mother and children, acknowledged the prevalence of family forms and living arrangements that were characteristic of matrifocal settings where father figures were absent in most instances. Moreover, the concept of the 'domestic group' was expected to capture family units in which extra residential unions were pivotal to the sustenance and well being of the respective members.

5   The World Bank (1996) indicate that the proportion of the population below the poverty line was 17% in St Vincent and the Grenadines, 35% in Belize, 33% in Dominica, 43% in Guyana and 25% in St Lucia.

6   The figures in parentheses represent the proportion of elderly persons in the respective populations: Antigua and Barbuda (8.2%), the Bahamas (4.7%), Barbados (11.8%), Belize (4.2%), the BVI (5.6%), Dominica (8.8%), Grenada (7.7%), Guyana (4.1%), Jamaica (7.4%), Montserrat (13.5%), St Kitts and Nevis (9.8%), St Lucia (6.5%), St Vincent and the Grenadines (6.5%) and Trinidad and Tobago (6.1%).

7   This project was conducted by the Institute of Social and Economic Research, The University of the West Indies, Barbados. It was executed in two phases, the first of which permitted the collection of data at a regional level and the second taking the form of fieldwork. The fieldwork targeted a random sample of 1,600 women aged 20–64 who responded to a questionnaire. The work was carried out in three countries: Barbados, Antigua and St Vincent and the Grenadines. Phase 2 also took the form of life history interviews with 38 women and six sector studies exploring specific issues in Barbados, Guyana, Jamaica and the Eastern Caribbean.

8   This discussion focuses upon the findings of a National Survey of Family Life conducted in Trinidad and Tobago during 1994. The project was commissioned by the Ministry of Social Development, The Government of Trinidad and Tobago and executed by the Institute of Social and Economic Research, The University of the West Indies in Trinidad. The findings were based on a nationally representative sample of 4,624 persons aged 15 years and over. The individuals were members of 1,974 households.

9   The Eastern Counties include the following: St Andrew, St David, Nariva and Mayaro situated on the eastern half of the island of Trinidad.

10   The study was based on a quantitative sample survey that was conducted during January, 1995 and data were collected from 400 persons aged 15 years and over and living in the community. Overall, 201 households were visited in order to interview eligible respondents about a broad range of social issues including those akin to the family as an institution.

7 Narratives of Caribbean families in Britain and the Caribbean

Mary Chamberlain

Introduction

This chapter is based on two case studies of Caribbean families drawn from the wider sample of families interviewed as part of the research undertaken by Harry Goulbourne and myself on *Living arrangements, family structure and social change of Caribbeans in Britain*[1] (as outlined in the Preface and Chapter 1 above). Our research argued that the diverse features of Caribbean families found in contemporary Britain and the Caribbean indicate the processes of adaptation and I argue that 'indigenisation' has long been a feature of Caribbean cultural life, in the Caribbean and elsewhere. This chapter engages in a micro-study of two families which illustrates the diversity of family form and models, the linkages between family and wider cultural values, the power and reconfiguration of customary values. They also demonstrate how family structures were adapted to meet the needs of migration and the migrant, the continuing influence of the Caribbean in the culture of family life, and the diverse responses to migration by successive generations. But they also caution against the difficulties of broad generalisations, and illustrate the need to investigate the particulars of any situation.

We located our profile of Caribbean families in Britain within the historical and cultural context of both the Caribbean, where there is important intra- and inter- island variation and in the migration and settlement process in Britain. Migration we considered, given its prominence historically and contemporaneously within Caribbean, was a continuing process rather than a final adventure. As such, its values were culturally and socially supported (Richardson 1983; Thomas-Hope 1992), and migration was enabled by family and neighbourhood (Barrow 1986; Chamberlain 1997).

We based our research on life-story interviews across three generations of sixty families (180 interviews in total) who originated in Jamaica, Barbados and Trinidad and Tobago. This enabled us to

117

establish patterns and lineages across all generations, including the migrant generation to Britain, to investigate in some detail the patterns of family organisation and living arrangements and to suggest family models which were transmitted, or transformed by settlement and regeneration in Britain. Informed by the theoretical possibilities of trans-generational life story narratives (Bertaux & Thompson 1993; Chamberlain 1997) and by the possibilities of some of the insights generated in family systems theory therapy – notably the nature of the relationship of the individual to the collective, the social construction of meanings, and the link between intergenerational patterns and meanings and contemporary interaction (Gorell Barnes et al. 1998) – we sought to explore the inner dynamics of families and the subjectivities of those involved.

> It is in the interaction between life cycle and intergenerational patterns and beliefs that the most fruitful understanding of family dynamics and equilibrium can be made (Gorell-Barnes et al. 1998:30–31).

Of course, such life stories are grounded in memory, and provide rich empirical data for the processes and evolution of Caribbean family life, in the Caribbean and as it has evolved in Britain. But memory provides more than empirical detail. The French sociologist, Maurice Halbwachs (1980), pointed out that memory is never 'purely' singular or idiosyncratic. The memories of others and about others enter into the memory of any one individual; memories are thus both inherited and transmitted and form one of the central planks in the process of socialisation. What is prioritised or what is repressed relate at varying levels to the permissions or prohibitions of social, cultural and, as Alessandro Portelli (1990) points out, political values. They have a didactic value. Memory is also part of a social dialectic as its emphases and resolutions shift with the vagaries of the life cycle, and that of others, responding to generational change and fashion, including representations of the past. Memory is equally structured by the shared cultural forms around it, in the languages, the images and the values. Located as it is in social form, memories are also subject to both narrative and genre (Tonkin 1992; Chamberlain & Thompson, 1998; Portelli 1998), which shape the imaginative structures through which memory is recalled and recounted. They represent shared values and modes of expression, which the scholar can identify and helps inform a historical understanding. Yet the recollection and recounting of memory equally responds to the audience and its questions, whether the questioner is the social investigator, or a member of the family. Any interview is therefore constructed by both interviewer and interviewee. The impurities, pluralities and volatility of memory – once considered evidence of its unreliability as a source – now provide considerable value for the social historian. Memories, in other words, require interpretation if their full richness is to be fully exploited.

Family 1

Samuel was born in Barbados in 1952, and came to Britain with his younger sister in 1968 to join his mother, Avis, her husband and his four younger (British-born) siblings. He had not seen his mother for twelve years; he had never met his stepfather, or his siblings. 'I want,' he says, 'to give you a true picture, which would identify with the research that you want.' (BF123/2 1/1/2) During his mother's absence, he and his sister had been looked after by her mother. Samuel's grandmother had twelve children, now dispersed 'all over the world'. Individual family members who went abroad could rely on communal family care for the children left behind. As a consequence Samuel's grandmother had, as she put it, 'reared enough grands'. Avis returned remittances regularly to her mother to support her children and contribute to the domestic economy of her family.

This arrangement was familiar to most of our informants, directly or indirectly, and may be considered to be one of the ways in which families enabled and supported the migration of its individual members. They, in turn, were required to support the well-being of the family members left behind. Each exchange reinforced the links between the two communities.

Avis was the second oldest of her mother's twelve children and had migrated in 1956 and her memories of her mother were vivid. She was a 'wonderful woman,'

> I remembered her as being very beautiful, and with long hair and we always used to be sitting down playing with it, you know. For some reason, she doesn't really like long hair, and we used to plait it over the ears ... and she'd always be poking it back, poking it back. (BF069/2 1/1/1)

It is an image which is sensual and textual and suggestive of the intimacy offered and shared between herself, her siblings and her mother. Indeed, the quality of relationships is often provided as much in the extraneous detail as in the adjectives or metaphors chosen.

Her maternal grandfather was one of seventeen sons, her mother the only daughter in a family of ten. The family was musical. Her grandfather invented the foot harp – 'they were all into the music', either as instrumentalists or, like her mother, as singers. This grandfather was a mason 'who travelled a lot'; her father was a carpenter/joiner who also had part-shares in a fishing boat. The family lived well on the fish and the produce from the land and food and sharing were also part of the leit motif of this family. As with other informants, the neighbourhood was peopled with kin and close neighbours: 'I remember her always sharing whatever she had'. (BF069/2 1/1/2) When Avis left for England, her mother continued to send food packages of sweet potato, cassava, corn meal and hot pepper sauce. It was a way of retaining both family connections and a potent reminder of the culture and its values of support and sharing. There was, in the words of Walter Benjamin (1997), a 'compressed fullness' in those packages. The exchange was not confined to food. One uncle, who had no children, and who lived in Trinidad, fostered Avis' eldest sister. The family was 'loving'. Her mother,

> used to make us know every cousin, brother, uncle, distant, whether it was fourth, third, sixth. She used to tell us who had what, who had how many sons, what daughters, what children, who they were, where they lived … to pass that knowledge on to her children. (BF069/2 1/1/11-12)

Avis was as close to her grandparents as to her parents, to her uncles and cousins, as to her brothers, childcare and support crossing generations, and transversing kin. Individual family members who went abroad could rely on communal family care for the children left behind, bounded within a neighbourhood of friends, godparents and kin. Its topography was, as Avis says, 'a map of my childhood'. (BF069/2 2/2/32)

When Avis was eighteen, she 'had a boyfriend and had a son'. (BF069/2 2/2/4) A few years later, she had a daughter, by a different man. Her parents were, at the time, 'bitter', but nevertheless stepped in to help her so that when, in 1956, she left to join her then boyfriend in Britain, she was able to leave her children confidently in the care of her family, the loss minimized by a history of support. 'My love was with me, so that was a comfort in itself.' (BF069/2 2/2/9) (Many informants talk of the loss and absence of family in similar terms, conveying an abiding emotional presence. 'I carry my family within me' was how another informant described it.) Twelve years later, when her son was sixteen and her daughter fourteen, she sent for them both to join her and her (new) husband, in England. The reunion was 'wonderful' but marred by the discovery that her son was illiterate. 'I don't know why … it could have been the disturbance at losing the mum.' (BF069/2

3/1/5) Once discovered, he was sent to a special school, but after four years in England, he was returned to Barbados,

> He was being ... rebellious. We don't know for what reason. Who knows what goes through children's heads? ... sometimes children see themselves suffer, they see things that you don't see ... but ... deep down, he's a very nice chap, and we have a good relationship. (BF069/2 3/3/4)

Samuel now has a successful business in Barbados. Avis is 'proud' of his achievements, as indeed those of all her children. As a mother, she had insisted that her professional life (she was a nurse) be organised around their needs, that they were always fully supported, that time was always allocated to them, their friends always welcome:

> once I said to [my son], I said 'I don't understand it. Why would your friends from these lovely homes, rich, wealthy backgrounds, want to come and kip on my floor?' And he say 'Because, this is a home, and theirs is a house'. Big difference. (BF069/2 3/2/1)

Like her mother, she has always laid stress on the family lineages and links, and maintained close family contact with her siblings and cousins across time and the world. 'It's important' she argues, *'[family] is part of one's identity* ... [In Britain] we round them all up ... and make sure they're in touch with these children from other family [branches]' (emphasis added) (BF069/2 3/1/5) Indeed, the importance of siblings and affines was reiterated through all families. Siblings acted as confidantes, and formed an essential link in the migration chain, both for departing and returning migrants; siblings cared for siblings at home and abroad. Equally, uncles and aunts, older family members, and even neighbourhood 'fictive' kin, all shared a role in ensuring the moral and social well-being of the family. 'Everybody had a responsibility to bring up everybody else's children.' (JF022/2) Phrases such as living 'like family', friendships 'like sisters', support 'like brothers' indicate the importance of such roles in the early stages of migration, while the use of these metaphors indicates the vitality of family models and in particular that of sibling relationships in the shaping of networks (Chamberlain 1999). 'We help each other out' was a common comment, we 'trust'. While the social circumstances and city topography in Britain may have altered the context, the importance of churches and community activity may be seen as its inheritor.

Thus Avis has also been active in voluntary and community work, trying to extend 'the principles that we grew up with in the West Indies', to strengthen the generational links between the older members of the Caribbean community and the young, through clubs and other social, political and religious activities. Part of those principles derived from and returned to, the strong sense of family commitment, where the sibling and family metaphor informed neighbourhood behaviour. For instance,

> if you're an elderly person, and you have a bereavement, you might not be able to cope with the food and all that and we'll take the thing over for you and do it ... and assist you with the running around and things like that ... and give you x amount towards the flowers ... [so] you can buy a wreath and things like that. (BF069/2 3/1/3)

With the exception of Samuel, who has returned to Barbados, Avis' other children – and their children – remain in Britain, although her daughters and one son have divorced (as has Avis) and are raising their children alone, with the assistance of Avis.

As the Caribbean family extends into its second and third generation, many of the patterns experienced in the Caribbean (and first hand by the migrant generation) are now replicated in Britain. Avis' role as grandmother and mother, her sense that she is 'needed' in Britain, is the major impediment to her permanent return to Barbados.

This is Avis' story. Her son, Samuel, wanted to give a 'true picture'. 'I love my mum,' he said, but

> if I tell you my whole life story, I'll cry. And what I'm saying to you, I'm not telling you anything out of any kind of hurt and revenge or animosity for my mum. I love my mum. (BF123/3 1/1/2)

As Avis' story overflowed with love and incorporation, Samuel's was its mirror image, characterised by absence and loss. Samuel has no memory of his mother. He can only 'pick up' from when he went to Britain at the age of 16. His adjustment to Britain, the family and his mother was hard, and was compounded by his mother's 'hurtful' reaction to his learning difficulties. As soon as he left school,

> I was placed on an aeroplane back to Barbados ... I didn't get the opportunity ... like the rest of my brothers and sisters. Everything that I had and they wanted, it would be taken from me and given to them. (BF123/3 1/1/2)

Samuel's agenda was a catalogue of maternal neglect and exclusion, culminating in his peremptory return to his grandmother in Barbados. His narrative moves through cycles of explanation: his mother's memory of him was a 'still memory', and he had changed; his learning disability proved 'hurtful' to her, he failed to understand how someone could be so cruel. 'How can a mother love a son, how can a mother do this kind of thing?'(BF123/3 1/1/9)

Finally, his analysis comes full circle. Samuel never knew his father. He had been told he was dead. It was only on returning to Barbados, and a curiosity to discover his roots, that he made enquiries, discovered his father and established a relationship with him. His father never knew of Samuel's existence.

> She didn't want anyone to know that she had any kind of contact with him. Up to this day, she's still denying the fact that he is my father. Her would not say who my father is. (BF123/3 1/1/9)

On one occasion, when his mother was visiting Barbados, she saw Samuel with his father. She responded angrily,

> and everything clicked in my mind. I went back to England, and all the years that I spend in England, up to that particular time, last year, I wonder how it is that my mother, when she see me, she feel so excited about me, she talks ... even in England, she speaks highly of me, she's proud of me. And what is it that my mother treat me the way she treat me? And I thought, in my mind, that it was because I could not read. But it clicked then. It was nothing to do with I not being able to read. It was that I was growing in[to] the splitting image of the man that she was denying. (BF123/3 1/1/9)

Avis had glossed over Samuel's conception and birth: 'I had a boyfriend and then I had a son.' As Gorell Barnes et al. (1998) remind us:

> Intergenerational patterns are often invisible guidelines to family life which appear to indicate the way a family regulates its present interactions in response to what has gone before .... The recognition of avoidance or reversal as a form of intergenerational influence is particularly important.

Samuel attributes his success in Barbados to a desire to prove himself to his mother, and to seek her approval. His narrative is punctuated by the question he never dares pose to her: 'Why are you hiding? Why are you still, after forty years, why are you still trying to hide?' (BF123/3 1/1/15) His mother, however, remains 'in denial',

> [But] it has to be finished. It needs to be finished. She need to come and speak the truth. She need to tell me who it is ...

I want to know the truth. He tell the truth. But I haven't heard her say. (BF123/3 1/1/11)

While he waits for her answer, his response takes the form of a public exposition. He is an active and articulate proponent of the rights of fathers in paternity and parenting; he argues vehemently for the recognition of 'roots':

> Some families, when they accomplish a certain level of success ... tend not to want to identify with there they came from ... if ... identifying with their past would have some kind of negative effect on how people in their social bracket look at them .... I know where I come from and connecting with my roots cannot take nothing away from me .... I was invited to lecture at the Community College on 'How can we empower our community?' .... I said ... we have people who are successful from the villages and ... are migrating ... to the heights and terraces and parks ... [and] don't want to identify with the village any more .... In the past, in the villages, we had teachers, we had policemen, we have inspectors ... that ... youngsters coming up ... can look at ... as role models ... people [must] understand that, because you are rich ... have degrees ... [it] give you the licence ... that you don't want to identify. (BF123/3 1/1/17)

He actively and positively maintains contact with his family in Barbados, Britain and North America; he is active in the education and school life of his daughter. On the surface, his public persona is in the image of his mother, a committed family man with a strong sense of civic duty. But, as he says, 'I take it and turn it all around'. (BF123/3 2/1/33)

Family 2

Valerie was born in 1963 in Jamaica, migrating as a child to Britain with her mother and other siblings to join her father who had settled in Birmingham. Valerie is a university graduate. She works full time, though she lists as her current occupations 'a) part-time lecturer, b) a co-ordinator for supplementary school. And c) I work part-time at British Gas and d) I'm also a housewife and a mother'. (JB008/2 1/1/1) As Modood et al. (1997) suggested, young Caribbean origin women in Britain have greater success in education and employment than their male counterparts.

Valerie is unmarried and has two children by different fathers, neither of whom make financial or other contributions to their children's welfare. She had her first child when she was seventeen. She, her children and her boyfriend (whom she plans to marry, who is not the father of either of her children) live together in her parents' house. Given the equation in the British (and some of the Caribbean) literature between education, class and family type, her status as a salaried professional woman should suggest a pattern of domesticity and lifestyle which conforms to an European model of family life. It is relevant to look therefore at the life choices made possible, and more particularly, at the cultural and family directives which helped shaped them.

Valerie is close to her family: 'I get along with all my brothers and sisters very well, I really like my brothers and sisters'. (JB008/2 1/1/16) Her concept of family extends both vertically and horizontally, embracing grandparents, cousins, uncles, aunts and close family friends – 'it felt like we could trust each other'. (JB008/2 1/2/18) Valerie's parents were both active Christians and had married before giving birth to their children. Her father's parents had similarly been married (her paternal grandfather was a Pastor) and had successfully raised 24 children, including one born 'outside'. According to Valerie, her paternal grandmother 'made a good family, they're so close. That close Mum couldn't even get into it'. (JB 008/2 1/2/12) Her mother's parents, by contrast, had not been married. Her maternal grandmother 'was very fair, half white, half black' and colour may have been one factor in determining the shape of this family.

> Her story is more of a sad story, though because it would have been difficult for her mum to have a relation with a black man in the first place, at that time. And she (grandmother) was brought up to feel that she was better than anyone who was darker skinned … I think she felt a bit alienated, and also didn't fit in. I don't know if it was not fitting in because she felt she was better, or whether or not she would fit in because other people wouldn't allow her to … the house was left to her by her mum … and she just stayed there. Then she went with my grandad who was a bit of a rogue and she fell in love with him and … she married before, and her first husband died, and it's as though she never quite really recovered from losing him. And then, with my grandad, he just wasn't the settling down type of person anyway. And so she had a couple of children for him … you see, on my mum's side of the family there's the children from my gran, then there's also the children from my

> grandad ... still blood related, because of the dad. And so in my mum's family, to be quite honest, I just lumped everybody together, if she's my auntie, she's my auntie ... I can't really say who belongs to who. (JB008/2 1/2/9)

Despite the diversity of family form, both Valerie's parents, Aleric and Norman, in their recollections of their respective families of origin, stress comparable values. The legality of the parental relationship was of little importance compared to the quality of that relationship within the broader context of kinship. Despite her parents not cohabiting, Aleric described the relationship between them as 'very good friends', Norman 'like sisters and brothers, even though they were wife and husband'. Aleric lived with her mother and her aunts 'like one family' (JB007/1 1/1/10) and both stressed the closeness of the relationship with the wider family 'we're all a big circle together, big family, happy family, together'. (JB007/1 1/1/5) The model of the wider family, and clear parental instructions – 'we couldn't do anything wrong with each other because mother and father was very strict in that, because they want us to grow up loving and nice and gentle to each other' (JB007/1 1/1/10) – ensured an environment of obligation, responsibility and family support. Both Norman and Aleric grew up in the same neighbourhood in Jamaica, characterised by mutual support

> when we have a funeral in that district, it's everybody's funeral ... there is no strain on the immediate family who got the loss. Everybody from the neighbourhood, from as far as you can remember, they come in with food. (JB007/1 1/1/13)

The family in general, and the sibling relationship in particular, acted as a metaphor to describe and proscribe neighbourly behaviour and relations. 'The district was like one big family' (JB007/1 1/1/12). Family was not only a description of kinship, but a powerful model and measure of human relationships, of love, kindness and trust, reinforced by and through the neighbourhood. Values such as these are reiterated and repeated throughout our narratives. There may be an element of the pastoral in such reminiscences (see Samuel and Thompson 1990), which may be particularly acute in the memories of migrants for whom time, distance and migration necessarily leads to a measure of comparison between the golden 'then' in the Caribbean and the tarnished 'now' in Britain. Equally, our informants may have taken comfort in recalling their family history as if were or recounting it as it should have been, what Portelli (1990) describes as 'uchronic memory'. Such descriptions, which stressed family support and love, may be seen nevertheless as a ranking of family priorities and as an aspect of cultural prescription for the nature and meaning of families and family life. The values highlighted may be seen as being as important as the validity of the description offered.

In this family the support expected, and provided, by the network of kin, affines and neighbours enabled Norman in due course to leave Aleric and their first two children while he went to work in America. Equally, the 'closeness' of family, the elements of love and trust, were values reiterated by Valerie, and repeated by her two children, 'Our family is very close … if you never had family, then … there'd be no one to live with and care for us or nothing, and so we'd be just lonely'. 'If I never had a family, I wouldn't know what to do and *it makes me feel like someone* … People just stick up for me and they're very kind.' (emphasis added) (JB009/3 1/1/6–7)

While support is one powerful family dynamic, there is also a powerful counter narrative. Norman returned from America, and migrated to Britain in 1952. Aleric joined him after four years, then returned to Jamaica after two, returning again two or three times before finally taking all her six children back to Britain to join him in Birmingham. The family travelled by ship, docking in Liverpool. Norman was not there to meet them at the dock. Nor was he at the station in Birmingham. Nor did he answer the door when they arrived at his house. The family waited outside.

> About two hours later, my dad opened the door …. He didn't want us to come in. He didn't want us. That's all it boiled down to … when we went into the house … there was evidence of another woman being there … we started disliking him from that night … for me, it was turning something different, from not really knowing the man, to thinking 'I hate this man'. (JB007/1 2/1/31)

Norman failed to support his family. Aleric found a job to provide food, but Norman did not pay the rent, and the family were evicted. Aleric left him and she and the children moved elsewhere, first to a (substandard) council house, and then to a larger house rented from a Jamaican friend. The balance in the family shifted dramatically and the narrative assumed a fresh and heroic dimension. Aleric gave up her work in the factory, and returned to her original trade as a dressmaker which enabled her to work from home.

> The business took off in a good way. And with that we knew that Mum couldn't do any housework, no cooking, no cleaning, no nothing, she just … didn't do none of that, she just sewed all the time. And we kids … we managed the house … so that she could just sew. (JB008/2 2/1/33)

Indeed, Aleric was so successful that in time the house was re-furnished, she learnt to drive, bought a car, and was buying a house with the help of her eldest son.

> Everything was going well. We'd managed, with the effort of my mum, my brother and us pulling our weight as children, and we'd managed … it felt great. (JB008/2 2/1/34)

At this point, when Valerie was thirteen, their father returned. To the children's dismay, their mother took him back:

> Mum was saying to us that when we grow up and we leave her, then she'll be on her own … we could understand that … and that she was going to find it in her heart to forgive him and hope that we would do the same too, and give him another chance. (JB008/2 2/1/35)

Norman moved in,

> with a paraffin heater and a tea pot … that's all it was … he'd worked the whole time. So we couldn't understand where his money is, we didn't get none, he's working, so what's he doing with it? And come back with just those two items? … we haven't got a clue … everything went down after that. (JB008/2 2/1/36)

In her parents' narrative, this period – of five or six years – is not alluded to. There may be structural reasons for this, but their secret is the silence which Valerie inherited also. Before her father's return, she was close to her mother. After his return,

> we started to go our own ways, and each of us in our different way gave her a different kind of trouble … we wouldn't have dreamed of doing it before, but it was like rebellion. But never against Mum, because we understood. Well, we were part of the whole struggle, so we wouldn't have done anything to hurt her, but she had hurt us … instead of calling him Dad, we called him Norman and so for a long time we avoided calling him altogether … we didn't know what to say … until my brother came up with the word 'Pops' … but never Dad. (JB008/2 2/1/36)

Valerie became pregnant. She did not love the child's father. She went with him 'on the rebound. I … had sex … once and once only and fell pregnant … it was a rebound situation that should never have happened'. (JB008/2 2/1/39) Shortly after, she and her son left home to cohabit with another man, 'and all I had in my mind was my mum telling me that if I ever left home, or left church, I was going to become a prostitute and end up in the gutter'. (JB008/2 2/1/39) This relationship ended, as did the marriage she subsequently entered into, because both men were 'over possessive'. (JB008/2 2/1/40) She has now met, and intends to marry, her current boyfriend. In between, however, she returned to studies, and took a university degree.

One reading of Valerie's behaviour is a simple teenage rebellion. The 'simple' is, however, misleading. That her rebellion assumed the form of motherhood is both psychologically and culturally meaningful. This family placed a high premium on marriage – Aleric and Norman are active Christians, her mother is now a pastor in a Pentecostal church. For them, marriage was a lifelong commitment. Throughout the separation from Norman, Aleric did not become involved adulterously with another man, nor was the question of divorce ever raised. Fidelity, loyalty and forgiveness were values which she cherished, along with an abiding commitment to her children. They also placed a premium on marriage as the necessary precondition for having children, a condition which Valerie flaunted alongside cohabitation and divorce (from the father of her second child). But remember also that her own grandmother had born children outside of marriage. More, as Kerns (1984) suggests, the importance of lineage – of whose continuity mothers and their children are living proof – is a powerful directive within the Caribbean and may help explain both the occurrence of high levels of births outside of marriage, and the apparent tolerance of them by families.

Valerie has never become close to her father. Her other relatives 'swear blind that my dad has other children … if I ask my dad, he says, well, there isn't any'. (JB008/2 1/1/5) Given the mystery surrounding his disappearance and reappearance and the breaking of the bonds of respect, love and trust, rebellion may be an appropriate explanation for Valerie's pregnancy. It may not be the most significant one. Valerie considers her role model to be her mother: 'I think I just do [model myself on her]. I think I just do it without … I think most of it is subconsciously'. (JB008/2 1/1/5) Although her mother was 'disappointed' by Valerie's behaviour, and disapproved particularly of the man with whom she cohabited (who was twenty years her senior), Aleric had demonstrated both heroism and stoicism in her commitment to her children and their joint struggle for survival and success in Britain. What emerges in Valerie's narrative is a comparable story of heroism. Despite the demands of motherhood, the complications of her relationships with men, and the need to work to support her children, Valerie completed her education, and her university degree. She is now a college lecturer; she has co-founded a supplementary school; she has proved as successful as her siblings, who all went onto higher education or became trained professionals. As Aleric said, 'people say to me, "It's because you're motherly", and I'm proud of that'. (JB007/1 2/1/31)

Despite the travails and traumas of Valerie's teenage years, Aleric stood by her daughter. She, her children and her partner live with her parents, emotionally supported by her siblings, cousins, uncles and aunts. She supports her children, and her children echo the sentiments of family, of caring values, which make you 'feel someone'. Those values, what Angelita Reyes (1996) described as the 'olden ways of kinship', die hard. Perhaps in thinking about the Caribbean family (or, indeed, any family) in a British context, it is as well to remember that the conjugal relationship is but a passing moment in the history of the family.

Discussion

Given the diversity of family structure, and the individuality of the family dynamic, focus on the values instilled in and by family members both explained the vivacity of kinship links, and may prove a fruitful avenue to explore in terms of nature and meaning attached to family life. At the same time, individual case studies may temper any tendency to romanticise that family life. Nevertheless, some generalizations from the data can be made. Obligation and responsibility were themes stressed in the case studies, which were repeated in the wider data, and were considered values which ensured family cohesion and loyalty and demanded reciprocity. Indeed, one might argue that these narratives contained within them 'genres', of which stories (particularly childhood recollections) of mutual caring and sharing was one example. Thus, a 'happy childhood' was one explanation offered for these linkages, 'the way we were brought up' another. Another informant, who is 'as close' to her half and step siblings, as her full siblings (even though they are in Jamaica, Canada and America) retained the links for her children because 'I have to let them know everybody, much as possible. All the family, everywhere, every one. Because the way we grow up, our family was so loving … and kind and everything else. Why shouldn't you want to know them? We have nothing to hide'. (JF020/2)

All informants regarded the discipline experienced in childhood as vital to ensuring these values, while the religious, 'spiritual' qualities of, or overtones in, the language used to describe family relations is indicative of the respect and status accorded to family members in general, and elders in particular. Such language suggested also the importance of lineage in family affairs, and of women as bearers of that lineage (Kerns 1984; Chamberlain 2000). Mothers, especially, were 'saints' and 'angels'. Dead relatives 'lived' in the living. 'Is them me get me blessing from' (JA140/1) was how one elderly returnee explained the sense of obligation and responsibility she had felt while in England towards her family in Jamaica, continuing 'God helping me and spare my life to go there and God spare my life to come back. So me have to give thanks'. Another (Trinidadian) informant spent his retirement savings to pay for his brother to come to Britain for a series of operations,

> but we said it's a life and we couldn't let him die … if my parents hadn't sent me to England I would not have been in the position to do what we have done. So it stems back from the original attitude of my parents, their unselfishness, the sacrifice that they have made to send me here. (TJ073/2)

The majority of our informants detailed precise ways in which both emotional and material support has continued across the generations and across the oceans (Goulbourne 1999), confirming the resilience of Caribbean family and kinship. It is perhaps the transmission of those values which characterises familial success, more than conformity to a particular code of sexual or conjugal behaviour. The continuing contact with the Caribbean, and within Caribbean families worldwide, both demonstrates and replenishes those values, while their ability to withstand or overide particular challenges (as both the case studies demonstrate) contributes to their strength and vitality.

In looking at Caribbean families in Britain, therefore, it may be more profitable to explore the values which underpin what people constitute as family, to explore 'nature and meaning', than to draw up family typologies or examine family structure. Families, indeed, make you 'feel someone', and are an integral part of identity. The diversity of family forms already remarked upon in the Caribbean are being replicated in Britain, a diversity which includes apparent changes across the generations. Such a statement, however, places the conjugal unit as the defining centre of family formation. Once, however, the family is approached from a horizontal, rather than a vertical axis, and once life stories, life-cycles, and the generational framework of the family are taken into account, then other family relations and relationships assume prominence or are given priority at different times. Thus, for instance, for our migrant generation, siblings and cousins formed an essential link in the migration chain, and in the migrant networks so essential for survival in Britain. They remain an important link:

siblings can be assumed to outlive parents, and it is often to siblings that people turn for support in Britain and to ease the transition on return to the Caribbean. At the same time, as the Caribbean community in Britain extends into second and third generation, some family roles, such as grandparent, can begin to assume an importance denied to the migrant generation whose parents, for the most part, remained in the West Indies.

Conclusion

Families are never static, but are reconfigured from generation to generation, in response to need, circumstance and convenience. At the same time, values proved by custom to be efficacious, and family models, which come in all shapes and sizes, are also part of the cultural capital transmitted, and transformed, across generations. It is the generation of this capital which is, perhaps, the most valuable function performed by families, providing the individual with a sense of value, and the community with a shared and distinctive culture and identity. It is, perhaps, the nature and transmission of this capital, rather than the haphazard formalities of family construction, which should direct family research, just as it drives family unity.

Notes

1   This research is based on H Goulbourne and M Chamberlain <u>Living arrangements, family structure and social change of Caribbeans in Britain</u> financed by a grant from the ESRC to whom grateful thanks are given. All sources refer to our data set. Summary of sources used in this chapter as below:

BF123/3	JB008/3
BF069/2	JA140/1
JB007/1	TJ073/2
JB008/2	JF020/2

Letters refer to family; number to interview and generation (after slash). Additional numbers in text after these prefixes relate to tape number, side number, and transcription page reference.

8 | Caribbean fathers in family lives in Britain[1]

Tracey Reynolds

Introduction

The support female members in Black families provide to mothers, and the relationships between them, have been strenuously documented over the years (see Stack, 1974; Bell-Scott, 1988; Hill-Collins, 1994; Stack and Burton, 1994; Roschelle, 1997). In direct contrast, support provided by Black male family members, whether it be as husband, fathers, brothers or uncles, has received little attention. It has proved very difficult to locate British literature on Black men in 'the family' (see Lewis and O'Brien, 1988). It is almost as if Black men have been written out of discourses and debates on Black family life. Instead, discourses on Black men tend to restrict them to the specific realms of urban youth culture, sport, music and entertainment. In this discourse 'hyper-masculine', 'hyper-sexual' and 'hyper-aggressive' (Mercer and Julien, 1988; Back, 1996; Alexander, 1996; Blount and Cunningham, 1996; Sewell, 1997) Black masculinised identities are celebrated. Notions of Black men as 'carers', 'emotional', 'affectionate' and 'loving' (traits usually identified as 'feminine' or 'motherly') act as a direct anti-thesis to traditional characterisations of Black men within Black masculinised discourses.

Where images of Black men in the family exist in media and policy debates, stereotypical representations prevail, and these do little to engage a critical understanding of Black men's familial experiences. Conventional constructions of Black fathers by media and policy-makers posit them as absent or marginal from the family home; 'feckless' and financially irresponsible (see Reynolds, 1997a). Not only are these men supposed to be emotionally uncommitted to their female partners, but they are said to lack concern about, or to be uninvolved in, the care and well-being of their children. The mothers' perceptions of the Black men in their families, whether it be their children's fathers, their partners, their own fathers or other male relatives, challenge these representations[2]. First, they recognise Black men as being actively involved in their family lives. Second, the mothers acknowledge that irrespective of Black fathers' absence or presence from the home, these men inform their mothering identities and contribute to their social realities. The aim of this chapter is to provide a detailed analysis of Black fathers in Black family lives by documenting these mothers' claims. The analysis will begin with a brief literature review of studies assessing Black fathering and detailing what are the common concerns. This is then followed by an exploration of the key findings which emerged in the mothers' discussions concerning Black fathers in family lives, and the role they play in their mothering experiences.

Black fathering

In the USA there have been attempts to redress the lack of available research on Black fathers. However, as noted when there is an attempt to voice Black fathers' experiences stereotypical assumptions guide much of the analysis. The focus is very much on highlighting and understanding Black men's absence from the home and the problems they have in fulfilling family responsibilities (Staples,1985). A causal relationship between Black male absenteeism from the home and wider economic factors is identified by many authors on this issue (see Wilson, 1987; Bowman and Forman, 1997). William Julius Wilson (1988) attributes the perceived marginalisation of Black men in the family to the high percentage of Black female-headed households (Wilson, 1988). He argues that the alienation of Black men from the labour market produced alienation from marital and familial relationships, leading inevitably to Black men leaving the home or being forced out by their female partners.

In a later study Wilson (1996) explores the psychological effect on fathers who experienced years of unemployment. He concludes that when the father's role as economic provider and breadwinner erodes, and the wife/mother assumes this position, Black men struggle to find alternative ways to define their masculinity and role within the family, resulting in psychological distress and self-alienation. The 'psychological distressed' state of the 'new urban [Black male] poor' re-affirms debates of old, where the current social and economic position of Black men is blamed on female-headed households and female dominance in family networks (see Frazier, 1948; Moynihan, 1965; Murray, 1985). Employing the notion of the self-fulfilling prophecy it is argued that Black women by going out to work fail to undertake women's 'traditional' home-based role. This results in the emasculation of Black men who are displaced as the main provider. To survive,

Black men must leave the family home, taking with them the greater potential earning capacity. Furthermore it is argued that fathers not being at home to supervise the children, leads their children to failing educationally and falling into a life of crime and other deviant activities (see Frazier, 1948; Moynihan, 1965 and Murray, 1985).

These debates about the role of Black fathers in families are embedded in the specific historical, cultural experiences of African-Americans. Political agendas lie behind their arguments, because in placing blame on Black women for the plight of poor urban Black men, attention is diverted from the social, political, and economic factors that cause societal inequalities. However, I draw upon these debates here because apart from media and commonsense belief there is a lack of substantive literature available in Britain investigating Black fathering. Also, despite the specificity of this debate to the USA there are many attempts to directly translate them to the African-Caribbean experience in Britain. For example, Black and White based newspaper articles alike employ the 'baby-father' syndrome[3] as a rationale for high rates of female-headed households within African-Caribbean families (see Song and Edwards, 1997; Reynolds, 1997a).

Studies which identify diversity among Black fathers – beyond the stereotypical characterisations of absent/marginal, irresponsible, young, possessing multiple children by multiple women – are few and far between. John McAdoo (1988) is one of the few theorists to document the experiences of Black fathers from relatively affluent socio-economic backgrounds. McAdoo compares fathers from different ethnic groups who share similar socio-economic backgrounds. His conclusive findings are that these Black fathers are no different to those of other ethnic groups. They are just as actively involved in childrearing and enjoy warm and loving interactions with their children and families. Where there is diversity in attitudes and involvement in childcare, it is factors such as class, age, location, family upbringing, relationship with wife/partner or children's mothers which inform these differences.

The mothers' perceptions of fathers in their families, their own fathers and their children, when I interviewed them supported this viewpoint.[4] All the mothers had children by Black partners. It was not my intention to secure only mothers with Black partners. That this was the case I attribute to the locality in which I undertook the research: areas with a high density of African-Caribbean households and also the fact that I obtained interviews through my own personal networks. With the exception of two mothers all the male partners were of African-Caribbean descent/origin.

The key findings to emerge from the mothers perceptions' of Black fathers/men in 'the family' are as follows. First, Black men are active participants in childcare and family life. Second, absent fathers assume an 'absent presence' in 'the family'. Third, Black fathers possess power and authority within 'the family', negating claims of 'matriarchy' as culturally specific to Black family life. I shall now go on to explore each of these findings in detail.

Public discourse of mothers' perceptions of Black fathers

When the subject of Black men's position in the family was first broached, the mothers' initial discussion was influenced by the public discourse which presents Black fathers' involvement in the family as marginal or absent. To an extent these negative public images of Black fathering have filtered into the Black mothers' perceptions of Black fathers in Black family life at a general level. Therefore it is important to document these debates (informed by the public discourse), before I go onto assess the mothers' discussions (informed by private experiences), of Black men in their specific families:

> *Nizinga*: If he [Black father] can't get a job he's feeling frustrated because of how the system's treating him, he's taking out on you because the system is not giving him a chance to be a provider or whatever. The ones that are decent are either married, gay or into White women, so that's one of the reasons a lot of Black women are on their own. They [Black men] want the children but they don't want the responsibility that comes with it. We're [Black women] seen as strong, we're always seen as strong and holding the family together. [Nizinga, age 31, single-mother: second generation mother]
> *Maxine*: You see a Black couple now and all you see is the children, no ring, no house unless she went out and got it herself. I tell you, anyone remotely decent, well they're snapped up long time ago. So if you're a single Black woman much less a single-mother, well forget it. As for the rest, let me see who we're left with, those who don't know the meaning of work, those on drugs, the ones in prison, men who have children scattered all over the place. [Maxine, age 29, single-mother: second generation mother]

These comments by Nizinga and Maxine which identify the bulk of Black men as 'worthless', unemployed, in prison, on drugs, or as having multiple children by multiple partners are reminiscent of those debates first propagated by policy-makers in the USA such as Frazier, Moynihan, Wilson and Murray, who connect the absence of Black men in the home to the rise of the Black underclass in urban America. Thus, it is significant that the mothers should draw upon these debates in their general perceptions of Black men in Black family life. How these American policy models of Black fathering come to be found in these mothers narratives could be explained by the influence of both the White and Black media (especially newspapers)[5], which has appropriated these USA debates, negatively stereotyping the fathering role of black men in Britain as well. For example newspaper reports by the *Voice*, a Black owned newspaper, which is targetted at the Black community in Britain and the *Guardian* and *Sunday Express*, two mainstream newpapers suggest of Black men that:

> For far too long Black men have failed to support women and our children, a reality that all Black men and women must seriously reflect upon. (*Voice*, 24 August 1993:6).
> and
> If today's Black women has brought credit to her race, the Black man is a different story. Not only does he have a tendency to opt out when the patter of tiny feet comes along, he is over represented in prisons and the dole queue. (*The Guardian*, 21 March 1995, section 9:3).
> also
> The 'Linford Christie syndrome' of one-parent families is now disturbingly ingrained in Black society .... Young Black males have adopted societal norms and are a lot more carefree in their responsibilities. (*Sunday Express*, 13 August 1995:2).

Private experiences: the mothers' perceptions of Black fathers

These negative characterisations of Black fathers construct them as an homogeneous group. The individualistic nature of these men and their familial relations are denied. Yet when the mothers' discussions turn to their private experiences and the actual men in their families, a different image of Black fathers emerges to that of the generalised public discussion of Black men in family life. Generally, the mothers in my study spoke of their own male familial members and the children's fathers with warm affection, and identified them as positive influences in their lives. Even Nizinga whom I earlier quoted as speaking so disparagingly about Black men in general, presented quite a contrasting view when discussing her relationship with her own father and her daughter's father who does not live in the family home but nonetheless assumes an active participant childcare role:

> I'm the apple of his eye [father]. When I was pregnant with [daughter], it was my dad who was sort of fussing over me the most and I suppose [daughter's father] dotes on her too, he does his bit.

And later on in discussions Nizinga confirms this active participant role of her daughter's father:

> *Nizinga*: He buys her clothes – if I say to him she needs this, then he will buy it. I'm quite happy with him in that respect, she knows who her dad is, he takes her out places and he buys her clothes, he helps out. [Nizinga: age 31, single-mother: second generation mother]

The negative viewpoints concerning Black men expressed by Nizinga in an earlier quote, is not evident in defining her personal relations. Her comments above re-affirm the argument that the mothers' own experiences in relation to Black fathers often contradict the public discourse.

Black men as active participants in family life

There are many examples in the data of the mothers' recognition of the active role Black fathers assume in 'the family' and childcare. Later in this chapter I will discuss in detail the four primary roles Black fathers' assume in 'the family'. These are economic provision; childcare; guidance and advice; protection and security. Of course not all Black fathers' perform each of these roles. Also the level of participation by Black men in 'the family' varies according to each individual circumstance. However, as Anne Roschelle (1997) argues, that despite the existence of a significant gender difference between men and women involving childcare provision (women devote considerably more hours to this compared to men), there appears to be no significant ethnic difference between Black and White fathers concerning the amount of childcare they provide. This presents a direct challenge to the discourses on black fathering which identify Black fathers as assuming a marginal or absent childcare and family role.

Roschelle's study also suggests that the amount of time fathers give to childcare has increased in the last ten years for both Black and White men (Roschelle, 1997). This increased activity and participation in the family by these men is seen by some commentators as representative of a new movement by all men, from all ethnic and racial groupings, towards 'greater psychological involvement in family life', (Taylor et al. 1997:248). As a result of great insecurity in work, men of all ethnic groups are said to be placing increasing emphasis on family rather than work (ibid.). Ambiguity and confusion shrouds these men's attempts to reconcile greater involvement in home life and childcare with that of traditional normative constructions of father: as 'breadwinner', workers, with non-involvement in childcaring (Furstenburg, 1988). Both of these arguments have very similar undertones to the 'New Man' rhetoric championed since the late 1980s.

The concept of the 'New Man' has been criticised elsewhere as little more than a media gimmick (see Chapman, 1988). The idea that activity and involvement by Black fathers in the home is representative of a 'new Black man' is also problematic for a number of other reasons. Taylor's (1997) suggestion that these fathers are desiring and actively choosing to place less emphasis on work, denote privilege and élitism. A privileged power position in which 'choice' arises does not exist for the vast majority of Black men in Britain. Furthermore, Black fathers involvement in family life is not a recent phenomena caused by an attitude change concerning a fathers' role in the home. Rather as the data shows this involvement has always existed.

As a result of the difficulties first generation mothers encountered in combining childcare and full-time employment during early post-war migration to Britain (see Reynolds, 1998), these first generation African-Caribbean mothers depended very much on their husbands to share in childcare and other domestic activities:

> *Enid*: With my eldest boys, I worked nights and I would rush home to get their breakfast ready for them whilst my husband got ready for work. When [husband] came home in the afternoon we would eat. I would then leave for work and he would look after them until the next morning. [Enid, age 69, married: first generation mother]

Other male members of the family such as uncles, grandfather and brothers, also played an active role in childcare during this period:

> *Jamilla*: My earliest memory was living in [area]. My grandfather came to live with us for a while. I remember he used to look after me, because my mum and dad was working, mum at nights and my dad late. My grandad used to have me during the day. I remember him feeding me soft boiled eggs, and he taught me how to ride a tricycle. I just remember that

he was always around and my being very spoilt by him.
[Jamilla, age 25, single-mother: second generation mother]

Today, Black family members and Black fathers are portrayed as just as active in family life and childcare as in the older women's accounts. I identified four key roles these men assumed within the home, in their position as fathers. These are economic provision; childcare; guidance and advice; protection and security.

Economic provision

Economic provision has long been recognised as an important fathering function central to fathering identities (Lewis and O'Brien, 1988). This function is regarded as equally important for Black fathering identities (Cazenave, 1981; McAdoo, H, 1996; Taylor et al., 1997). The mothers claim that whilst the men in their lives believe they should contribute to family and household expenses, these mothers themselves should also assume some economic responsibility:

> *Tanya*: Both [Tanya and ex-husband] of our mothers worked, so you kind of assume that I would do the same thing as none of us had any experience of doing things differently. I know he [ex-husband] just thought I would return to work after maternity leave. It was never 'are you going back to work', but 'when are you going back to work?' [Tanya, age 40, partnered single-mother: second generation mother]

Tanya's account convey the implicit, almost taken for granted, expectation many Black men appear to possess with regards to their wife/partner economically contributing to the family income. This expectation of women's role in 'the family', shared by Tanya's ex-partner/son's father derives from a combination of historical, cultural, and economic factors. African-Caribbean women have a tradition as workers both in Britain and across the Caribbean, undetermined by factors such as maternal status, class factors, urban or rural living (see Reynolds, 1998). This culture of African-Caribbean women as workers ensures that many fathers, especially second and third generation ones, have been raised seeing their mothers in full time employment. As a result, they encounter less ambiguous expectations in terms of mother's dual domestic and economic role in the family. For many White, middle-class, fathers today, their own mothers did not contribute financially to the family, and so this was not part of their childhood experiences. Increasingly, in today's society more White mothers are engaged in full-time employment and possess a greater share of economic provision to the family. In these circumstances it could be argued that concerns about interweaving work and family pose greater adjustments for White males than African-Caribbean men (Duncan and Edwards, 1998).

The experience of African-Caribbean women (including mothers) as workers is deeply ingrained in Caribbean and African-Caribbean identities through economic necessity as well as cultural expectations (see Reynolds, 1998). There are higher rates of unemployment among young Black men and young Black women under the age of 25. Also both Black men and women are over represented in low security and low pay employment (Bhavnani, 1994; CRE, 1997; Modood, 1997). This ensures that many Black mothers cannot realistically expect their male partners to act as sole economic provider. In comparing first generation mothers' accounts of raising a family with young children during the late 1950s with second and third generation mothers' experiences today, I found the lack of Black fathers' acting as the sole economic provider to 'the family' is a relatively unchanged phenomena:

> *Pearl*: I had to go to work because there was no question of me staying at home because he [husband] wasn't earning enough. Those times were really hard, we hardly got to spend any time together, when he was going out, I was coming in or it would be the other way round. [Pearl, age 61, married, first generation mother]
>
> *Denise*: At one stage neither of us could find work and we didn't feel right just living hand to mouth on the dole. We decided that because I was a qualified hairdresser and being a woman, it would be easier for me to find work. [Denise, age 22, partnered single-mother: third generation mother]

Denise is living with her partner Michael, who is currently unemployed. Therefore, it is Denise's salary as a hairdresser they depend upon for an income. Denise's experiences represents a growing trend within younger two-parent families. Higher rates of unemployment for Black men as a result of racial inequalities in access to employment means that in some households Black fathers have a limited economic provider role. Denise and Michael have had to re-negotiate a fathering identity for Michael, which moves away from traditional constructions of father as economic provider towards one where his contribution to the family is still highly valued:

> *Denise*: During the day Michael looks after [son], he takes care of everything so that when I get home I just really have

to give him his bath and put him to bed. I don't know how I
would cope if it wasn't for him, it would be a real struggle.

Far from absenting the home as a result of unemployment and his
inability to contribute to the household financially, Michael has built
additional functions and areas of responsibilities into his fathering
identity. Moreover, he is perceived by Denise as very much involved in
the family. There appears to be an acceptance by these mothers that
due to present economic conditions and racial inequalities in employment, the fathers of their children will in all likelihood encounter
periods of economic inactivity. Therefore the re-negotiation of Black
fathering identities allows for fathers to remain at home, and undertake
some aspects of childcare, whilst the mother acts as the primary/sole
breadwinner.

The position of such fathers directly opposes the claims which
suggest the impact of economic marginality for Black fathers results in
absence and marginality from the home and family, and diminished
fathering responsibilities. As Denise's comments about her boyfriend,
Michael, clearly illustrates, the inability to act as primary economic
provider in the family does not make a man any less of a father or less
responsible and committed to his family or children. In order to move
away from constructions which pathologise Black fathers who are
unemployed or on low-income, and which minimise their importance
to the Black family, analysis needs to look beyond this narrow
identification of fathering as economic provider, and investigate other
valuable functions and roles they perform in the family. For instance,
the mothers highlighted other activities and responsibilities Black
fathers undertake, which are just as vital to the family. These are childcare, guidance and advice, protection and security.

Childcare, guidance and advice

The physical, emotional and psychological care of the child(ren) is
identified by the mothers as a key responsibility undertaken by their
children's fathers. I should stress that this is purely in a supportive
capacity, as primary responsibility for childcare remains with these
women. Furthermore the degree to which childcare occurs among
Black fathers varies according to each individual family's circumstance. In Lydia's instance, for example, the childcare her children's
fathers provide is virtually negligible. However for those fathers who
are actively involved in childcare, this care involves fathers deputising
for mothers as primary carer when these women are away from the

home (Backett, 1988). It also constitutes these fathers setting aside specific time to spend with their children and carrying out activities with them. They are also involved in everyday matters pertaining to their children's welfare or, where absent from the family home, kept informed of these.

In all childcare tasks except one, the mothers in this study describe the fathers performing tasks that parallel those performed by White fathers in other studies (see Lewis and O'Brien, 1988). The one exception is in terms of guidance and advice. Guiding children through the everyday trials and tribulations of life as they learn to become adults is something with which parents of all ethnic and class groups have to contend. However, as parents rearing Black children in Britain there is a racialised element to this guidance and advice, precipitated by the systems of racial inequalities and systems of injustice that exist in Britain. Elsewhere (see Reynolds, 1998) I highlight the way that preparing children for racism and providing them with strategies to cope with racism is an important mothering function. Black fathers are also actively involved in this too:

> *Anita*: If you're White, male and middle-class, you're always going to remain at the top. White women benefit from this too, as Black parents you think about these things, White parents take it for granted their children are going to be successful; we know our children are seen as failures before they've entered the world, so it's our job to make sure they don't end up fulfilling these expectations. In a sense we're starting out parenting from two opposite ends. I think we try to be fair, get a balance with them [children], but [husband] is much harder on them, he's pushes them more, motivating them to try harder, to try and be the best, he'll sit down and talk to them about why it is important for them – he says is if he doesn't sit down with them and make them understand about the world then no-one else is going to bother with them. So that's his thing really. He much rather do that, he feels that's more important than working all hours for more money. And he's right, the children's well-being is more important, so they should come first. [Anita, age 43, married, first generation mother]

Anita's comments are specific to her husband and the way in which he perceives guidance and advice to his children as his most important fathering responsibility. Many of the mothers support Anita's claims. Whether it be their husband/partner, children's fathers, own father, brother, uncle, or even a close male family friend, these women recognise the important role Black men possess in the family in terms of assisting them with guidance and advice around issues of 'race', racism and other systems of inequalities the children will encounter. This is especially so for their male children. As a result of particular concerns facing African-Caribbean young males in the wider public domain such as in educational underachievement, schools exclusion, police harassment and incarceration, racial violence and Black on Black male violence (Gillborn, 1995; Back, 1996; Alexander, 1996), there has been a particular concern in the parenting of an adolescent son. Providing them with the necessary guidance and advice to resist systems of racism and inequalities is seen as a central role (Reynolds, 1998).

Protection and security

In the mothers' narratives fathers as a source of protection and security for the home and family constitute another element to Black fathering identity. This involves protecting children from external threats and dangers and offering them security against this. This racialisation in terms of the protection and security provided to sons, primarily involves keeping them safe from physical violence, racially motivated or otherwise. Protection for daughters centres very much around her sexuality, whether it be protecting girls against sexual violence or securing and controlling (and thus safeguarding) her sexual virtue. Issues of 'possessiveness, a desire to preserve her innocence, the implicit threat presented by male competition for their daughter's affection,' (Sharpe, 1994:85) are also common aspects of the father-daughter relationship.

In discussions about their own childhood and relations between their daughters and fathers today, the mothers identify the way female sexuality underpins father-daughter relations, either explicitly or implicitly. Zora, a second generation mother when discussing her partners response to his two daughters arriving at adolescence, comments:

> *Zora*: He's already really possessive towards them now, so I dread to think what he's going to be like when they get older and start wanting boyfriends. As far as he's concerned, they're his little girls and that's how it's going to stay, he's already said they're not allowed to have boyfriends until they're 25 [laughing].
> *TR*: 25, You're joking, right? [laughing]

Zora: I'm not joking, he's serious. It's no man until 25 and even then he's not sure. I've told him that's not going to happen and you can't really expect it, and he says why? I know for a fact he had girlfriends from when he was 14 but he says it's different. Then he just gets all ignorant and vex [upset], and says 'I don't want to talk about it' or he'll say 'because I'm a man, I knows how man stays and at that age any boy sniffing around his daughters is up to no good, that's why no man troubling them until they're 25'. It's a bit of a touchy subject, so I bring it up sometimes just to wind him up because I know he'll get annoyed and start huffing and puffing about the place. [Zora, age 26, partnered single-mother: second generation]

Although Zora talks about her angry partner's response to any mention of his daughters' future sexuality in a quite light-hearted way, I think it is interesting that she recognises he perceives his daughters as his 'possessions', even at their very young age. It could be argued traditional constructions of patriarchal relations which incorporate issues of male ownership of the female are informing this relationship (Walby, 1990; Walkerdine, 1997). This is significant in the context of Black fathering and the African-Caribbean family because typical representations of Black family forms posit them as female-centred or 'matriarchal', with Black men very much on the periphery and possessing little power within Black family life.

Power and authority of Black fathers

Traditional constructions of Black families in the Caribbean, the USA and Britain define them as 'matriarchal'. In the literature (Stack, 1974; Sutton and Makiesky-Barrow, 1985; Senior, 1991) 'matriarchal' in this sense refers to maternal female power and authority which results in the emasculation of the Black man and situates him in a marginal familial role. The structurally powerless position that Black women and mothers occupy in society ensures the notion of the 'Black matriarch' is a problematic construction (Wallace, 1978; Davis, 1981; Staples, 1985). It also acts as a controlling image for dominant groups in society, whereby Black mothers and their family forms are rendered deviant (Hill-Collins, 1991). Nonetheless, some Black feminist theorists have embraced this term to celebrate their mothers (for example Bell-Scott, 1988). The mothers in the study also do so. Ironically, while celebrating this traditional image of Black mothers as strong and powerful when describing their own mothers, it is their fathers who emerge as possessing the greatest source of power and authority in the mothers' accounts. The following comment by Jamilla, single-mother age 25, illustrates this:

'She's [mother] the backbone of the family, she's the work-horse in the family, she's knows whats what. If anything needs asking or doing ask mummy. I think my dad is there as her support, her backup.'

Jamilla then goes onto reflect:

Having said that my dad was the disciplinarian in the family, I remember if I was getting into trouble, then he would punish me. It didn't reach the stage where he would hit me, all he would do is look at me and I would crumble. I can't recall much of it but I think what used to happen is that she [mother] would say 'go to your father' and then that would be it for me, I would be wetting myself. It was my dad that I was scared of, his physical presence.

She also remembers:

My mum would sit down and work out what bills were to be paid where, but all the major decisions and big things like moving house, buying a new car was joint. Well daddy had more input really.

Jamilla's thoughts are crucial in that they effectively sum up the contradictions and ambiguity in the power relations between Black mothers and fathers. The construct of the 'Black matriarch', as central to power relations in the Black family, provides an inadequate framework to explore these contradictions and ambiguities. Jamilla acknowledges her mother as the 'workhorse' in the family and her father as the 'backup' in specific day to day domestic activities. Here, her mother is dominant and her father provides a purely supportive role. This mirrors traditional gender divisions within the home, where the father or male figure supports in childcare and domestic duties but is not the primary figure. For other (perceived) major household issues, such as discipline, purchases of expensive household goods, however, Jamilla talks about power and authority remaining with her father. Nevertheless, Jamilla conflates her mothers' role with the notion of 'Black matriarchy', whilst overlooking her father's equally dominant position, and his physical presence. Why does this occur?

The 'Black matriarch' has come to be seen as the quintessential characteristic of Black mothering. This is so much the case that the construct of the 'Black matriarch' is universalised as normative for all Black mothering and Black family forms without detailed interrogation and acknowledgement of diverse family patterns. I noticed that in most two-parent first generation families, traditional gendered power relations inform household relations. The reality for these two parent households is that within the home the fathers appear dominant even if they hold little economic power. This suggests a contradiction between Black family ideology (matriarchal families) and social reality (see Mirza, 1992). The notion of the 'traditional' family (which posit men as dominant and women and children as subordinate) inform these family forms at an ideological level. However the social reality of cultural and economic adaptations within Black families which occurred take account of Black men's structural and economic subordinate societal position. Thus, Black fathers dominant position and authority in the family is not dependent on him acting as the sole or primary economic provider (ie. the breadwinner) within the family. Angela, a married mother in remembering family life growing up within their homes, comments:

> *Angela*: Definitely we had greater respect for dad than mum. He wasn't really there [at home] that much and when he was he was always very ... very ... I suppose very aloof would be the word. I mean he was there and everything and he would talk to us about things but he wasn't really there, if you get what I mean? He was a man who came and went, so he was part of the family but not really part of it, if you understand? When he was at home, everything was about him, we tiptoed around him and would be whispering to each other, to not disturb him if he was at home sleeping for example. And if it was anything major, like to go on a school trip, mum would always ask him and then she would tell us his decision. [Angela, age 27, married: second generation mother]

These recollections are indicative of the fact that, disempowered in wider society, home is often the place Black fathers can feel they have a sense of power and authority, and they exercise this over their wives and children (McAdoo, 1988; hooks, 1997). This is despite the fact that the mothers also work, creating a degree of financial autonomy for themselves. There would appear to be greater equity today between the second and third generation men and women in the home in terms of decision-making. However, the persistence of inequalities in the gendered division of labour within homes ensures gendered power relations still persist.

Absent fathers in Black family lives

At present 51% of African-Caribbean families are female headed households by a single-mother (Modood, 1997).[6] As a result of the high number of female headed households, and perceived male absence, the 'baby-father' syndrome dominates characterisation of 'absent fathers' and constitutes a key representation of African-Caribbean masculinised identities. The 'baby-father syndrome' champions the idea that Black men have multiple children by multiple partners, without pause for care and responsibility of the child. Although attempts have been made to challenge this characterisation (see Song and Edwards, 1997; Reynolds, 1997), its common sense appeal remains.

A substantial proportion of single-mothers in my study (about two-thirds of them) did state that their ex-partners/children's fathers have additional children from subsequent relationships. However, most of these men exist at any one time within stable, conjugal relationships with their partner. In addition, despite this 'absence' it is clear from these mothers accounts, that their children's fathers still actively partic-ipate in childrearing and childcare, and this shape these women's mothering experiences.

> *Maxine*: The children's fathers helps out. Even if you're single, the father can still be around, so they can help with the upbringing if they want to. [Maxine, age 29, single-mother: second generation mother]

Maxine's comment is indicative of the way fathers' absence from the home does not automatically exclude him from childcare and family life. In can be argued that 'absent' fathers in fact assume an 'absent presence' in family life. They are absent in terms of no longer living within the households, but they are still present and very active in their children's and mothers' lives. The majority of single mothers I spoke to had regular contact with their children's fathers. Only Lydia, age 28, a single-mother with two children by different partners, and Joy, age 39, a single-mother with five children, again with different partners, have very limited contact with these men. The men's access and involvement with children is agreed informally by both parents. Only in the case of Michele, a single-mother, age 28, did the legal system intervene to secure father's visitation rights on terms that are agreeable to both of them.

These 'absent' fathers have regular contact with their children and are active in childrearing, either visiting the family home or arranging to have the children spend time with them, primarily at weekends and during school holidays. Many of the activities and responsibilities which these mothers describe as performed by these 'absent fathers' are identical to those where the father lives in the family home. Describing the relationship with 'absent' fathers and their involvement in childcare, the following mothers note:

> *TR*: Does he [your daughter's father] play any part in raising her?
> *Nizinga*: Since I split up with him yeh – he has become far more interested in [our daughter]. Before I left him, I was always doing the buying, doing the providing. Now he helps out. If he's not doing anything in particular he will take her overnight, and, she stays with him some weekends. He buys her clothes – if I say to him, she needs this, then he will buy it. I'm quite happy with him in that respect. She knows who her dad is, he takes her out places and he buys her clothes, he helps out. [Nizinga, age 31, single-mother: second generation mother]
> *Tanya*: He's a good father, I can't really fault him on that. He gives him money to buy clothes and those computer games. It's nice because it takes the pressure off me to provide everything for him. I'm glad he's there for [his son], that he's a responsible father. [Tanya, age 40, partnered single-mother: second generation mother]

What is so interesting about Nizinga's and Tanya's accounts is that they each identify these men as playing a more active role in child care and childrearing after the relationship with their children's fathers broke down and these men left the family home. Prior to separation, the men spent less time with their children. Neale and Smart (1997) in their studies of divorced fathers active participation in child care report similar findings. One could therefore argue that fathers' presence in the home does not guarantee greater time devoted to child care.

In the same way 'absent' fathers can be said to assume an 'absent presence' within the family, fathers who live within the family household home but are away from it for long periods of time, can be said to assume a 'present absence'. Diane Reay (1998) found that fathers who are present in the home, actually do very little child care and domestic tasks. It is ironic that whilst the latter type of fathering is celebrated as normative, the former, is vilified.

'Absent present' fathers are still considered to be important part of the family by the mothers, even after the men have departed the family home:

> *Jamilla*: Sometimes I want to rely more on [her daughter's father] – alright yeh, things didn't work out between us and

he left. He's not here all the time but I still see him as family, as part of my family. [Jamilla, age 25, single-mother: second generation mother]

Maxine: Well he is his dad, so there's not much I can do to stop him. It's he's like family really, you're stuck with them. When you have a child with the man, if he decides he's going to be one of those dads that stick around then you're stuck with him too. [Maxine, age 29, single-mother: second generation mother]

To Jamilla and Maxine, both of their children's 'absent' fathers are perceived as family. Relatives of these fathers, such as parents, brothers and sisters, uncles and aunts, also provide support to these single-mothers reinforcing claims that these 'absent' men and their kinship networks constitute family.

In addition to the 'absence presence' role these fathers provide in terms of child care and childrearing, as 'absent present' fathers they also have a very real effect on the way these women experience mothering. The single-mothers operate around the notion of men in their lives even if they are absent (see Pulsipher, 1993). The single-mothers also still question their position as 'single-mothers' in relation to the normative yardstick of a 'present' father and husband. This is evident by the way in which they discuss their children's well-being in relation to the perceived benefits of a father's 'normative presence':

Jamilla: Sometimes I wonder whether she's [my daughter] losing out, whether I'm enough. Sometimes when her dad comes round, even my dad or my brother, she's really clingy to them and I wonder whether she's bored with me, the female and if she's missing that male influence in her life, well [her father] is an influence is her life but I suppose I'm talking about that permanent influence, a father who is always here for her all the time. [Jamilla, age 25, single-mother: second generation mother]

Jamilla's discussion on the necessity of a male presence and the earlier accounts by the second-generation single-mothers who expressed the need for male role-models in their children's (but especially their sons') lives reinforce a normative 'yearning' for 'traditional' family forms, rather than getting on with the business of overtly recognising the value of their lived 'alternative family' forms. Although these mothers describe their 'alternative' single-mother family status, they still use the language of 'traditional' family ideology when in actual fact their family form has progressively changed.

All of these factors negate the marginal influence 'absent' fathers are said to have on family life and childcare, and which is usually identified in studies on single-mother families.

Conclusion

Black fathers are active participants in parenting and child care. Traditional representations of Black families, where Black fathers are marginal/absent fail to acknowledge this. In this chapter, from the mothers' accounts, I have identified four key functions performed by Black men in the family. The first, economic provision is largely perceived as a 'traditional' fathering role. The others – child care, guidance and advice and protection and security – constitute a re-negotiation of fathering identities by these men to encompass other roles. Thus, those fathers who are unemployed and therefore unable to financially contribute to their families can still undertake a significant role in family lives.

Many of the fathers who live outside the home assume an 'absent present' position, rather than disappearing from 'the family' altogether. Sadly, studies such as Moynihan (1965), Wilson (1987) and Bowman and Forman, (1997) tend to equate the high percentage of single-parent mothers with male absenteeism. These studies also suggest wider structural inequalities such as higher rates of Black male unemployment and low incomes are responsible for the Black father's absence in the family. This misrepresents Black fathers' positions. I am not suggesting that mothers and 'absent' fathers enjoy a 'perfect' relationship. There can be tensions, hostilities and problems, as with any relationship that has broken down. However, most do the best they can within the means and time available to them. They often arrive at arrangements that are agreeable to both parties for the sake of the child. It is a fallacy to assume that the fathers' 'absence' from the home means that he disappears altogether or is marginal in children's and mothers' lives. Whilst 'absent', his presence is very much felt by both of them. As I illustrate in this chapter, fathers assume an active participant role in childcare, and the way mothers still perceive these 'absent fathers' as family means the men inform the women's mothering identity.

As in the case of the 'absent father' misrepresentation, it is also too simplistic to say that Black family forms are matriarchal. The term 'matriarchal' is contentious in itself. If we take this to mean female economic independence and authority within the home (see Moynihan, 1965; Joseph and Lewis, 1980, Wilson, 1987), there are indeed examples where this does exist. Nevertheless, associating matriarchy in this form as culturally specific to Black families does not allow for express-ing diversity in family structures. Evidence exists in this chapter that within some of the first generation two-parent households, the fathers held the greater power and authority despite the fact that the mothers worked and they were economically independent.

In my study, contrary to the homogenising tendency within studies to stereotype all Black men as the same there was much differ-ence and diversity between fathers. In documenting the experiences of mothers who enjoy supportive and positive relationships with Black men within their families I recognise that all relationships are not like this. Many Black mothers can and do encounter negative and abusive experiences. There is no single construction which encompasses all of these men's experiences. Unfortunately, within the public discourse of Black family lives Black fathers are either invisible, pathologised or presented as absent from the family home. The experiences of Black fathers who live within the family household and also Black middle-class fathers are under represented. It is only when difference and diversity of Black fathering is recognised and that Black men consti-tute an active part of family life (whether they are present or 'absent present' in the family and also irrespective of class and income levels) that their experiences can be accurately documented and the construc-tions of Black fathering can remove itself from the negative debates.

Notes

1 I would like to thank Heidi Mirza, Rosalind Edwards and all of the mothers who participated in the research upon which this chapter is based.
2 In challenging these negative representations of Black men in 'the family', it is not my intention to present Black men as a homogeneous group. Vast differences exist between Black men and their relationship to, and with, their families. There are instances where Black men provide a negative contribution to the family (see Mama, 1993 for example). However, there are also many more instances where Black men's contribution to the family is positive. Nonetheless in the discourse of Black men in the family, but especially Black fathers, this is very rarely seen. Thus, the central aim of this chapter is to make visible this latter group of diverse Black men who make a positive contribution to the family.
3 The term 'babyfather' is a Caribbean colloquial term to describe Black men who have children outside of wedlock. Both the Black and the White press have appro-priated this term (also 'babymother') to document Black male-female relationships and the high incidence of single-mother households amongst African-Caribbean families. This notion of the 'babyfather' was further popularised in Patrick Augustus' bestseller *Babyfather* (1994). Over the years, however, the 'babyfather' and 'babymother' have increasingly been criticised by members of the Black com-munity for the negative way in which it stereotypes Black familal relations and the way they resonate with slave images which confine Black people to 'breeders'.
4 During January 1996 to January 1997 I interviewed 20 African-Caribbean mothers across South London. The interviews formed part of my doctoral thesis which

examined the experiences of African-Caribbean mothers in Britain. To ensure that I had a diverse sample the mothers that were selected for interview came from differing socio-economic groups and spanned a wide age range (from 19–81 years) (see Reynolds, 1998).

5 See Song and Edwards (1997) and Reynolds (1997a) for White and Black based newspaper examples which persistently negatively characterize Black fathers.

6 This figure also includes mothers who are living with male partners in a non-marital conjugal relationship. It is estimated that 32.% of single-parent families are the sole adults within a household (Owen, 1998).

9 | Middle class kinship networks in Guyana

Trevor Noble

Introduction

Levi-Strauss (1977: 20) argued that a kinship system '… exists only in human consciousness; it is an arbitrary system of representations, not the spontaneous development of a real situation'. In the same vein in his account of kinship in Guyana and Jamaica, RT Smith contrasted the relative stability of these cultural conceptions of kinship and the changeable social process which they mediated and instituted (1988: 2) But the data he described was collected over twenty years earlier in 1967 and while the systemic characteristics of kinship may be more or less unchanging, their relation to the actual social processes of kin knowledge, interaction and maintained contact is a contingent one. Social relations with kinsfolk may be a great deal more subject to the influence of changing social, economic, demographic and even political circumstances. To focus our attention on kinship systems is to give emphasis to relatively stable cultural norms while the actual size and configuration of people's actual kinship networks might be undergoing a variety of changes.

Background

Some of the extensive literature has proposed the existence of distinctively West Indian cultural patterns in family and kinship organisation. Much of this material, however, was gathered when most Caribbean societies were still colonial territories. The economic and demographic changes which have taken place since independence have had extensive but not fully explored repercussions for many aspects of culture, including family norms and behaviour. Cultural values may sometimes reflect a remoter history, it is true, but everyday relationships are made and remade within more immediate circumstances. Smith's study *The Negro Family in British Guiana* (RT Smith, 1956, 1953, 1955) vividly

154

described the life of the most economically insecure and least skilled Afro-Guyanese families in three rural villages in colonial times. Smith and Jayawardena (1958, 1959) examined Indo-Guyanese family life on two sugar estates and in a rice-growing area (see also Jayawardena 1960, 1962; Robinson 1970). We should not, however, assume that these traditional patterns of village family life either were then or are now generally typical. Traditional ways neither indicate the direction of change, nor do they always represent the experience of all or even the majority. Smith himself suggests that the pattern of family life he distinguished in British Guiana was mainly confined to the lowest status group even within the villages (1988, pp 253–4).[1]

Since independence in 1966, Guyanese society has gone through many vicissitudes politically, economically and demographically (Singh 1979, Barber and Jeffrey 1986, Thomas 1988). These have had substantial consequences even for those not personally involved in the extensive social mobility consequent upon political independence.

The group who provided information about their kinship networks described in this study included men and women, Afro-Guyanese and Indo-Guyanese; single, married and divorced. Their ages ranged from 27 to 46 years which meant that all had more or less come to adulthood in the post-colonial period (that is, since 1966) and had lived through much the same historical circumstances.

The respondents came from a variety of backgrounds in terms of parents' occupations and place of origin. All were lower middle class by occupation and mainly employed in the public sector as junior managerial, administrative and clerical personnel or minor professionals, mostly teachers, librarians and social workers of various kinds. Though all the women who provided information were economically active, there is no obvious reason why women in employment should have fewer relatives than non-employed women. They may have less time to spend with them, but this would mainly affect interaction with close relatives. The group was homogeneous not only by their own occupations however but also by education. All were current or former mature students of the University of Guyana and were studying or had studied part-time. This is a less restrictive factor than it might be in many other societies (Searwar, 1970). Until 1991 education in Guyana was free and open to all citizens up to and including university degree level, and the availability of all university courses on a part-time basis meant that many people who were unable to continue their studies immediately after school returned to do so later. While the children of more prosperous professional or business upper middle-class families generally tend to go into higher education overseas, mostly either elsewhere in the Caribbean or in North America, this element of educational selectivity

in my respondent group increases the degree of similarity of class position amongst them.

The class homogeneity of the group means that any diversity
amongst them has to be attributed to other factors than class differences. But the selection of well educated middle-class respondents has
other methodological advantages as well. Obviously the question of
accessibility was a consideration; much more important however was
the intrinsic interest in gathering data on a structurally significant but
under-researched stratum in any post-colonial society. The professional
and administrative cadres in newly independent societies are not only
critical groups in political and economic development but are arguably
more acutely exposed to the processes of personal social mobility and
general social change than peasantry, proletariat or political elite. A
large and growing sector of society, this stratum is where the balance
of inherited cultural tradition and adaptation to changed social conditions is likely to be especially critical.

While respondents were socially homogeneous in terms of their
class, age category and education this of course was not true of all their
relatives. On the one hand any diversity among their kin would be
likely to blur the distinctiveness of any class or age-linked pattern that
might be found. The inclusion of Afro-Guyanese and Indo-Guyanese
within a class-homogenous set of families makes it possible to estimate
the relative importance of cultural tradition against common socio-
economic circumstances. The comparison of men and women of
similar educational and occupational status also provides us with an
indication of how much is attributable specifically to gendered differences rather than the result of being in paid employment instead of
being confined to a purely domestic role. Thus by considering groups
significant in their own right but also constituting critical cases, it is
possible to look for the limits of generalisations that have been or
might be made about kinship in Guyana.

The data on kinship networks was gathered graphically, that is, by
asking respondents to complete, or rather to help the investigator complete a chart showing relationships of marriage (including non-married
unions) and descent amongst those they considered their relatives or
'family'. The respondents almost all found this a helpful and enjoyable
way of recording information which simultaneously served them as a
memory aid with the help of which they visualise the spread of relatives and sometimes recall groups or individuals who had not at first
sprung to mind. This, it should be emphasised, was a form of self-
prompting and the content and context of the kinship chart or diagram
was determined entirely by the respondents themselves. They were
asked only to include all those they regarded as relatives or 'family'

with whom they maintained some degree of contact. Deceased relatives were included in the diagrams only where necessary to show the connections between living members and were not counted in any of the numerical comparisons reported here.

From the investigator's point of view this graphic method of recording data has other advantages beside the enjoyment or interest it gave respondents and the consequently probably enhanced comprehensiveness and accuracy of the results. It also lends itself to a very straightforward second order analysis.

By referring to 'effective kinship networks', I mean then, the set of relationships which people maintain with living relatives rather than a notional 'genealogical universe' which includes all those living and dead with whom they might be helped to trace some connection regardless of whether in fact they have any contact with those indicated or not (R T Smith 1978, 1988). A genealogical universe inevitably embraces large numbers of people who are not currently members of the respondent's effective kinship network. Of those kin included in the genealogical universes Smith described, 29 per cent were dead (1988: 50, Table 5) and with 25 per cent of the consanguines identified, the respondents had no contact whatsoever (ibid. p 76). In many cases his respondents did not know either the names or even the sex of those they included and neither recognised nor acknowledged them as family, though connections were traced in the course of the research questioning (ibid. p 49 N 1). Clearly, a genealogical universe is a much larger thing than the world of living family ties and obligations, of lived relationships, in which everyday conduct is shaped. Those are the components of the more limited, if not always precisely bounded, group which may be described as a kinship network. However, it is not possible to distinguish such groups within Smith's data as so far published. In setting out to describe their effective kinship networks I asked the respondents to determine for themselves whom they acknowledged as being members of their 'family'.

Network size

In total my twenty-three respondents identified 1750 relatives distributed through 627 households. The median kinship network comprised 72 members in 28 separate households. There was no significant difference in network size as recorded by men and women, but the two ethnic groups did differ. Afro-Guyanese women acknowledged more kin than Afro-Guyanese men did, but the opposite was true amongst the Indo-Guyanese. However with a median size of 82 Indo-Guyanese kinship networks were larger than those reported by the Afro-Guyanese with a median size of only 56, a difference statistically significant at the five per cent level ($x^2 = 4.49$ df.1).

To represent the sample as a whole without being led astray by extreme cases, let us to begin with, consider the array of median values. The 'typical' respondent was a married woman of thirty-two. One of a family of six brothers and sisters, at the time of her interview she herself had one child. Four of her siblings were married and she had eight nieces and nephews. She acknowledged her sisters' and brothers' husbands and wives as members of her family but none of their other affinal connections. Our median respondent recognised more relatives on her mother's side than her father's, 26 as against 16. Of the total tally of 71 acknowledged kin with whom she maintained some degree of contact more than thirty per cent lived overseas. As a general picture of middle class kinship networks in Guyana there is little here that would seem distinctively Caribbean or, with the exception firstly of the large number of overseas kin and secondly the relatively large ego's sibling group, that would sharply distinguish Guyanese family patterns from the average in North America or West European societies. However, as is to be expected, the median case can be a misleading guide to a diverse population and we now must consider the data in a little more detail.

I argued earlier that social change may have led to changes in kinship behaviour, as represented in the composition of the kinship networks people maintain in practice, while cultural values may endure with little modification. This relates to the question of external structural constraints as against cultural tradition as the major determinants of family and kinship systems (Hoetink 1961). If the politico-economic character of post-colonial society has played the major role in shaping kinship and family patterns then we should expect there to be little or no difference between families in a similar class position regardless of their ethnic origin (Comitas and Lowenthal, 1973; Whitehead, 1978). Marked differences of family and kinship patterns between different ethnic groups regardless of similar class location would in contrast indicate the continuing influence of distinctive cultural tradition even into post-colonial society.

For men and women in both ethnic groups, ties of common descent are considerably more important than ties of marriage. One woman included only consanguines in her chart, excluding all affines, except for her eldest brother's wife, on the grounds that they were not relatives of hers. The exception was unexplained. While she was an extreme case, most respondents recognised only a small proportion of affines as relations, usually no more than the spouses of their own and their parents' sibling groups and, if married, their own spouses' parents. Affines account for only about one in four relatives for respondents in each gender and ethnic group. Many affinal connections indeed are not acknowledged as 'family' at all.

Effective kinship networks in the Guyanese middle class rarely go beyond three generation in depth or beyond first cousins in range. Ego's siblings and their children together with his/her aunts, uncles and first cousins account for about two thirds of all kin. When first cousins' spouses and children are added 88 per cent of all acknowledged kin are accounted for and there are apparently no differences in this regard between men and women or Afro-Guyanese and Indo-Guyanese. Effective kinship networks then are generally shallow in generations and narrow in range. Contact appears to be maintained within and through a group of siblings.

As the parent generation dies off, contact is lost with cousins and the depth and range of the network is retained at more or less the same level for each succeeding generation. There is, however, an interesting difference between the numerically larger and smaller kinship networks here which runs counter to what might have been intuitively expected. While there are no differences in the proportion of kin represented by close relatives, that is, siblings and spouses plus their children in the ego and parent generations, cousins' children and spouses unsurprisingly represent a much smaller proportion of kin in the smaller kinship networks. What was less expected was that more remote kin account for a significantly greater percentage of relatives, almost one in four, noted by respondents with smaller kinship networks as compared with only about one in fourteen in the largest networks. (largest: smallest networks x^2 10.53 df.1 p <0.01) Whether this represents a yearning to retain even remote contacts on the part of those with fewer relatives round them or some sort of kin overload on the part of those with many is a matter for further investigation. It would be especially interesting to know about threshold levels in either case.

Elementary and extended family households

The residential group of a couple living together along with any children they might have or of a lone parent and (usually) her children is commonly described as the nuclear or elementary family on the grounds that it is the nucleus or elementary component of wider kinship structures. This is the usual residential grouping among the Guyanese middle class. Of the households identified in the kinship charts 55 per cent were nuclear families and only eight per cent were extended family households where this nuclear pattern is extended by a generation or by marriage.

These proportions, however, are misleading. The remaining 37 per cent of households include not only single persons living alone but also those where relatives were co-resident with others not acknowledged as kin. In such cases this might either reflect my respondents' limited knowledge of other members of some households or the effective limits of their acknowledged kinship. Logically the latter must always be the case though the former may not always be so. That is to say, as we have seen, in some cases members of a household could be identified but were not recognised as relatives and were therefore excluded from the chart whilst in other instances my respondent simply did not know anything about other possible members of a relative's household. Such unknown co-residents were clearly de-facto also outside the range of acknowledged kin.

It seems reasonable to assume that knowledge of ego's, ego's siblings', parents' and grandparents' households would be reliable. Among the households within this more narrowly circumscribed group, 75.8 per cent were nuclear families as defined above, 18.5 per cent were by the limited definition employed here extended family households, and only 5.6 per cent were single person households. We have no grounds for believing that these proportions should be confined to close kin alone and would not be evenly distributed across the whole kinship networks. Consequently, it can be inferred that, after identifying nuclear and extended family households in the reported kinship networks and allowing a consistent proportion of single person households, the remaining 31 per cent of households contain kin plus persons not acknowledged as relatives. At the periphery of a significant proportion of middle-class Guyanese kinship networks, therefore, it is clearly not the case that kinship ties always link household with household (cf. Firth 1956: 62–63, Firth et al. 1970: 197) but that they very often take a more individually selective form. Extended family households were more common in the Afro-Guyanese networks with a ratio of extended to nuclear households of 1:5.2 compared with 1: 16.3 amongst the Indo-Guyanese, but that still means less than 15 per cent of Afro-Guyanese households and only a little over five per cent of the Indo-Guyanese could be described as extended.

Matrilaterals and patrilaterals

Regarding Caribbean families, as RT Smith observes, 'there is general agreement that … women play an unusually prominent role in the domestic and kinship domains' (1988: 2). There have been a number of disagreements about why this should be so (Cohen, 1956; Herskovits, 1960; Hyman, 1961; Massiah, 1983; Manyoni 1977; Monagan, 1985; Rodman, 1966; Whitehead, 1978) and whether the explanation is primarily cultural or structural. Much of the empirical material on which the view of the predominance both of women as kinship agents and of matrilateral kin ties is based, refers to disadvantaged and localised communities (Manyoni 1980) and it is worthwhile asking whether it is equally valid a picture of kinship amongst the less disadvantaged, the more mobile or indeed amongst more recently investigated groups. Thus, the question arises whether the dominance of female kin connections and matrilateral ties is characteristic of a persistent Caribbean family culture in general or perhaps, alternatively, only of those least privileged rural groups at a particular historical phase of development which have been the subject of the great bulk of the ethnographic investigations.

As we have noted, respondents on the whole included more matrilateral relatives than patrilaterals on their kinship charts and this was equally true for all men and all women for Afro-Guyanese and Indo-Guyanese respondents taken together. However it should be noted that while in two out of three families matrilateral kin predominated, in one third of cases patrilateral kin predominated and in one fairly small network there was an exact balance.

The general picture masks a considerable amount of variety amongst individual networks. It was least amongst Indo-Guyanese men. Their networks ranged in size only between 74 and 90 acknowledged kin but, contrary to expectations from traditional Hindu family patterns, in this middle-class group in only one case did patrilaterals outnumber matrilaterals 30 to 26. There was much greater diversity amongst the Indo-Guyanese women with Rashmee Narayan[2] identifying 106 members of her kinship network but only one of them a patrilateral. At the other extreme Laksmi Kanhai counted only 29 in her widely scattered kinship network with patrilaterals outnumbering matrilaterals 16 to 10. Mrs Narayan's father was an only child, her grandparents were all dead and there were no known patrilateral cousins or other relatives. Though she identified all her matrilateral first cousins she knew few of their children as only one uncle and his family remained in Guyana. Since 29 of the 31 households in her kinship network were located outside Guyana, one might conclude this had become a Canadian family with only the slenderest Guyanese roots surviving. Of the nine separate households in Laksmi Kanhai's kinship network at the opposite numerical extreme, many were located overseas too: two in the USA, two in Australia and one, her late mother's cousin's family, in India. This was the only instance in the sample of a contact maintained with India and the cousin in question was a Guyanese whose mother had emigrated after the interracial conflicts of the 1960s. With the exception of the overseas marriages of emigrants from both groups, the Indo-Guyanese are quite as exclusively West Indian in their kinship as the Afro-Guyanese. Ms Kanhai lived with her late father's mother and kept in touch with the families of four of his cousins and all their children.

Amongst Afro-Guyanese women we can contrast Martha Lyle (married aged 32) with 70 patrilateral kin and only 26 matrilaterals with Judy Worthington (single aged 31) acknowledging only ten patrilateral kin but 58 matrilaterals. Mrs Lyle's network stretched no further than the children of her first cousins with no 'outside' children at all while Judy Worthington counted her maternal great uncle's great grandchildren, her maternal great grandmother's and grandfather's outside children's grandchildren and, on the patrilateral side, her paternal uncle's outside daughter, his former wife, present common-law wife but not the mother of his acknowledged and co-resident children. It is nonetheless the case that amongst Afro-Guyanese women, in seven cases out of ten, matrilaterals outnumbered patrilateral kin. There was no such obviously predominant pattern in the Afro-Guyanese men's kinship networks. Robert Kaplan (divorced, aged 45) acknowledged 167 relatives up to first cousins' children including outside children and, altogether, more than twice as many patrilateral as matrilateral relatives, 109 against 40. Thomas Austin on the other hand reckoned only 42 in his kinship network with twice as many matrilaterals as patrilaterals, 14:7.

Matrifocal families

The Caribbean family has been described as having high rates of illegitimacy and low rates of marriage, as matrifocal in structure with wide and strong kinship networks particularly on the matrilateral side (see, for example, Davenport, 1961; Dubreuil, 1965; Ebanks et al., 1974; Greenfield, 1962; Hoetink, 1961; Otterbein, 1965; Rubenstein 1983b; Schlesinger, 1968a,b; MG Smith, 1957, 1962; RT Smith 1963, 1988; Solien, 1960). This characterisation has formed the basis of a well established stereotype not only for the region but related also to the families of the Caribbean Diaspora. An extensive literature has grown up beginning with the early studies of Black rural matrifocal family life by Henriques in Jamaica (1949, 1953) and Smith in British Guiana (1953, 1955, 1956) in the 1940s and 50s. The general picture that emerges is of what Monagan (1985) calls 'the West Indian mating system'. She describes a Trinidad village in 1970 where women tend to have their first children while still living at home with their mothers, marrying only much later while men generally only marry when their own mothers have died. Rubenstein (1980) found that exactly two thirds of the households in the village he studied deviated from the nuclear family pattern with a widespread acceptance of extra-marital mating and parenting in the lower class. This confirms the findings of Rodman's (1966) Trinidad study which indicated an inverse correlation between acceptance of non marital unions and social class. Outside the region itself in his ethnographic study of a dozen West Indian families settled in the English West Midlands, Driver (1982) discovered a wide variety of structural patterns both within the nuclear family and in wider kinship networks. He concluded, however, that for some time mother-centred households were likely to be a persistent feature of West Indian family life, though adapted in various ways to their changed circumstances after migration. This was confirmed by the Labour Force Surveys for 1987–9 which found that 44 per cent of all West Indian families in Britain with dependent children were headed by lone mothers and another five per cent by lone fathers in Britain compared to the proportions of 16 per cent and two per cent of all minority groups taken together (Haskey 1989; see, also, Owen in this volume).

Manyoni (1980) and Schlesinger (1968a and b), however, have questioned the limited range of reference in Caribbean family research which, they argue, has tended to focus almost exclusively on the least privileged segment of society to the detriment of a full understanding of the social processes involved. Manyoni, nevertheless, concluded from his 1977 survey in Barbados that extramarital relations and parenthood were more common than those within marriage.

Revisionism on this question is, however, now itself of some antiquity dating at least from WJ Goode's sceptical 1960 review of the literature on illegitimacy in the Caribbean (1960). More recently Gardner and Podolefsky (1977) found that amongst peasant and proletarian males in Dominica in the 1970s, although cohabitation tends to be about as common as marriage up to their mid thirties and marriage tends to be late (modal age 43 years) almost everyone marries eventually. MacDonald and MacDonald (1973) found little evidence for a general pattern of matrifocal families and large numbers of children born out of wedlock in Trinidad and Tobago. Similarly Charbit's findings from his surveys in Guadeloupe and Martinique (1980) indicate that residential matrifocality was only a marginal phenomenon and nuclear family structures were the most frequent. While the British Labour Force Survey referred to of course confirms that a majority of

West Indian families with dependent children there involved married or cohabiting couples (*ibid* Table 4: 38).

There are problems of operational definition to be confronted before all this can be examined empirically. For example a widow and her children cannot necessarily be regarded as a matrifocal family in the normative sense, although of course even before the death of her spouse in some cases that might have been the case. However, though as a consequence we may very slightly underestimate the prevalence of the type, we can define the matrifocal famly as a household containing a mother and her children plus any other relatives except the children's father (but not when he is deceased). Out of all households identified by these respondents, 6.5 per cent could be described as containing matrifocal families by this definition. In the Afro-Guyanese networks the proportion was nine per cent as against only 1.8 per cent in the Indo-Guyanese (p<0.01). The difference between male and female centred networks was small and not statistically significant. Even if every widowed mother and every mother with an unrecorded partner (that is, not treated simply as a partner not acknowledged as a relative) were to be counted as matrifocal families, clearly an overestimate (Monagan, 1985; Valee, 1965), the proportion of matrifocal families among the networks of these middle class respondents would rise only to 13.2 per cent over all. Even amongst the Afro-Guyanese networks the proportion would rise only to 14.4 per cent of all families or almost 19 per cent of all nuclear families as defined above, and 14.6 per cent of nuclear families amongst the Indo-Guyanese. Whilst the networks described here were all focused on middle class respondents, not all their relatives were middle class. In a set of networks focused on respondents of lower socio-economic status it is conceivable that the proportion of matrifocal families could have been higher. However, the attention this pattern has received in the literature as a distinctive feature of Caribbean family life may seem to be greatly misleading when we contemplate the other 80 per cent plus of families reported here.

While the majority of middle-class Afro-Guyanese and Indo-Guyanese live in non-matrifocal nuclear family households, the small differences between the two communities in this respect would appear to be strongly associated with differences in the prevailing attitudes towards marriage. Amongst the Indo-Guyanese respondents and their relatives, conjugal relationships are more likely to be characterised by legal marriage and to be more long enduring than among the relatives of the Afro-Guyanese respondents. Afro-Guyanese kinship networks as a result include a higher proportion of severed conjugal ties ($x^2 =$ 33.38 df. 1p<0.01). It has been suggested that the fewer interruptions in their conjugal unions may account for the slightly higher fertility in the Indo-Guyanese group (Nevadomsky, 1985; Roberts 1975; Schwarz, 1965; Singh, 1979) and possibly thus their slightly larger kinship networks. Marital instability was notably more frequent amongst Afro-Guyanese with 34 per cent of all Afro-Guyanese unions severed (not counting deaths) compared with seven per cent amongst the Indo Guyanese. Similarly 16 per cent of Afro-Guyanese consanguines were related as half-siblings, more than three times the proportion noted amongst Indo-Guyanese (p<0.05) while multiple unions were more than twice as common at 18 per cent of cases for the former group as amongst the latter. If the Indo-Guyanese hardly appear to conform to the supposedly Caribbean type of family at all then, no more than a small minority of the relatives of the middle class Afro-Guyanese do either, and scarcely in such numbers to distinguish amongst them a Caribbean type of family significantly different from patterns found elsewhere in the populations in the industrialised countries.

Overseas kin

From census data we know that less than one per cent of the population as a whole were born outside Guyana, most of them elsewhere in the Caribbean. Emigrants, in contrast, mainly head for North America. Seventy-five per cent of the households containing relatives overseas identified by my respondents were in the USA or Canada. Another 14 per cent lived in the UK and only seven per cent elsewhere in the Caribbean. Thirty-nine per cent of all acknowledged kin lived outside Guyana. Three out of four networks have more than 25 per cent of their members living overseas and, in 26 per cent, more than half were living abroad. Although the balance of migration has been consistently outward since about 1916, the rate of emigration increased sharply with the deterioration of the Guyanese economy after the early 1970s (Thomas, 1988, pp 251–265). Between 1965 and 1985 per capita GDP fell by a third and a cautious estimate of net migration in the period since World War II (Noble, 1991) suggests that around a quarter of a million Guyanese are now living out of the country. To put that in some kind of perspective, that is equivalent to over 30 per cent of the presently resident population, a proportion only a little short of the Lebanese living abroad after that country's disastrous civil war (*The Economist*, 3 April 1993: 78).

When we refer to relatives overseas, then, in Guyana we are referring to emigrant Guyanese. Indo-Guyanese families on average contain a higher proportion of overseas kin than Afro-Guyanese families. This suggests the former are more likely to emigrate than the latter, though, having on average slightly larger total networks, it may be that they are also more likely to keep in touch with their emigrant relatives. The reason for the even more marked differences in the proportion of over-seas kin in the networks of women compared with men in both ethnic groups is harder to explain. The average size of men's and women's kinship networks is much the same, but the explanation probably lies not so much in the character of the networks described here as in the respondents themselves. The mean age of these respondents was just under 34 and in the 1980s, two-thirds of Guyanese emigrants had left the country by then. As women generally emigrated at younger ages than men (United Nations, 1987; Daly-Hill & Zaba, 1981) by the time they had reached the age when they were interviewed, those who described their kinship networks to me were less likely to emigrate than the men. The lower proportion of potential emigrants amongst the women makes them in comparison a more residual group who have remained behind while a higher proportion of their relatives have migrated. This is not then a matter of chronological age but of the phase in the family cycle of migration which they had reached.

The continuing importance of relatives overseas to those remain-ing behind is difficult to quantify but has at least four important strands. First, overseas kin are a source of regular or occasional remit-tances in times of hardship, for those without a regular income or when the costs of medicines, doctors or dentists bills have to be met (Brana-Shute & Brana-Shute 1982; Rubenstein 1982). Although this kind of subsidy is sometimes from parents to children left behind, or between siblings, it seems most commonly to be from emigrant adult children to ageing parents (see Stark & Lucas 1988) and, as such, was only indirectly experienced by the respondents in this study. Second, over-seas kin may send back consumer goods, clothing, electrical appli-ances, spares, even some manufactured foodstuffs unavailable or prohibitively expensive in Guyana – the so-called 'barrel phenome-non'. This type of benefit is much more widely distributed and involves a wider range of kin relationships than direct money remittances. Third, overseas kin represent a range of potential sponsors for overseas visiting or further emigration. Fourth, of course they are family and ties of affection or family loyalty may remain strong even without a material interest sustaining them.

Conclusion

The amount of individual variation within ethnic and sex of ego groups is greater than that between them. Their considerable diversity is one of the most striking features of these kinship networks. Generalisations made about aggregates will frequently be very misleading in individual cases. Makers of family policy and those agencies and professionals active in its implementation need to be much more aware of the tremendous differences that make each family unique. In general the socio-economic circumstances of both groups appear to shape generally similar, though individually diverse, patterns. The class homogeneity of the respondents, however, suggests that such small though significant differences as do emerge from this evidence attest to the persistence of ethnic cultural differences sufficiently important to moderate generalisations about West Indian or Caribbean patterns of family life when these, in so far as they are sustainable at all, apply perhaps only to the Afro-Caribbean population.

The extent to which kinship amongst any members of the Guyanese lower-middle class conforms to the stereotype pattern of 'the West Indian family', however, appears to be slight. Notwithstanding the nostalgia for the village community apparent in much recent Guyanese literary fiction and in some of the academic studies of family life in the Caribbean zone, we need to recognise the emergence of a more urbanised, more bureaucratised, society and its associated new social classes in the post-colonial period. The new attitudes and values may be reflected in the very diverse but collectively similar nuclear and extended family life of men and women regardless of their ethnic background. Cultural traditions are not dead but give way before the similarity of historical circumstances, life-cycle, education and class position. The degree of selectivity in relationships, at least with remoter kin, is a further sign, not merely of the greater geographical dispersion of present day families but, along with changes in marriage patterns parallel to those in Europe and North America, (Brockman, 1987), of the growth of a more individualistic set of attitudes too.

Notes

1   For autobiographical material see, for example, Roy Heath 1990; Grace Nichols 1986).
2   In this discussion all original names of respondents have been anonymised.

Part 3

Issues of Living Arrangements, Social Provisions and Policy

The dynamics of return migration to St Lucia

Frank Abenaty

Introduction

For St Lucians, like many others from the Caribbean, the dream of returning 'home' was the vital ingredient which sustained them during their long sojourn in Britain. Increasingly, having acquired the where-withal, a significant minority are returning to St Lucia. Some wait until they have either reached, or are close to, pensionable age, but others return and take up employment in a range of occupations. The attempt of these returnees to come to terms with St Lucian society in the post-return milieu is the central concern of the discussion in this chapter. The data drawn upon here is from a larger study of St Lucians in England and St Lucia, using a life-story approach, in 1996. It is based on life-history interviews conducted in St Lucia in 1996. The returnees in the sample included 15 women and 13 men who returned to St Lucia between 1972 and 1994, having spent an average of 27 years in Britain. Their ages ranged from 51 to 71, and 21 of them returned five years or more before they were due to retire in England.

The context of St Lucian return migration from Britain

The phenomenon of return migration has been a long established aspect of Caribbean societies, whereby successive waves of out-migration have produced a corresponding stream of returning migrants (Rubenstein, 1979; Thomas-Hope, 1978). The migrations of the late nineteenth and early twentieth centuries to destinations in Central America, Haiti, Cuba and the Dominican Republic, as well as those from the Eastern Caribbean to Aruba and Curaçoa in the 1940s, took place on the basis of recruitment either for a specified period, or for work on a specific project such as the Panama Canal, after which the migrants were expected to return to their respective countries.

The movement from Britain, on the other hand, has represented the largest voluntary return of migrants from a single destination which the Caribbean has witnessed. Peach, extrapolating from demographic trends, estimated that the Caribbean-born population in Britain, declined from 330,000 in 1966 to a 1988 figure of 233,000 (Peach, 1991, p 2), and he attributes this discrepancy, largely to the re-migration of West Indians from the UK to their country of origin, with Jamaica and Barbados experiencing the highest levels of this, as Chapter 9 of this volume demonstrates.

The number of St Lucians returning from Britain can only be estimated, as few official figures exist in that respect. Nevertheless, their presence has been highly visible and contentious on this small island, with a population in 1991 of 133,308 (Government of St Lucia, 1991) and estimated in 1997 to be around 158,000 (Chamberlain, 1997). Of the estimated 10,000 St Lucians who migrated to Britain in the 1950s and 1960s (Midgett, 1977: 163), Peach has tentatively suggested that around 2,800 of these would have returned between 1966 and 1988 (Peach 1991: 13), a figure which would have been augmented since then. The Pensions and Overseas Benefits Directorate, in Newcastle-Upon-Tyne, has also produced statistical data which provide some insight into the return process in St Lucia. Their data are related only to those who are receiving retirement and widows pensions and, for the period 1996/97, for example, payments were made to 1120 pensioners and 22 widows. These figures only partially reflect the process, however, since many migrants return before reaching retirement.

The contradictions and expectations of return

It is appropriate to begin the discussion of returnees' experiences with the advice given by Jim Warner, who had migrated to Britain in 1957 and returned to St Lucia in 1989. He advised that:

> Coming back [to St Lucia] has to do with one's perspective. Do not expect anything and you will find it far better; expect nothing....The great problem is one's expectations (Interview with Jim Warner, 8.4.96).

Given the negative experiences recounted by many of these returnees, this advice would seem to be reasonable. In human terms, however, it is not a realistic proposition since, arguably, in returning to the place where they spent their formative years, it would be unusual not to have expectations. To have none would entail wiping away the memories of the past and having a neutral perception of space, time and events.

Both returnees and local St Lucians had expectations of each other, which, in the context of their different experiences, were unrealistic. The returnees considered themselves to be returning 'home', either to work, deploying the skills which they had acquired in the metropole, retire, or simply to luxuriate in the Caribbean sunshine. However, after an absence of 20, 30 and in some cases 40 years, they were not only returning to a very different environment, but they themselves were not the entities they were in the pre-migration period. They would have been exposed to a very different way of life and through the process of acculturation, would have most likely imbued certain characteristics, and values, which in some instances conflicted with those of St Lucian society. The encounter has, therefore, spawned ambiguities and contradictions.

Local St Lucians, for their part, harboured contradictory expectations in respect of these returnees, who were expected to display some outward manifestation of their success. Yet, many respondents complained that they were resented if they bought a plot of land or built a house. This aspect was seen as particularly contradictory in St Lucian terms, because earlier returnees from destinations such as British Guiana, Curacao or Aruba, who returned with little to show for their efforts were accused of having *maltwaray*, which is an extremely pejorative Creole term, denoting worthlessness and a spendthrift attitude to life. Mindful of that, some returnees have felt a sense of frustration at this local display of resentment. Richard Soames, who was in the process of returning to develop a tourism-based business was critical of that attitude.

> We can go home and build a house and there's a certain resentment from people home. Doesn't that create conflict? I went home and I managed to buy a piece of land. I showed a relative of mine the land and straight away the girl is telling me that everybody from England is coming here and buying land. We work, we stay for a little while, we work hard and we go home and buy a piece of land. What I'm saying is that there does exist a certain attitude home that we face (Interview with Richard Soames, 21.01.96).

Some of the expectations of the respondents stemmed from the logistics of the move. Most of those wishing to return from Britain, would have had at some stage to trust either a member of the family, a builder or lawyer and, investing this trust, engendered an expectation that whatever had been agreed, would be carried out according to their wishes. While many of these transactions seemed to have been accomplished satisfactorily, in a sizeable minority of cases, the dream of return was soured by the dishonesty, incompetence or both, of those entrusted to execute those transactions, resulting in heavy financial loss.

Mr Winston Preece, whose house was built in his absence, outlined some of the problems which he encountered:

> The 10,000 gallon tank placed in the ground started leaking and the whole place was flooded; the whole tank had to be drained. Then about seven or eight months after, cracks started appearing all over the place ... The builder didn't put ring-beams and the wall started cracking all over (Interview with Winston Preece, 08.04.96).

It cost Winston and his wife a further $63,000 EC (about £14,000) to rectify these faults, and without substantial additional savings, their plight could have been extremely grave.

Some family members, too, proved to be both a boon and a bane in the process and, in the case of Mr Adrian Price, one proved to be the latter. Adrian, aged 55, returned in 1990 and was involved in the importation and selling of plastic furniture from Britain. His account was that just before he was due to return to St Lucia, he engaged the services of his uncle to paint the house which had been built a few months earlier. The uncle was to be paid an agreed sum. Adrian then sent several gallons of paint to St Lucia which, in his words, 'was enough to paint three houses because I asked him to give the walls three coats as it was a new house' (Interview with Mr Price, 02.05.96). On his return however, he found that, not only had his uncle given the walls only one coat of paint but he also claimed that the paint had been insufficient to complete the task. Adrian had to purchase additional paint in St Lucia, at considerable extra cost. He had not spoken to his uncle since the episode. The uncle's attitude, however, would seem to be reflective of a widely-held view among the non-migrant community in St Lucia, that these returning migrants are well off financially and can easily afford the added expense.

These inauspicious reintroductions to 'home' have not only soured many family relationships, but as the news filters through to returnees and potential returnees, an atmosphere of distrust towards local tradesmen and providers of goods and services has ensued. For others, however, this part of the transaction went relatively smoothly. Joyce Green, for example, seemed to have had remarkable faith in a family member. This was her account.

> From the time I came my house was nearly finished because I have a very good uncle and he's the one who see to things

for me whilst I was still in England ... I did not see where I
was going to live until I came down. I had seen the area and
some of these houses going up but he bought the land and
built me this lovely house (Interview with Joyce Green,
15.04.96).

Questions of identity

Apart from the logistical difficulties identified above, the respondents
were disconcerted by the challenge to their identity. St Lucians, it
would seem, have been quick to question the identity of those who
have left to live or work elsewhere, even when this is within the
Caribbean region. For example, a few months before winning the
Nobel Prize for Literature in 1992, Derek Walcott was involved in a
campaign to prevent the building of a 115-room, all-inclusive, tourist
resort called Jalousie, between the pitons[1] in the town of Soufriere,
which is situated in the south of the island (*The Star*, 5 October, 1996:
6). Over the years, Walcott, despite having lived for a time in Trinidad
and later the USA, never lost contact with St Lucia, had paid regular
visits and written extensively about the island and its people. Yet,
because of his vociferous opposition to this development which he and
others considered to be inimical to the environment, was referred to as
a 'Johnny-come-lately' by the then Tourism Minister, Romanus
Lansiquot (*The Star*, 10 October, 1992).[2]

If someone who had contributed so much to St Lucia and the
wider Caribbean was treated in this way, St Lucians, returning from
Britain, who in some cases had maintained only minimal contact, were
unlikely to be embraced by the community at large, without a challenge to their 'St Lucianness'. Rita Floyd, who suffered some hostility
particularly in the workplace, explained it in those terms; she stressed:

> I think it was initially that there was this girl from England.
> Because when you've lived and worked in England for a
> while and you come down, your very friends don't even see
> you as a St Lucian but as an outsider (Interview with Rita
> Floyd, 01.04.96).

The challenge to their identity was related partly to the fact that many
of these returnees dressed differently, projected different body languages and had what local St Lucians call 'an accent', which immediately marked them out. But it was also because they were prepared to
question certain practices, particularly in relation to the provision of
goods and services. These difficult encounters were also experienced

by those returning from locations other than Britain. Carl Simonds, a returnee from Canada, although not one of the sample, explained the point in these terms:

> When one returns to St Lucia it's as though people, and the administration in particular, expect you to be humble. It's as though you don't know anything about anything and must therefore take whatever comes and keep quiet. Well, I'm afraid that I'm not prepared to do that (Interview with Carl Simonds, 12.05.96).

More importantly, they condemned what they perceived as the widespread practice of being overcharged in these transactions. Tina Charles observed that

> Here in St Lucia, they know when you come from another country ... They know that you come from England or America or Canada ... and especially if you go to the market. If you ask them for the price of something, if they are going to sell it to the locals for $5 they will charge you ten ... (Interview with Tina Charles, 18.04.96).

Indeed, some returnees have boycotted the main market in central Castries, where fresh fruit, vegetables and ground provisions were readily available. This was partly because they perceived they were being overcharged but also because buying at the market usually involved a process of bargaining, in which those returnees who were able to communicate in patois or Creole,[3] generally fared better than those who could not, or did not wish to. These returnees, therefore, preferred to shop at the various supermarkets, where everyone paid the same price for whatever commodities were purchased, rather than face the uncertainties of this haggling process. While this action may indicate that these returning St Lucians had, to some extent, become accustomed to a certain lifestyle in the UK, it would seem to be related, to a large extent, to their resentment at being overcharged simply because they came from Britain, and are presumed, therefore, to be wealthy.

Competing values

In common with returnees in other locations, these St Lucians have returned with attitudes and approaches to life which have bred resentment from some members of the local community. In the sphere of work, for instance, most respondents were critical of what they perceived to be a lack of professionalism on the part of working

St Lucians. Ruth Myers, returned to St Lucia in 1989 having spent 27 years in Britian and before her departure, was a Senior Housing Officer with the an inner London local council authority. At the time of the interview, she was employed as an executive accountant with the St Lucian branch of the Organisation of Eastern Caribbean States. This was her response:

> The attitude of the employees is very much different from what I'm accustomed to. They are not committed to their jobs at all. The two institutions that I worked for in England were of such high standards that I came here with the approach that I had disciplined myself into. And when I find that people are slapdash in their work I find that difficult to cope with (Interview with Ruth Myers, 02.04.96).

Pauline Redburn too, now secretary to a firm of lawyers and despite having returned since 1979, had not come to terms with, what she saw to be, the poor attitude to work which prevailed in St Lucia.

> My point of view where work is concerned is completely dif-ferent. You'd be on time, because having lived in England as far as I'm concerned I have come to work and at the right time I leave and go home. St Lucians don't really work that way (Interview with Pauline Redburn, 04.04.96).

However, it would seem that these views were also shared by some employers, who perceived returnees to be far more positive in their attitude to work, and were prepared to employ them in relatively senior positions, if they possessed the necessary skills. 'I find that in the three jobs I've had, the appreciation of my work has always been with the bosses rather than ordinary workers,' remarked Rita Floyd (Interview with Rita Floyd, 04.04.96). This has given rise to resent-ment and petty jealousies on the part of local employees, leading to non-cooperation in some cases, particularly if new ideas were being proposed and formulated. Mary Nugent concluded that:

> If there's something which they've always done and you try to do it differently because you think it's a better way, they criticise and tell you that's not how we do it in St Lucia. It's like a one-man band because they're not really interested in implementing changes here (Interview with Mary Nugent, 19.04.96).

Peter Clifford had worked in St Lucia for most of his adult life and was employed by a large, privately owned organisation, which employed a substantial number of expatriates as well as some returnees. When asked about St Lucians' attitude to work and the related factor of their relationship with returnees in the workplace, this was his reply:

> In England or America you are a number as far as work is concerned. Here we are people orientated. We talk to each other; we ask each other about home and family and that does mean that we may actually not work the full amount of time we are supposed to in a day (Interview with Peter Clifford, 27.05.96).

As far as Mr Clifford was concerned, the presumed efficiency of returning St Lucians was largely chimerical, and he could see no reason why they should presume to dictate to local St Lucians in the workplace.

Whilst some of the literature on return migration points to the extravagance of returnees in some localities, particularly in relation to house building (Dahya, 1973; McArthur, 1979), the phenomenon was not apparent among the respondents in this study. That some returnees, especially those who returned in the 1970s and early 1980s, have built large homes is an empirical fact,[4] but this was not the case for the overwhelming number of respondents. Although nearly all possessed what seemed to be well-built and relatively spacious homes, only five (18%), all of whom had returned before 1990, would be considered to have substantial homes of four bedrooms or more. Most of the other homes contained three bedrooms and given that these were, in the main, utilised by a wife and husband only, and in four cases by a single individual, there was still an abundance of space in these homes. On that basis, and given the escalation in land and building costs particularly during the boom years of banana production in the 1980s, these returnees viewed the building of extravagant homes as wasteful and injudicious, as Ruth Myers pointed out:

> ... When I told a St Lucian that we'd got one of the houses on this development, I could see the look of disappointment on her face; but I know when we both go to bed at nights we are quite happy because we don't owe anybody. We have a three bed-roomed place here but we don't use it and if my son and his wife or friends come down from England there is plenty of room for them ... As a matter of fact it is the local St Lucians who own the biggest homes here (Interview with Ruth Myers, 02.04.96).

Indeed, when asked what they considered to be some of the main changes which had taken place in their absence, many identified the pursuit of materialism which they considered was now endemic in

St Lucian society and pointed out that ostentatious consumption was, in the main, the preserve, not of returnees from Britain, but of the local *nouveau riche*. Roy Rodriguez[5] was in agreement, and observed that 'materialism in St Lucia had become an obsession probably fuelled to a certain measure by a shift in cultural terms towards North America' (Rodriquez, 1995).

This ostentatious demonstration of their wealth and the encroaching Americanism seemed at odds with the less demonstrative, Anglicised and less materially orientated sensibilities of those returning from the British cultural environment, and some respondents seemed to have chosen to live their lives in opposition to this ostentation. Ruth Myers' attitude to home ownership was a case in point, and a similar attitude prevailed as far as car ownership was concerned. Those who owned a car had either purchased a modest vehicle in St Lucia, or simply brought with them the one they owned in England. This was exemplified by John Gould, who was still in possession of the Volkswagen Golf which accompanied him in 1989 and with which, as he explained, he was quite satisfied.

> It's not that I cannot afford to buy a new car ... but what's the point? This is a perfectly good, reliable car which gets me from A to B (Interview with John Gould, 08.04.96).

There was a further contradiction related to the material development of the island. This had fostered certain expectations, because the overwhelming number of respondents had expected that social progress, or at least their version of it, would have accompanied this upsurge in materialism. They were therefore critical of what they perceived to be a mismatch between these material rewards, and the relevant inter-personal skills and attitudes which should accompany them. Mr Pritchard expressed his disappointment in an interesting way when he stated that

> St Lucia has advanced considerably. There is a lot more money and prospects, but the people has allowed the money to go ahead of them and they remain behind ... They even have this big house but cannot manage it in the way that they should (Interview with Simon Pritchard, 24.04.96).

This tension between some returnees and the emerging *nouveau riche* is indicative of the changing class structure of St Lucian society, wrought to a large extent by the advent of bananas as an export commodity. This has occasioned a transformation in both the economic and social structure of the island (Barrow, 1992), enabling many more people to gain access to wealth, as well as creating the climate in which some sections of the business community have prospered.

Consequently, the class structure of the society is a much more fluid one than in the 1950s and 1960s, when many of these returnees left St Lucia. It is now centred more around wealth as opposed to colour or family background, although these factors still have a residual impact. To an extent, therefore, some respondents, who themselves, returned with notions based on British middle-class values, have found it difficult to come to terms with what they perceived to be the stridency and abrasiveness of this new elite.

The continuing British connection

It could be argued, therefore, that many respondents returned with a new set of cultural influences and a value system which they expected to be the norm. The realisation that this was not the case has led to disillusionment and an element of 'cognitive dissonance' (Festinger, 1957), which reflects the psychological dislocation and ambiguity which result when our expectations are at odds with the reality around us. In that regard, they perceived that they had a greater affinity with the British way of life than with the St Lucian one. Indeed, some local St Lucians have labelled returnees from Britain 'ex-pats', and what is more, some returnees have, themselves, embraced this appellation. Particularly during the early months of return, some were apt to make comparisons between St Lucia and Britain in a number of spheres. Understandably, local St Lucians tended to adopt a defensive attitude to such comparisons. The constant reference back to Britain proved to be a source of irritation, and their advice to these returnees, was that they should return to England once more. John Gould who returned seven years previously, expressed some sympathy with this view and was prompted to give this advice:

> When you move from one country to another, whether it be St Lucia or anywhere else, accept that country for what it is … you cannot therefore physically live here and mentally live there. You've got to accept that you've come back for whatever reason and that's it. You've got to put up with certain things. You cannot hanker after England (Interview with John Gould, 08.04.96).

While it would seem that John had made a successful transition from Britain to St Lucia, an enduring aspect of the return for most respondents has been the desire to straddle the two traditions by maintaining contact with Britain whilst, at the same time, attempting to come to terms with life in St Lucia. John himself, when asked later whether he read or received information from England, underscored the contradictions and anomalies inherent in the return experience with this reply:

> All the time; through the *Sunday Telegraph*, the *Sunday Times* and maybe a copy of the *Daily Telegraph*. I get that sent from England on a weekly basis (Interview with John Gould, 08.04.96).

John was the only respondent who received newspapers from England, but the vast majority of those in the study kept in touch with events in Britain. Ruth Myers, in response to the same question, was almost apologetic in admitting that she did maintain contact.

> I speak with my children all the time on the phone and on TV you can get the World Service all day long. I just have to put the TV on and hear an English voice and I'm there. Unfortunately, I'm afraid, anything to do with England. . . Right now I'm following up this meat business (the BSE crisis) with interest. I must say I do keep in touch a lot (Interview with Interview with Ruth Myers, 02.04.96).

For two respondents, however, the return process had been so difficult and traumatic that they stated that, if circumstances permitted, they would have returned to England. Mr and Mrs Pritchard, a retired couple who had lived in England for over thirty years, returned to St Lucia in 1988, principally because Mrs Pritchard felt that she could no longer stand the cold English winters. There were added complications because Mrs Pritchard suffered from diabetes, and her husband had a minor heart condition. He had returned reluctantly and emphasised this quite forcefully, when he stated:

> Personally I loved everything in England up to today, and personally up to this moment ... I don't want to be in the West Indies (Interview with Simon Pritchard, 24.04.96).

Their account was one of regret, isolation and despondency. Their medical bills amounted to at least $200 EC (about £45) a month, having escaped the cold they found the heat unbearable, and they generally felt isolated. Mrs Pritchard explained that:

> We don't have friends because the people our age we know are dying or are abroad and the young people is not us they want for friends (Interview with Elizabeth Pritchard, 24.04.96).

This sense of dislocation would seem to have been experienced to a greater extent by Mr Pritchard, who, in the seven years since their return, had visited England, where their three children reside, on four occasions, compared to his wife's single visit. Returning to England, they felt, was not a realistic option at this stage in their lives. Mrs Pritchard summed up by saying that:

> Death is all about and if I really knew the tough time we would have in St Lucia I would not have bothered to come (Interview with Elizabeth Pritchard 24.04.96).

Some perspectives on the experiences of women returnees

In the context of this study, Mr Pritchard's disillusionment was unusual in terms of its persistence over time and from the point of view of other male respondents, most of whom seemed to have reached a *modus vivendi* with St Lucian society. This was not the case with the majority of the female respondents, however, eight (53%) of whom expressed strong reservations about living in St Lucia, reflecting some of Gmelch's (1983) findings, in his study of returnees to Newfoundland and Ireland.

Tina Charles, a seamstress (sewing machinist), returned in 1985. She explained vividly the difficulties she faced during the initial stages in the following terms:

> ... It was very hard uprooting everything I had in England because when I left here I had nothing and after a couple of years in England I sent for my children and living in England for twenty-six years where you're settled and have a family. It was very, very, hard to uproot all that and leave your children behind, which was a tragic thing. And when I got over here, all I could think about is my children, my my children, my children [sic]. It took me about six months before I stopped crying ... but eventually I settled down alright because I have my brother and my sister here. It took me a good three to four years before I really got England out of my system, but what got England out of my system completely was I had to go back there. When I went back on holiday, it's as though I went in search of something I don't know what. And when I got back there I realised there's nothing left there for me except my children and we're always in touch on the phone and they come on holiday all the time. So I thought to myself you're not really missing anything (Interview with Tina Charles, 18.04.96).

One facet of the process which prolonged the adjustment in the above case, and in others, had been the deep attachment which these women felt towards their offspring and grandchildren in England. Tina later conceded that the constant longing for her children had, for a while, put a severe strain on her marriage because, as she recalled,

> I used to take it out on my husband, always arguing with him and each time I would say to him I'm going back, I'm to meet my children ... (Interview with Tina Charles, 18.04.96).

Her account of having to revisit London on more than one occasion in order to 'exorcise' the ghost of London from her system, was a poignant reminder of the extent to which many returnees had grown accustomed to life in England. Tina's experience also illustrates the importance of time as a factor in the adjustment process, concomitant with the building up of social contacts, becoming known and generally feeling more at ease in the 'new' setting.

The problem of boredom, after having led a relatively active life in Britain, is one which many returnees, especially the retired, have had to address; but this would seem to have been a particular concern for some female respondents. First, they considered there to be a lack of the variety of public entertainment which they felt able to attend on their own. For example, there was not a public cinema anywhere in Castries, the St Lucian capital. Second, the means of getting to what little entertainment there was, were not always available, for, while public transport was improving, it remained at a fairly basic level. Third, only three (20%) of these women were driving at the time of the study and not being able to drive, or being disinclined to do so, imposed severe restrictions on their freedom.

The issue of safety on the roads was of paramount importance to most of them as expressed by Claudia Burns, who, although owning a car in England, had no inclination to drive in St Lucia, even though, as the following statement suggests, she recognised the value of so doing.

> The only thing that keeps me back a lot is not bringing my car down from England. It means I have to depend on my husband a lot and sometimes he's not around. But I'm petrified of the roads here because the drivers have no care for life. I will not drive here (Interview with Claudia Burns 15.04.96).

Rita Floyd, approaching retirement, and actively considering the prospect of dividing her time between England and St Lucia, put the point this way:

> Life here is very different from England. There's a lot more
> to do in England as far as the arts are concerned. We've got
> just one theatre here, the Cultural Centre. We do hear of con-
> certs in other parts of the island but because of the mad
> driving one is scared to leave Castries to go to perhaps Vieux
> Fort, if ever there was one. In London you can hop on a bus
> or get on a train in safety. There ain't many places that one
> could go to during the day and relax ... One has to think very
> carefully I would say, before coming here and deciding to be
> a full-time housewife because it can be very boring
> (Interview with Rita Floyd, 04.04.96).

The hot weather, too, while affording greater opportunities for outdoor
activities in some respects, restricted the leisure activities which some
returnees had enjoyed in Britain. For example, Barry and Patricia
Jackson, who returned in 1994 immediately on Barry's retirement, had
been keen gardeners, and the hobby kept them occupied for several
hours during the summer months; but although they still kept small
vegetable gardens in St Lucia, they had been unable to pursue the
hobby to the same extent. Patricia explained the effect which the heat
had had in curtailing her gardening activities, when she stated that:

> We've always been ardent gardeners but the heat plays a big
> part. That's why we can't do gardening. We had a beautiful
> garden in England, but we couldn't take the heat (in
> St Lucia), so we turned the whole place into a fruit orchid
> (Interview with Patricia Jackson, 07.05.96).

The evidence from this study suggests that married couples from
Britain, in the main, accompany each other much of the time to occasions such as going to church, and attending public and private gather-
ings. However, during the free time available on an individual basis,
the leisure activities which some of the men engaged in, such as visiting the rum shop, swimming in the sea, or playing dominoes, were
those which, on the whole, tended to exclude women, or indeed, those
in which they had no desire to partake.[6]

The factors identified above have combined to create a level of
dissatisfaction whereby slightly over 50% of the female respondents
were either so dissatisfied with life in St Lucia, even after an average
of four years' residence there, or missed England to such an extent,
that three were actively contemplating dividing their time between
Britain and St Lucia, while the others would gladly return to Britain,
were it not considered imprudent to do so. These women had con-
sented to return to St Lucia, but there were many clues, as well as

explicit statements during the interviews, which suggested that they had returned mainly because of the strong desire of their husbands to do so and some of the men, themselves, acknowledged that fact.

These female returnees did not, however, represent the majority of the respondents, but comprised 53% of the women interviewed and 29% of the total sample. Conversely, only one male respondent, Mr Pritchard, felt so disillusioned, that he would return to Britain had this been practicable. While having many reservations, therefore, the majority were pleased that they had returned and come to accept St Lucia as 'home' for the foreseeable future. Peter Bates considered that life was qualitatively better for him in St Lucia than it would have been in England.

> Yes, I'm quite happy and as I say, it depends what you make of it … Because going back to England on the past three or four times, looking at it in the area where I last lived and some of my old friends there in my age bracket, I see they all stand by the street corner and telling me, boy, things ain't so nice at all. It was just like back in the 60s when we first came. So I'm quite happy (Interview with Peter Bates, 22.04.96).

Similarly, Pauline Redburn, who seemed to have had little difficulty in adjusting to St Lucian ways, expressed the view that

> St Lucia is not a paradise. There are many problems here, but I'm a lot more relaxed here. I'm happier here because this is my home (Interview with Pauline Redburn, 28.04.96).

However, even for those who may have been unhappy initially about having returned, the logistics of remigrating to Britain were fraught with difficulties. First, all the respondents had sold their homes in Britain to help finance the move, and would have had to reverse the process, which may have proved to be extremely traumatic and costly. Second, given that these returnees were, in the main, in their mid-50s and early 60s at the time of the interviews, and given too, the state of the British economy, finding worthwhile employment could have been very difficult. Third, the cold weather was cited by a substantial number of respondents as a factor in their decision to return to St Lucia. It would now seem perverse, therefore, to return to these same conditions in Britain, especially, as they were now older than when they first left. These considerations have helped to concentrate the minds of both female and male returnees, on adjusting to their 'new' life in the old country.

Having fulfilled the dream for which they had laboured in Britain, all the respondents faced difficulties in adjusting to life in St Lucia.

Some had adjusted more readily than others, however, and the women, in particular, seemed to have had a harder time of it. These difficulties stemmed from three main sources. First, they returned with views and perceptions, some of which were at odds with those inherent in St Lucian society. Second, they attempted to maintain a foothold both in St Lucia and in Britain and made, what locals considered to be, unfair comparisons between the two locations. Third, the ambivalent attitude of the St Lucian community, towards those who had lived abroad, compounded the matter. In the view of the respondents, it was an attitude which ridiculed those who had failed in their quest for material success, yet, was antagonistic towards others who had progressed.

Re-assimilation or integration?

Adjustment did not mean that these returnees had come to accept fully the values of St Lucian society. Moreover, because of the length of time that most of them had lived in Britain, and the acculturation to British ways which evolved over that period, re-assimilation remained a distant prospect. While these respondents were prepared to embrace aspects of St Lucian society which were considered to be worthwhile or progressive, what was being demanded was that they reconfigure their thoughts, actions and experiences, in ways which were acceptable to St Lucian society. A similar expectation confronted Norwegians returning from the USA, when, according to Eikaas, in order 'to be truly accepted in Norway, the returnee must give up his American identity and see the world through Norwegian lenses' (Eikaas, 1979, p 109). However, none of these respondents were prepared to abandon the central values which governed their lives. On that basis, it is argued that these respondents sought not re-assimilation, but 'integration'. They wished to be able to balance the demands of St Lucian society against the values and attitudes formed during their stay in Britain, retaining those which they now considered to be the right and proper ones to hold.

The essence of the process which these returnees had undergone was perceptively captured by a returnee who was not a respondent. Rupert Stevens returned to St Lucia 15 years earlier and runs a highly successful restaurant business. As far as he was concerned, 'those of us coming from England, have adopted the rhythms of our adopted country and those rhythms stay with us' (Interview with Rupert Stevens, 24.04.96).

The attachment to Britain was born of cultural, emotional and instrumental ties, for despite the difficulties many endured during their sojourn, it was there that these returning migrants had spent much of their youth. Crucially, too, they had established families, reared children and grandchildren and developed strong emotional ties with them. It seems natural, therefore, that they would wish to maintain those links on their return to St Lucia. Additionally, those who were receiving pensions, or hoping to do so in the future, had a vested interest in Britain's economic prosperity and more particularly the strength of the pound, since this determined the number of Eastern Caribbean (EC) dollars they received, with a strong pound adding appreciably to their level of income. In matters of health, too, some returnees travel to Britain to obtain treatment for their ailments and, sometimes those visits were extended, in order to renew personal contacts with family and friends. It is evident, therefore, that the fortunes of returning St Lucians are inexorably linked to those of Britain and there is likely to be, for the foreseeable future, a continuing relationship with their former 'home'.

Conclusion

These on-going interchanges mean that the process of return migration from Britain to the Caribbean, ought not to be interpreted in the same unilinear perspective which characterised the involuntary returns of a previous era, but in terms of its flexibility and dynamism, whereby West Indians and their offspring share varying amounts of time together, either in the UK or the Caribbean. Within that flexible perspective, the returnees in the study, 25 (89%) of whom were British passport holders, had the option too, of returning to Britain at any time.[7]

Notes

1   The two pitons, named Gros Piton and Petit Piton, are the two most prominent peaks visible in approaching the town of Soufriere by sea. The area between them is thought to have been an Amerindian settlement.

2   Attitudes to Derek Walcott are very different now. The main square in the capital, Castries, formerly known as Columbus Square, has been renamed Derek Walcott Square. Ironically, Walcott has, himself, become an icon for tourists.

3   While English is the official language, for many St Lucians, particularly in rural areas, Creole (patois or patwa), a language which combines elements of French, African and local forms, still governs their daily lives.

4   For some St Lucians, a fortuitous set of circumstances combined to provide them with the wherewithal to acquire land and property in St Lucia. Those fortunates, who benefited from the inflationary boom in house prices in Britain in the 1980s, were able to return and not only build large homes, but purchase additional land and property, given the relative cheapness of these at the time.

5   Roy Rodriguez is a Dominican but lived and worked in St Lucia oven an extended
    period. He is currently chief economist at the Commonwealth Secretariat, London.
6   The members of three households involved in the study had formed a domino club,
    which met at alternate locations each Wednesday evening. The women all took part
    in the games.
7   Joyce Green has returned to England and, based on current information, is the only
    one of the respondents to have done so.

11 Family structures and domestic conflict in Jamaica

Elsie Le Franc, Don Simeon and Gail Wyatt

Introduction

Traditionally, the family has had a very high socio-cultural value in most societies. Harmonious family life is in many cases almost an 'object of veneration' (Miller 1990). The belief in the integrative functions of the family unit is therefore a well established one – with one of its most recent expressions being the positive linkages drawn between 'enmeshment' on the one hand, and good mental health, proper health seeking behaviours, beneficial learning habits, and superior educational accomplishments on the other (Green & Werner 1996).

In recent years there has been increasing concern (especially in policy-making, and social development circles) about the fate and integrity of the family in the urban and post-modern society, and the anticipated consequences of family breakdown and the growing numbers of children being brought up in single-parent (usually a female) households for a range of social and political problems. The higher levels of instability among cohabiting couples (as compared with marriages), the higher levels of economic disadvantage among cohabiting couples with children, the levels of 'welfare dependency' among lone-mothers, poor educational performance, the possible increase in the number of children (especially males) who are irresponsible, problem-prone or even criminal are the problems most frequently highlighted (Lewis & Kiernan 1995; Morgan 1995; Buck et al. 1994).

In Caribbean societies, and among persons of African descent in the UK and the USA, where the phenomena of single parenthood, common-law unions and visiting relationships are especially prevalent, there have long been suggestions that those family forms account for many of the social and economic problems currently being experienced by those societies and communities. Barrow's review of the literature traces the movement from beliefs that these family forms were dysfunctional and pathological aberrations, to ones which suggested that they could be positive adaptations to existing social and economic realities (Barrow 1996). The study by Louat and Groshe provides some support for the more benign perspective: examining data from surveys of *Living Conditions in Jamaica* they concluded that certainly with regard to specific health outcomes (the incidence of diahrreal disease among children) the female-headed household was not necessarily a risk factor (Louat & Grosh et al. 1995).

In the Caribbean, while most of the attention has been given to female-headship and single parenthood, it must be recognised that there are a number of other features that need to be considered. These include the much discussed phenomenon of multiple partnering (Chevannes 1993), and therefore the possibility of frequently changing household composition. Data from a national survey of sexual and partnering behaviours in Jamaica have shown that the partnering process may not be (or no longer be) as linear nor progressive as traditionally believed. Rather, the current partnering process has a short-term, shifting or perhaps serial character. The majority (61%) of the partnerships (among individuals aged 15–50 years) lasted three years or less, with the means for the different types of relationships ranging from 2.7 to 5.9 years (Le Franc et al. 1994). Thus, while female household headship may, by itself, not be a critical factor the possible impact of general family instability and constantly changing household boundaries on specified social behaviours must be considered. This paper seeks to explore that matrix of relationships between changing household structures and family types, and a specific type of behaviour, namely, domestic violence.

Abuse and violence

Domestic and household violence inclusive of child sexual and physical abuse have come to be recognised as a major social problem. Most of the prevalence studies on child sexual abuse have been done in the USA where rates ranging from 27–45% have been found (Russell 1983; Wyatt 1985). In the UK child sexual abuse, expressed as a percentage of the general child abuse cases recorded, rose from 1% in 1980 to 17% in 1992 (NSPCC 1984; Woodroffe et al. 1993). Another report on the studies based on self-reports noted that some estimations were as high as 54% of all the children surveyed (Regan 1979). In Jamaica, our study found that 15% of a sub-sample of females (aged 15–50 years) reported at least one childhood sexual abuse incident. This translated into a prevalence rate of 152 per 1,000. While somewhat low in comparison to that found in other countries outside of the

Caribbean (Wyatt 1985; Heiss et al. 1995), it is higher than that found for any other Caribbean country.[1]

With respect to domestic partner violence, its fairly widespread character has also been the focus of increased and more intense scrutiny. With data emerging from societies as different as the USA, UK, France, Nigeria, Colombia, Nicaragua, Mexico, Kenya, and Papua New Guinea reporting incidence levels that range between 20–70% it has not been difficult to conclude that the family is in reality a 'violent place' (Mama 1989; Nazaroo 1995; Schuler 1992; Carillo 1990; Miller 1990). While there has been no hard data on the actual prevalence rates for domestic violence in the Caribbean, there are general reports of increasing levels of violence against women since the 1970s (Mama 1989). Community-based studies also report high levels of violence (Chambers and Chevannes 1991). A recent examination of family and gender relations (Bailey & Branche 1997: 43) found that sexual relationships were 'adversarial, aggressive and predatory' (p 41), and further, that:

> there was both an assumed societal context of violence as well as understanding that violence was a natural part of the human interaction process. Violence was especially tied up to man/woman relationships (Bailey & Branche 1997: 43).

Family systems and abuse

The temptation to trace these social pathologies to dysfunctional family structures and relationships is almost irresistible. Even if family dysfunction and lone motherhood may not be a direct cause, it is at least expected to compound the problem (Groves & Soothe 1996). Bailey and Branche (1997) argued that dysfunctional families without any sense of commitment become cause, sustenance and effect: 'outwardly directed boys' brought up without the assumed benefits of an internally meshed household express the stresses in aggression (p 21). Woodroffe et al. (1993: 59), writing about the increase of child sexual abuse in the UK sought to link the problem with the condition of the family unit. They stated that:

> Child abuse is closely linked to deprivation, family breakdown and parental stress owing to unemployment and financial problems even though they also concede that the actual prevalence is unknown.

In spite of the increasing awareness of the severity and high prevalence of violence and abuse there is still however, a great deal of conceptual confusion in respect of the causal relationships between family structures, social ideologies, socio-economic status and violence. The current debate appears to be between those who would focus most attention on the demands and consequences of patriarchy, where violence represents a form of control and/or punishment of females; those who place more emphasis on external factors such as socio-economic class and occupation; and those who argue that the problem is really one of violent individuals (Nazaroo 1995; Schuler 1992; Carillo 1990; Mama 1989). Studies which have found that females may be as, or even more likely than men to perpetrate violence (Strauss et al. 1980; Strauss 1983; Nazaroo 1995), or that domestic violence crosses all class, racial, ethnic, ideological and national boundaries (Carillo 1990) have compounded the problem, and effectively delayed conceptual clarity. There have been attempts to identify 'families at risk' of child abuse (Howe 1992), but by and large we are still without a definitive framework for conceptualising domestic violence and therefore how to prevent it (Schuler 1992).

Focus on the demands of maintaining a patriarchal society will help to identify the rationale and tools used by individuals utilising violence as a conflict resolution tactic; it may also indicate which societies may be more prone to violence against females. Since not everyone in this social environment uses violence to resolve a conflict it is however necessary to distinguish between perpetrators and non-perpetrators, and to try to identify that which may become a *casus belli*, or act as a triggering mechanism. In any case, patriarchy cannot explain the female perpetrator phenomenon where her acts are not on behalf of the dominance and control of some males.

Elsewhere we reported data which show that in Jamaica child sexual abuse reported was, in the majority of cases, perpetrated by someone known to the victim; that the main perpetrators were relatives as well as friends and acquaintances of the individual and individual's family; and most important, that the families most at risk of child sexual abuse were both-parent households and those where the principal 'upbringers' were fathers or relatives of the father. Since fathers or step-fathers accounted for very low percentage (approximately 4%) of the abuse reported, that left the both-parent household as the main locus of the problem: that is, 'normal' both-parent family structures did not appear to be any more protective of children than alternative family structures (Wyatt et al., submitted for publication).

Given then the apparently close association between violence and the partnering process, as well as the findings on the child abuse, the next basic question seemed to be: might there be a relationship between household types and domestic violence in general? In this paper we wish to specifically explore those risk factors associated with spousal/partner violence. Focus will be on those acts of violence used to 'settle' spousal/partner conflicts. Questions that will then be tackled are: what might be the relative importance of social and economic deprivation, family dysfunction, breakdown or instability for the incidence of domestic violence? In other words, are there particular types of family or household structures that are more prone to violence as the medium of social intercourse? Further, where individuals in a household have experienced child sexual and/or physical abuse can any long term effects be deduced from any associations found between those experiences and current violence-oriented practices? Two main hypotheses will be tested. These are that:

i) *persons in 'dysfunctional' families will experience higher levels of domestic/household violence regardless of educational, economic and occupational status*

and

ii) *persons with a history of child physical and sexual abuse will be more likely to experience/practice domestic/household violence.*

The sample

Two-stage probability sampling was used to obtain a sample of males and females, ages 15–50 years which was generally representative of the Jamaican population. The sample was drawn by the Statistical Institute of Jamaica (STATIN). The island was divided into 217 sampling regions and from these a random sample of 145 regions was selected. Two enumeration districts (EDs) were selected from each sampling region with probability proportional to size. Households were selected using a circular sampling technique with a random start. Anticipating a 30 per cent fallout due to possible demolition or vacancy of selected households, as well as the likelihood of drawing households that did not have persons in the desired age range, 4,350 households were initially identified. This was expected to yield the desired sample size of 3,000 households. Fieldwork began in March 1992 and was completed in February 1993. Upon completion, it was determined that 826 households had no-one on the required age group, 365 were vacant, and 158 demolished. Of the remaining 3,001 households, 219 refused to participate, and for another 202, appointments made were repeatedly canceled or avoided. The final sample size is therefore 2,580 individuals, with an overall refusal rate of 14% (18% percent for males and 11% were females).

When household met the age criterion (that is, having persons in the 15–50 year age group), all members of the household were listed. Day and month of birth were also ascertained for all the household members aged 15 years or older. The person aged 15–50 years with the most recent birthday was selected as the respondent. The age and gender distributions of the final sample are set out in Table 1 below. These distributions are also compared with those of the national population, in order to illustrate the representative character of the sample.

It will be seen that both set of distributions are generally similar. There is however, slight underrepresentation of both female and males adolescents (15–19 years). Also, males in the 40–49 year age group are somewhat overrepresented, as are females in the 30–39 year age group. The general underrepresentation of adolescents is no doubt due to the difficulties in obtaining parental consent for all persons under the age of 18 years – a requirement of the Human Subject Protection protocol. Where, and whenever necessary the appropriate weighting procedures have are carried out.

The questionnaire which consisted of 679 questions, included both open-ended and pre-coded items, covered a wide range of social, psycho-social, cultural, issues and topics deemed pertinent to sexual behaviour, decision-making, and practices. The questionnaire also contained four sub-files on specific high-risk (i.e. for HIV/STD infection) factors: sexual abuse at or before the age of 15 years (the age of consent in Jamaica), sexual abuse since the age of 16, and sex with same sex and with the opposite sex. Respondents answering affirmatively to screening questions were asked about the circumstances of high-risk behaviours.

Every effort was made to ensure privacy and confidentiality. Informed consent was obtained prior to conduct of the face-to-face interview, and respondents were interviewed in locations convenient to

Table 11.1   Percentage distribution of sample and national populations by age and gender

	Age group	National (1992) Males	Females	Sample Males	Females
	15–19 years	21	20	16	14
	20–29 "	39	39	37	39
	30–39 "	25	26	27	32
	40–49 "	15	15	20*	15*
Total	634,880 (100.0)	635,360 (100.0)		977 (100.0)	1,599 (100.0)

*Age group = 40–50 Years
Age missing: Males = 2; Females = 2

them – usually in or around their homes. Average interviewing time was three hours. For questions requiring multiple, closed-ended responses, respondents were given sets of 5×7 cards. Other devices, such as ladders, were also utilised as visual aids for responses to scaled items that required ratings. These procedures were designed to facilitate the interview process, especially in cases where literacy levels were less than functional. Since pilot testing had showed that interviews by mature females (i.e. over 25 years) produced the best results, the interview team was comprised of females only.

Inter-rater reliability tests done during the interviewer-training period, as well as the data collection phase showed over 90% (kappa coefficient of .92) agreement on all the questions asked. A 5% sample was also randomly selected from the 2,580 completed questionnaires, to establish validity. The coding error rate was 0.7 per cent, and the data entry error rate was 0.7 per cent.

Also referred to as 'punishment', child abuse as a variable is based on self reports and recollections of 'upbringer' response to childhood wrongdoing. In the Caribbean sexual abuse is defined as the sexual exploitation of a child through violent or non-violent molestation. It includes a spectrum of behaviour from violent rape to inappropriate touching or seduction. Since this subject has been extensively explored and analysed elsewhere (Wyatt et al. submitted for publication), in this paper only the simple indication of abuse will be reported and incorporated into the analyses. A prevalence rate of 152 per 1,000 was reported. The categories used to indicate union status, and occupational status are those in standard use by official and academic researchers in the region. (Jamaican Census 1991, Labour Force Surveys; Roberts and Sinclair 1978). Respondents were classified on the basis of who was responsible for their upbringing (up to the age of 14 years). The categories used were 'both parents', 'mothers only or mother's relatives', 'fathers only or father's relatives', and other arrangements, including employment status, which refers to whether a person is in full-time or part-time employment, is unemployed, or a housewife. The Educational status variable which indicates the level attained is a composite one made up of responses to questions about length of schooling, type of educational institution attended, and any certificates awarded. Relationship fluidity was derived by categorising respondents according to the frequency with which they changed their partners, or type of partner, over their recorded 'partnering lifetime'.

The main outcome/dependent variables are child physical abuse, and domestic violence. The independent variables are age, education, occupational status, employment status, current union status, relationship fluidity and family of origin. Child sexual and physical abuse are also used as independent variables. All data and analyses are disaggregatd by gender.

Childhood punishment

The levels of severe punishment for childhood misbehaviours were high: 50% were severely (for example, beaten, punched, pinched, hit with a heavy object) punished, 21% were moderately punished, while 20% received little or no punishment [N=1957]. There was no significant gender difference. Bivariate and multiple logistic regression analyses were carried out using all the independent variables indicated. This showed that among males the only significant association was the degree of relationship fluidity in later life. Thus, those who changed partners more than 4 times were almost twice as likely as those who had never partnered, or had never changed partners to have been severely punished as a child (see Table 11. 2).

Among females, more of the independent variables were significantly associated. Thus, respondents who had experienced severe levels of childhood punishment were also more likely to have been sexually abused (69%, p=0.001), to have a lower level of education, a higher frequency of partner change (fluidity), and lower occupational status. The data are shown in Table 11.3. The results of the multiple logistic regression indicated that the independent predictors – in order of significance were level of education (p=0.02), child sexual abuse (p=0.02), and fluidity (p=0.04). Family of origin was not significant.

Domestic/partner violence

Respondents were classified on the basis of whether they were perpetrators of a violent act in response to a conflict situation, were

Table 11.2   Pecentage of male respondents reporting severe childhood punishment, by partnering fluidity

	Percentage reporting fluidity
Never Partnered	41
Never Changed	46
Changed once	51
Changed 2–3 times	53
Changed 4+ times	70

N = 930
p=0.01

Table 11.3   % Distribution of females reporting severe childhood punishment by fluidty, education, and occupation

Independent variable	% Reporting fluidity
Never Partnered	33
Never Changed	44
Changed once	50
Changed 2–3 times	58
Changed 4+ times	67

p<0.001

Level of education	
Primary	55
Secondary	49
High	31
Coll/Univ.	33

p<0.001

Occupation	
Professional	43
Clerical	40
Self-employed	46
Service	67
Factory Worker	59
Unskilled	57
Unemployed	52

p=0.03

perpetrators and victims of a violent act, or were solely victims. The percentage distribution is shown in Table 11.4. There was no significant gender difference among the perpetrators nor among the combined perpetrator/victim category. Among victims only, there was a significant gender difference with 5.1% of the females (*versus* 3% of males) indicating a victim only status (p=0.02). That is, while if a respondent was a 'victim only' it was more likely to be a females, females were just as likely as males to commit or be involved in violent conflict resolution tactics.

Further analysis showed that, 66% of male respondents who were perpetrators said that their partners were also perpetrators; 66% of female respondents who said that they were perpetrators said that partners were also perpetrators; and 56% of the females who said that their partners were perpetrators said that they were also perpetrators. The general conclusion that may therefore be drawn is that while males may be more likely to utilise violence against his partner, the females are almost as likely to retaliate and/or be an aggressor.

Table 11.4 Percentage distribution of respondents by degree of involvement in domestic violence % reporting

	Males (n = 846)	Females (n = 1400)	Total (n = 2246)
Involvement			
Nevers	90.0	85.5	87.2
Perpetrators	3.0	3.7	3.4
Perpetrators & Victims	4.1	5.7	5.1
Victims only	3.0	5.1	4.3

(p=0.02)

The results from the bivariate and multiple regression analyses revealed that among male perpetrators the only significant variable was childhood punishment (p=0.02). Among females, however, a number of the independent variables were significantly linked. These were relationship fluidity, current union status, occupation, and the incidence of childhood punishment. The data are shown in Table 11.5. Although among females child sexual abuse is significantly associated with child physical abuse, sexual abuse is not significantly linked with later violent behaviours.

Among females, the independent predictors – in order of significance – were current union status

(p<0.001), relationship fluidity (p=0.01), and childhood punishment

(p=0.03). More specifically, the type of union with the most violence was the common-law union: respondents in these unions were twice as likely as those in legal marriages or visiting unions to report severe violence.

Among females, the independent predictors – in order of significance – were current union status (p<0.001), relationship fluidity (p=0.01), and childhood punishment (p=0.03). More specifically, the type of union with the most violence was the common-law union: respondents in these unions were twice as likely as those in legal marriages or visiting unions to report severe violence.

Among females, the only variable with a significant relationship after controlling for all other independent variables was current union status. Those married were most likely to be a 'victim only': that is 6% *versus* 5% for those in common-law union, and 3% for those in visiting union (p=0.004).

When involvement in violence (that is, as perpetrator and victim) was examined, among males the significant independent variables were current union status, family of origin, and childhood punishment.

Table 11. 5   % Distribution of female respondents reporting perpetration of violence by fluidty, education, and occupation

Variable	% Reporting
Fluidity	
Never Partnered	8
Never Changed	8
Changed once	9
Changed 2–3 times	14
Changed 4+ times	14

p=0.04

Current Union Status	
None	10
Married	7
Common-law	14
Visiting	7

p=0.002

Occupational Status	
Professional	5
Clerical	1
Self-employed	11
Service	15
Factory Worker	9
Unskilled	12
Unemployed	12

p=0.004

Persons in common-law unions were the most likely to report violent behaviour: the percentages are 9% for common-law unions, 3.2% for visiting unions, and 2.5% for those married (p=0.04). With respect to family of origin, the variation is as follows: both parent families – 3%, father/father's relatives 3% mother or mother's relatives – 6%, and others family arrangements – 15% (p<0.05). However multiple logistic regression indicated that none of the variables were independent predictors.

Among females relationship fluidity, union status and occupation were significant, with current union status being the main independent predictor. For union status, the proportions are common-law – 8%, married – 5%, and visiting – 3.2% (p=0.01).

With respect to relationship fluidity the percentage distribution is a follows: never changed partners – 3%, never changed – 4%, changed once – 5% changed 2–3 times – 9%, and changed 4 times or more – 6% (p=0.02). Finally here, those experiencing severe childhood punishment were twice as likely to be in a violent situation (9% *versus* 4%; p=0.004). The results of the multiple logistic regression analyses showed that the independent predictors in order of statistical significance were childhood punishment (p=0.001), relationship fluidity (p=0.02), and current union status (p=0.02).

Discussion

There are a number of interesting associations in the data obtained, and the findings are not entirely expected. There are four findings that need to be highlighted. The first is that partner violence is not a particularly male-dominated activity: females are giving almost as good as they are getting. Second, the structure of the family of origin had no predictive nor explanatory power. Third, there were important gender differences in respect of the predictive independent variables. Among males, the only factor that was significantly and independently associated with the use of violent conflict resolution tactics was the incidence of severe childhood punishment. It is not known if punishment by male *versus* female 'upbringer' would introduce any variation; this is an area worthy of further analysis. Among females, however, a wider variety of sociological variables – *viz* relationship fluidity, union status, education and occupation – were significantly associated. These associations among females are presented diagrammatically in Figure 11.1.

It could be argued that since relationship fluidity could be both cause and effect of partner violence, and that the relationship between

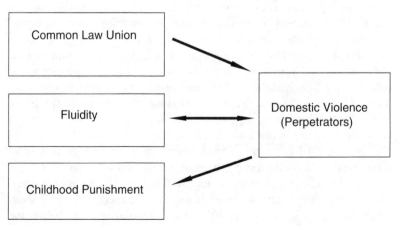

Figure 11.1   Domestic violence, fluidity and childhood punishment – females only

childhood punishment and later educational status could also be due to an earlier association between the educational levels of the 'upbringers' and the probability of physical abuse, then the really critical variables are childhood punishment and current union status. It may also be that while the respondents were children there were other socio-economic factors that encouraged the severe character of the physical punishment, and that these same factors are still helping to shape and influence the incidence of domestic violence. More in-depth examination of the relative importance of these factors is needed. But the fourth important finding from these data is that it is the common-law union (*versus* the lone-parent or more traditional marriages) that are most at risk. A cautionary note is necessary here: because the sample included persons aged 15–50 years, and since more marriages have traditionally taken place after the 5th decade of life (Roberts and Sinclair 1978), it may be that inclusion of older age groups could alter the patterns found. Balancing this possibility however, is another one: violence levels could be lower in the older age groups.

In seeking to understand the possible reasons for the higher levels of violence in common-law unions, it is useful to look more closely at some of the characteristics of this type of union. It has long been a dominant form in Jamaica, and most have described them as being relatively stable and long-lasting (Roberts and Sinclair 1978). In this sample 21%, 34% and 15% of all respondents were in a common-law union, a visiting union, or a legal marriage, respectively. This distribution is similar to that found by the recently completed *Reproductive Health Survey in Jamaica* (NFPB 1998). More recent analyses of partner relations in the Caribbean now argue, however, that there needs to be much greater recognition of the economic calculus that women bring to the process of partner formation, and the extent to which women see children and child-bearing as the gateways to men's incomes (Handwerker 1993; Le Franc et al. 1994). Resistance to the legalisation of stable cohabitation is therefore likely to be due to the reluctance of the female to have her resources or opportunities for maximising her economic gains curtailed and/or constrained (Le Franc et al. 1994). This line of argument could make it easier to understand why common-law unions would create arenas in which there may be limited sense of collective commitment, in which males feel most threatened, and where there is a constant conflict over access to, and the use of available resources. When all of this is played out in an environment in which unemployment levels are in excess of 17% (Labour Force Statistics 1996), some 30% of the population falls below the poverty line (Survey of Living Standards 1996), and male labour force participation rates have continued to decline, even while those of females have increased, it is important to understand some of the likely negative effects on male identity development, and the process of partnership formation.

The study on family and the quality of gender relations in Jamaica (Bailey and Branche 1996: 89,113) had concluded that especially in constrained economic circumstances the household is essentially a fairly fragile negotiating and negotiated entity. Entry as well as continuing membership are dependent on calculations of what can be brought in, and/or taken out. The young males studied saw females and relationships with them as the arena where power – psychological, symbolic, material, social and sexual – was necessary to secure for self the required status and values in a world in which the 'good' things of life were increasingly scarce *or had to be acquired through some kind of market relationship* (emphasis added) which communicated above all else the fundamental value of power . . . In the end there could be little doubt that relationships were seen as arenas of struggle – struggle defined by the gender ideologies on offer.

Given then what is now known about some of the features of gender relationships – especially in economically constrained circumstances, it is tempting to try to push further the analogy with the market alluded to above. It could be argued for example, that many partner relationships should be seen as contractual relationships based on and regulated by market principles. This is to be distinguished from the alliance, or corporate hierarchical structure that the family unit has been expected to be. If so, then it may be possible to describe and understand conflict, breakdown and violence in terms of dissatisfaction with the 'transaction costs' by at least one party, and/or in terms of the introduction of 'imperfect competition' as a result of advantages gained (or lost) for whatever reason. The reasons could be related to economic difficulties being experienced in the wider society, or to other contractual relationships established. It is interesting that the 'victim only' individual is most likely to be married.

In any case, it seems clear enough that males under threat do seek to achieve and acquire power and masculinity through violence and multiple partnering. However, although the tools provided by patriarchal ideology are being used, it is hardly a demonstration of dominance and control. Females on the other hand, are almost as likely to use the strategies on offer as they seek to carve out and establish their own domain of independence. The increasing willingness and ability to change the household boundaries if and when the situation becomes physically intolerable and/or there are diminishing returns only serve to compound the sense of instability and lack of cohesion which itself encourages conflict.

The hypothesis that persons with a history of child physical and sexual abuse will be more likely to experience/practice domestic/household violence was partially supported in that physical abuse was significantly associated with later domestic violence. It is interesting that this was significant for males only. The severity of childhood punishments and the later orientation towards violent conflict resolution tactics are then mutually supportive in a cause-and-effect spiral.

It may be recalled that this paper was stimulated by an earlier finding that with respect to the incidence of child sexual abuse the more traditional families were no more protective of children than the alternative family structures. The data presented here show that the hypothesis that persons from 'dysfunctional' families of origin – where 'dysfunctional' has been used to describe those female-headed, mother-centred households – will experience higher levels of domestic/household has not been supported; while those currently in those kinds of households are not the violence-prone ones.

There is much that still needs to be explored. This paper has only been able to draw out a number of significant associations with hints of causality. Since this sample was not able to collect detailed data on the families of origin[2] – such as their occupational, employment or status, it is not possible to exhaustively look for the range of possible influences there. Further, in light of the findings from case-study material (Chambers & Chevannes 1991; Bailey et al. 1998) it is likely that in this study there is be some underreporting of the incidence of violence. More work, utilising qualitative methodologies as well as quantitative ones with larger sample sizes are necessary before definitive conclusions may be drawn.

Conclusion

In this chapter we have sought to explore some of the relationships between different types of family structures, selected socioeconomic variables and violent behaviours. This search was originally stimulated by the somewhat unexpected finding that the more traditional family arrangements did not necessarily reduce risk when compared with alternative family structures. In trying to determine whether or not it might be possible to identify violence-prone households, and in looking for factors that could help us to better identify those persons who may be at greater risk, it was found that exposure to violent forms of childhood punishment and involvement in a specific type of union were critical. Very important, however, is the fact that partner violence is not really gender specific, and that there were critical gender differences in respect of the explanatory variables. Perhaps the most general conclusion that needs to be drawn then, is that it may be more useful to focus attention not so much on the formal form of the family structure, as on the character and quality of gender relationships, on the process of managing and establishing the 'market-type relationships', as well as on the capacity to manage and negotiate them. It also suggests that solutions targeted at adaptations, such as the single, female-headed household, instead of its causes may be inappropriate.

Notes

1   This could be due to the fact that the legal age of sexual consent (at 16 years) is lower than that of many other countries thereby affecting the number of incidences that may be classified as abuse.
2   This was largley due to problems of recall as well as the particular goals and objectives of the overall study.

The Caribbean family and the child welfare system in Britain

Ravinder Barn

Introduction

This chapter is concerned with Caribbean people of African ancestry in Britain and their experiences of the British child welfare system. It draws upon two empirical research studies carried out by the author (Barn 1993, Barn, Sinclair and Ferdinand 1997). The empirical findings from these studies are presented in the context of wider research in this area. A conceptual framework is developed to understand the experiences of Caribbean families by exploring demographic patterns, household and family structures, socio-economic circumstances, and the ideological framework of social work theory and practice. It is argued that a narrow conceptualisation of the structure of families of Caribbean backgrounds, and factors which impinge upon family life have resulted in the lack of development of child care services adequate for these families' needs in Britain.

The child welfare system

Child welfare agencies were created to fulfil a number of duties, namely to protect children from harm, preserve families whenever possible, provide decent care for children, and either return children to their birth families or find appropriate foster or adoptive families for them. In Britain, the child welfare system arose from the voluntary efforts of Victorian philanthropy. With the advent of the welfare state, children's departments were created in 1948 to provide help and assistance to families in need. Due to the disparate and fragmented nature of these organisations, a process of reorganisation took place in the early 1970s. Following the *Seebohm Report* in 1968, local authority social services departments were established to provide a more generic and comprehensive service to families. These included preventive help/family support (in cash or kind, family aides, counselling, etc.); respite care; foster care; adoption; residential homes; and day care.

The Children Act 1989, in England and Wales, placed a new statutory duty upon local authority social services departments (SSDs), 'to take account of race, culture, religion and language', with respect to social work with children (DoH 1991-1989 Children Act, sec 22 (5) (c)). Previous legislation, namely, 1976 Race Relations Act (sec.71) had imposed a duty upon local authorities to combat direct and indirect racial discrimination leading local authorities, as mentioned above, to formulate equal opportunity policies. The 1976 Race Relations Act, in spite of its weaknesses, and the 1989 Children Act represent important challenges for local authorities.

Early welfare experiences

The involvement of Black families with the social services is not a new phenomena. Since their significant arrival in Britain in the 1950s, and 1960s, social services agencies have concerned themselves with their presence. Although the social work literature does not always provide specificity of ethnic grouping, based on our current understanding, it would be reasonable to assume that much of the early research on minority ethnic families is implicitly about Caribbean families and children. In 1954, six years after the docking of the *Empire Windrush* at Tilbury a National Children's Home report documented the high number of 'coloured' children in residential homes in Britain. In 1960 the Family Welfare Association reported that the problems of 'West Indians' were no different to those of the indigenous population, and that this group was making adequate use of the services. Little recognition was given to racial discrimination in public services, as the problems of the new migrants were constructed within an ephemeral framework around newness and adjustment to 'host society'. Subsequent studies highlighted the problem of a growing number of Black children in residential homes and the difficulties of finding substitute families for these children (Rowe and Lambert 1973). Much of the early research adopted a problematic approach, and focused upon Black family structures and lifestyles to understand the situation of Black families and children involved with the social services (Fitzherbert 1967, McCulloch, Batta and Smith 1979). There was little or no attempt to explore the impact of structural racism upon Black family life, and the relevance or appropriateness of British social work theory and practice. The over-emphasis upon Black family structures, and the lack of understanding of the experiences of Black families and welfare institutions was largely the impetus for my own work in this area.

Methodology

The findings presented here are drawn from two research studies which explored the situation of Black children (including Caribbean children) looked after and those on the child protection register (Barn 1993, Barn, Sinclair and Ferdinand 1997). In Britain, there are currently no national or local statistics available on the number of Caribbean or other minority ethnic children in the public care system. National data are collated annually on the numbers, characteristics, and circumstances that lead children to be admitted into the care system, but this provides no information on ethnicity. Moreover, research studies have paid scant attention to exploring the circumstances under which Caribbean children come to be represented in the care system. This has resulted in a dearth of information in this area.

Data from two research studies carried out by the author are presented here to begin to understand the underlying factors which may contribute to these children's involvement with the personal social services. These included, first, a study of 'Wenford', an inner-city London local authority social services department. A cohort of 564 looked after children constituted the total 'in care' population. This cohort included 150 children of Caribbean origin, and 103 children of mixed-parentage background (Barn 1993). Although the majority of the mixed-parentage children represented a Black Caribbean/White mix; for the purpose of this paper we shall concentrate only upon the Caribbean children. This is largely due to the fact that the vast majority of the mixed-parentage children came from a lone parent family, where the sole carer was the White biological mother. A discussion of the circumstances of these mothers and their children is offered elsewhere (Barn 1999). The second study was of three local authority social services departments, where a total of 196 cases were examined, 35 of which were of Caribbean origin (Barn, Sinclair and Ferdinand 1997).

Both studies used a combination of quantitative and qualitative methods. There were three main components. First, there was the collection of quantitative data from case files. Barn (1993) took a snapshot of all children found to be in care at the time of the study; whilst Barn, Sinclair and Ferdinand (1997) examined the case histories of 200 allocated cases. Second, there was a sub-group study involving semi-structured in-depth interviews with social work practitioners, carers, families and young people. Third, analyses of departmental policies through scrutiny of policy documents and interviews with senior managers were conducted.

The first research study was conducted in the London Borough of Wenford, a fictional name used to preserve the anonymity of this inner-city local authority. At the time of research in 1987, about a third of the borough's population was described as being from the New Commonwealth and Pakistan; the largest minority ethnic group being African Caribbean. The borough experiences a high rate of deprivation and disadvantage – high unemployment, poor and overcrowded housing, poverty and family breakdown. Wenford is one of the poorest and most economically deprived areas in England, and the local authority is Labour controlled and attempts to combat deprivation through a range of service provision. At the time of the research, alongside the usual budget constraints the local authority was rate-capped by central government which imposed further restrictions on its spending power.

The second, a national research study, was undertaken in three local authorities in England, reflecting three authority types, including a shire county in the East Midlands, a metropolitan authority in the West Midlands, and a London borough. In part, these authorities were chosen because they served populations with substantial and diverse minority ethnic communities. In addition, the particular social work areas within those authorities in which research was located were, in the main, the areas with the highest concentration of Black people. For example, the two teams from the shire county served a part of the city where 60% of the child population is Black, although a very different pattern existed in the more rural area in county. The characteristics of the child care populations in these authorities are representative of their authority group as a whole. This would suggest that despite the higher than average Black population in these areas the findings from the study will have widespread applicability and the lessons from this research will be of relevance to other authorities.

Findings

Our studies included a group of 185 children of African Caribbean origin. Although there were roughly equal numbers of boys and girls in our first study (Barn 1993), our second study included more girls than boys. Due to the small number represented in this study (35), it is not possible to establish any firm reasons for this gender difference. Almost all the African-Caribbean children were born in Britain. The majority of children came from one parent families (82 per cent).

About one tenth of the children lived with both parents prior to entry into care, and the remainder were in extended families or with grand-parents, aunts and uncles. Lone parenthood is a typical characteristic of families involved with social services. Our research shows, however, that African-Caribbean children were more likely to come from a one-parent family than other groups.

A high proportion of the families were living in local authority housing, and our research shows that poor housing was often a concern for African Caribbean families. Indeed, research studies have shown that Black applicants and tenants frequently receive poorer quality housing than White applicants and tenants (Brown 1984; Lakey, 1977). Our research shows that black children were twice as likely to be admitted into care where poor housing was a contributory factor (Barn 1993).

The majority of the mothers were over the age of 25 (81 per cent); over half the sample represented the 25–45 age group. Most of these women were born in the Caribbean (91 per cent). We found that in comparison with other ethnic groups, including white, a higher number of African Caribbean mothers were in paid employment. They were also more likely to be found in a range of occupations representing lower middle class and working class backgrounds. With the exception of age, information on fathers was less readily available. We found that African-Caribbean fathers were older in comparison with the mothers in the study. Almost all the African-Caribbean fathers were over the age of 25 (96 per cent), and a high number were over the age of 45 (66 per cent). With respect to employment, information was only available in relation to 65 fathers. Of these 40 were in paid employment, mostly in skilled and semi-skilled occupations. Five fathers represented classes 1 and 2 (professional/managerial and higher white-collar). Most fathers were Caribbean born.

Our research shows that African-Caribbean children entered the public care system for a variety of reasons ranging from family relationship problems, to parental neglect, mother's mental health, poverty, and housing (for a detailed discussion of this see Barn 1993, Barn, Sinclair and Ferdinand 1997). We found that statutory agencies were much more likely to exercise a coercive role in the referral of Caribbean families. For example, African-Caribbean mothers were two and half times more likely to be referred by the police and the health service for concerns around mental health than White mothers. Also, Caribbean youngsters were twice as likely to be referred by the police for reasons of delinquency than White youngsters.

In our data analysis of admission patterns, we found that African-Caribbean children were entering the care system more quickly than any other ethnic grouping. In our recent national study of three Local

Authority Social Services Departments, we found that greater proportions of African-Caribbean children entered care within two weeks of
referral than any other ethnic group – 68 per cent compared with
59 per cent of mixed-parentage, 50 per cent of Asian, and 49 per cent
of white (Barn, Sinclair and Ferdinand 1997).

African-Caribbean children were also found to spend longer
periods in the care system, and less likely to be returned to their birth
family. Our recent study shows that 36 per cent of the African-
Caribbean children had been in public care for more than five years
compared with 24 per cent of children of mixed-parentage, 10 per cent
of White origin, and eight per cent of Asian origin (Barn, Sinclair and
Ferdinand 1997). Our research found that over two-thirds of the
African-Caribbean children entered the care system with parental
consent (63 per cent). That is, parental agreements were reached with
parents to avoid court action. The Children Act 1989 is clear that care
orders should be made only when not making a care order would be
detrimental to the child's welfare. In situations where children are
being admitted into care with parental agreement, the possibility of
working with the family to obviate entry into care is clearly a valid
approach. Our findings point to problems around social work assessment and engagement which prevented the development of a supportive approach that may have proved useful to maintain the child within
their own family.

Discussion

The above findings raise some important questions about the high
number of African-Caribbean children in the public care system, about
the above average number of Caribbean families involved with the
social services, about the circumstances which led to Caribbean children entering care more quickly than other ethnic groups, and about
the longer periods spent in the care system by children of Caribbean
backgrounds. In addressing these questions, it is necessary for the discussion to explore some relevant demographic patterns, household and
family structures, socio-economic circumstances and social work
ideology.

According to the 1991 census figures, and as analysed by David
Owen in Chapter 5 above, there are 493,339 people of Black-
Caribbean origin. This represents more than half (56.1 per cent) of
Britain's Black population of African, African-Caribbean and Black-
Other. However, as we can see in Table 12.1, self-identification and the
nature of ethnic classification are such that it leads to a variation in

Table 12.1   Great Britain Composition of the 'Black' and ethnic categories

Ethnic Group	Population	Percent
Black people	879,850	100.0
Black – Caribbean	493,339	56.1
Black – African	208,110	23.7
Black – Other	178,401	20.3
British	58,106	6.6
Mixed:Black/White parents	24,687	2.8
Mixed-Other	50,668	5.8
Other answers	44,940	5.1

Source: OPCS/GRO (Scotland) 1994 Country of Birth and Ethnic Group report (HMSO).

data recording. Given that a sizeable Black population may define themselves as African or Black-British suggests that in any discussions involving the use of census statistics, it is important to be aware of the problematic nature of data recording and interpretation.

A conceptualisation of the age profile is crucial in understanding the interactions of Black people with the social services departments. As Owen shows in Chapter 5 in this volume, a significant number of the Black people are represented in the young category. For example, half of all Black-Other males are aged under 15 years. We know that this includes Black British young people, but also those of Black/White parentage. Research has continually documented the high representation of African-Caribbean and mixed-parentage children (Foren and Batta 1970, Bebbington and Miles 1989, Rowe et al. 1989, Barn 1993, Barn, Sinclair and Ferdinand 1997). The census data also show that the Black-Caribbean ethnic group is, on average, older than the Black-African ethnic group. The significance of the growing elderly population for the Caribbean family and the social services has implications for family life and service provision (see Table 12.2).

Boss and Homeshaw (1974) found that African-Caribbeans were the only group who were over-represented as child care clients – 1.03 per hundred came for help during the year of the study. In providing an explanation for this phenomena, Boss and Homeshaw assert that:

> ...coloured families are predominantly young. They are therefore likely to be at the height of their child bearing years and will therefore have more dependent children. The chances of their needing child care help are thus, for demographic reasons alone, higher than average (Boss and Homeshaw 1975, p 355).

Table 12.2 Demographic characteristics of 'Black' and White groups in Britain, 1991

Age group marital category birthplace, migrants	White		Black – Caribb		Black – African		Black – Other	
	M	F	M	F	M	F	M	F
Population (000s)	25,066.4	26,807.4	239.5	260.5	106.8	105.6	87.5	90.9
% aged 0–4	6.7	6.0	7.9	7.2	11.8	11.8	20.9	19.7
% aged 5–15	13.8	12.2	15.2	13.5	17.6	17.4	31.2	29.3
% aged 16–24	13.0	12.1	14.6	15.1	15.8	17.4	18.2	19.7
% aged 25–44	29.8	28.2	29.6	35.6	41.6	42.7	23.1	25.2
% aged 45–59/64	22.8	16.6	26.2	19.2	11.4	8.5	.2	4.0
% of pensionable age	13.9	24.8	6.5	9.3	1.8	2.1	1.3	2.0
Median age in years	35.8	38.9	30.2	30.3	26.6	26.0	15.0	16.5
	percent aged 16 and over							
Single	29.5	22.6	47.2	50.0	46.9	43.3	63.6	64.2
Married	61.0	56.1	42.2	35.2	48.2	46.5	31.0	27.5
Widowed	3.9	14.5	2.0	4.2	0.8	3.2	0.8	2.1
Divorced	5.5	6.8	8.6	10.7	4.1	7.0	4.7	6.3
% born in the UK	96.0	95.7	53.6	53.7	35.9	36.9	84.1	84.8
% living outside UK one year before census	0.5	0.5	0.6	0.6	7.9	6.7	1.8	1.6

Source: Owen, D. (1994); 1991 Census Local Base Statistics (ESRC purchase); Crown Copyright. OPCS/GRO (Scotland) (1994) Country of Birth and Ethnic Group report (HMSO).

The demographic data show that Caribbean people constitute the largest grouping within the Black group (56.1 per cent). This amounts to less than one per cent of the total British population (0.9 per cent). A collective representation of all three Black groups amounts to 1.6 per cent of the total British population. The figure for the other significant minority ethnic grouping (Asian), in Britain, is considerably higher (3.4 per cent). Thus there are twice as many people of Asian descent than of African and Caribbean descent.

Research into children in the care system indicate the high representation of African-Caribbean and mixed-parentage children, and continue to point to the under-representation of Asian children (Barn 1993, Barn, Sinclair and Ferdinand 1997). Given their higher representation in the general population, one could expect to find more Asian children in the care system. However, this is not so. Barn, Sinclair and Ferdinand (1997) selected localities with high presence of Asian people, and yet did not find Asian children to be significantly represented in the care system. Table 12.2 shows that both Black-African and Black-Other groups have a younger population in comparison with white and Black-Caribbean. We know that Black-Other contains children of Caribbean parents as well as children of mixed ethnicity. Given this younger population, it could be assumed that more of these children become involved with the social services. However the low representation of Asian children in the care system is indicative of the fact that demography alone cannot explain the high presence of African-Caribbean children in the care system.

In Britain, there is a lack of accurate and comprehensive historical data on patterns of family and household sizes and structures for different ethnic groups. This is largely due to the recent settlement of minority groups, in any significant number, in Britain. Official surveys such as the Labour Force Survey (LFS), the *National Dwelling and Household Survey* (NDHS), and the *Policy Institute Survey* (PIS) have provided useful insights about the living arrangements of minority groups (Haskey 1989, Berrington 1994, Department of the Environment 1993). Whilst statistical data may provide useful information, there are interpretation problems associated with this. One such difficulty is the demographic profile differences between the white indigenous population, and minority ethnic groupings. The age structures of minority ethnic populations are generally much younger than average. The 1991 census figures show that there are substantial differences between the household and family patterns of minority ethnic groups in Britain (Murphy 1996). In particular, there are higher proportions of female-headed, lone-parent families among Black people (including African, Caribbean and Black people of mixed-parentage). Table 12.2 shows that whilst divorce rates are comparable to White people for Black-Africans and Black-Others, they are somewhat higher for Black-Caribbeans, with 10.7 per cent of Black-Caribbean women aged over 16 being divorced compared with 6.8 per cent of White women). It would also appear that a large proportion of Black lone-parent families have dependent children compared with white lone parent families (Owen 1994). Murphy (1996) argues that:

> among groups where extra-marital childbearing is common, and where potential husbands have very poor economic expectations, the conventional Western model of childbearing within a marital union by a couple able to set up an independent households with the husband providing for his family will not be an option in many cases (p 238).

Whilst recognising the range of problems associated with some non-traditional living arrangements within societal and social policy context, Murphy (1996) points to the socialisation repercussions upon children in the light of negative stereotyping of non-traditional families. He argues that if negative images of non-traditional families were racialised, the effects are likely to be even more substantial for those concerned. Gopaul-McNicol (1993) warns of the dangers of negative stereotypes, and their debilitating effect particularly on Black males and their ability to function as husbands, fathers, and workers.

Social work intervention

The experiences of many African-Caribbean families in Britain reveal a picture of disadvantage and discrimination in housing, education, employment and other public services (Lakey 1997; Eggleston 1986; Owen 1994; Modood et al. 1997). For example, with respect to male unemployment, Modood et al. (1997) found that the rate of unemployment among Caribbean men was much higher than whites, and Indian/EastAfrican Asian men. For example, 61 per cent of Caribbean men under the age of 35 (with no qualifications) were unemployed compared with 19 per cent of whites, 18 per cent of Indians/East African Asians, and 45 per cent of Pakistani and Bangladeshi men in a similar situation (Modood et al. 1997: 91). The social effects of this upon family life are enormous, and commentators have pointed to the debilitating impact of this upon Black males ability to function as husbands and fathers (Gopaul-McNicol 1993).

Research into housing and lone parenthood shows that lone parents are more likely to be tenants, or even in temporary accommodation than their partnered counterparts (Duncan and Edwards 1997a). Moreover, they have tended to get the worst housing, for example older properties, flats rather than houses, and higher floors rather than lower floors (Harrison 1983). Such housing situations, no doubt, create their own social and familial problems. As our research indicates, poor housing was a contributory factor in the referral and admission of Caribbean children into the public care system.

Our research documents the greater likelihood of African-Caribbean children being referred by statutory agencies and being admitted into the care system than other minority ethnic groups. Early social work intervention is crucial in providing family support to prevent disruption. Our research shows that African-Caribbean children enter care much more quickly than other ethnic groups. An analysis of the factors involved show that African-Caribbean children are not significantly 'at risk of abuse and neglect' as many of these admissions happen with parental consent. Child care legislation is clear about acting in the child's welfare (DoH 1991). Our research shows that admission into care is not necessarily in the best interests of the child. Lengthy periods in care, lack of stability, removal from family and community, and lack of preparation and training into leaving care have a detrimental effect upon African-Caribbean children (Ince 1998).

Fitzherbert (1967) in her study of 'West Indian Children in London' recommended social workers to adopt a 'tough' casework approach to prevent the flow of Caribbean children into the care system. She believed that African-Caribbean parents were willingly placing their youngsters in care as they perceived it to provide good training to equip them for life in England. Fitzherbert also held this conviction:

> They (the children) became 'socialised', and acquired habits and skills which equipped them better for life in England than would have been possible had they remained at home (Fitzherbert 1967: 72)

Fitzherbert's thinking is couched within an assimilationist framework where the care system is presented as a vehicle for instilling an 'English life style'. Her over-emphasis upon cultural lifestyles fails to explore the power dynamics involved in the process of social work decision-making, and the impact of the care system on children separated from their birth parents and community. The care system is presented as a benevolent entity in the process of assimilation. Liverpool, a Black practitioner, acknowledges elements of the 'culture conflict' theory but argues that:

> ... these factors were compounded by the responses of the Social Services Departments which failed to recognise the strengths of these families, and play a more supportive role (Liverpool 1986: 20).

Our research shows that African-Caribbean children were not only likely to be admitted into care more quickly than white children in situations of family relationship problems, and socio-economic difficulties, but also where allegations of child abuse had been made (Barn 1993). Social workers were found to be operating within a atmosphere of fear, panic and a lack of understanding. Arnold refers to the subtleties in family interaction and the meanings attached to language:

> The West Indian parent who threatens to beat the living daylight out of a disobedient child, or who asks him to leave 'if he thinks himself a man' seldom means to be taken literally. These are his or her attempts at imposing a discipline in the hope that threats will serve as a deterrent for the delinquent behaviour (Arnold 1982: 109).

Our research shows that problems in social work assessment and engagement were likely to be the result for the initial speedy admissions of African-Caribbean children in care, and the subsequent lengthy periods in the care system. Black and White writers in recent years have questioned the framework of assessment employed by social workers and it has been argued that lone parenthood in the African-Caribbean community has been presented as problematic (Lawrence 1982, Phoenix 1988, Stubbs 1988, Gambe et al. 1992). The African-Caribbean family is perceived to be inherently weak due to lone-parenthood. This is used as a convenient explanation in many areas such as 'delinquent children', 'underachieving children', 'children in the care system', and so on.

African-Caribbean mothers in our study were more likely to be in employment than their white counterparts. They were also more likely to be in lower middle class occupations compared to their white counterparts who were concentrated in semi-skilled or unskilled occupations. Data on fathers was sketchy, but we found that where this was available, African-Caribbean fathers were largely in skilled and semi-skilled occupations. A small number (five) were found to be in professional/managerial and higher white-collar jobs. Duncan and Edwards (1997b) in their study of lone mothers found that African-Caribbean lone mothers were better able to integrate motherhood and employment within their views than their White counterparts who viewed motherhood and employment as incompatible or separate activities. This suggests that African-Caribbean women face fewer conflicts in their mother/worker identity than their white counterparts, and attempt to confront challenges presented by this situation. There is, however, a dearth of literature about family support networks of African-Caribbean lone parent families. The perceptions of lone Caribbean mothers are polarised into 'Supermum', or 'Problem-mum', both of which are unhelpful in understanding the issues and concerns faced by these families. Such a dichotomy prevents the development of an adequate response to the needs and concerns of Caribbean lone parents.

Dutt and Phillips (1996) point to the 'under-interventionist', and 'over-interventionist' approach in social work with minority ethnic families, and the negative consequences of this upon families and children. The under-interventionist approach may be based upon fallacious views about Black families and their capabilities thereby absolving social services of their role and function to become involved to provide the necessary help and assistance. For example, the London Borough of Lambeth inquiry report into the death of Tyra Henry, a five year old who was killed by her father when her grandmother was unable to continue to look after her refers to the 'Supermum' figure:

> ... a 'positive', but nevertheless false, stereotype in White British society of the Afro-Caribbean mother figure as endlessly resourceful, able to cope in great adversity, essentially unsinkable ... we do think that it may have been an unarticulated and unconscious sense that a woman like Beatrice Henry would find a way of coping, no matter what, that underlay the neglect of Area 5 Social Services to make adequate provision for her taking responsibility for Tyra (London Borough of Lambeth 1987: 108–109).

It is possible that the child welfare system's inability to identify issues and concerns, and provide appropriate supportive help leads to crisis situations in which Caribbean children are particularly vulnerable and likely to enter the care system more quickly than other groups. The over-interventionist approach may be based upon negatively held beliefs about Caribbean families, as well as social worker inability to recognise the effect of race and ethnicity upon a given situation. There is little or no attempt to move away from this deficit model of the African-Caribbean family. To understand this situation, it is important to observe the nature and role of social work in Britain which is largely casework oriented. This results in the assessment and intervention of problems in an individualistic manner. There may be insufficient recognition given to the family's social network, and their structural position in society. Such an approach leads to partial assessment, and consequently to ineffective intervention. The casework approach is therefore limited in its potential for effectiveness, and improving the client's situation.

There is also a significant relationship between social work ideology and universality (see Barn 1998). The concept of universality operates within a framework of hegemonic ideals, for example, about family life/family structures, family roles and responsibilities. Social work knowledge base contains hegemonic ideals about child development, and child abuse and neglect. An understanding of the lives of Black families is approached from this perspective. A universalist framework which is anchored in the hegemonic framework fails to conceptualise the diversity of a multi-racial society. Thus, any deviation from the White British 'norm' is consciously or subconsciously perceived as problematic. The concept of family requires attention in the social work literature and in the British psyche which views family structure in extremely rigid terms.

Gopaul-McNicol (1993) emphasises the fluidity of family structure and life, and asserts that:

> The West Indian family is usually an extended family that encompasses not only those related by marriage and blood, but also godparents, adopted children whose adoption is informal ('child lending'), and in some cases even friends. The function of these non-related family members is to provide security for children and to offer help in crises ... The extended family is a source of strength for the couple ... [and] is particularly useful for women, who may rely on other women in the extended family for help with childbearing and household duties (Gopaul-Mcnicol 1993:22).

Recent qualitative research shows the importance of family ties, and the differing meaning attached to the family by Black people in Britain (Hylton 1997). An African-Caribbean woman, in her forties, echoed the sentiments of many other respondents in Hylton's study, thus:

> Well, I don't know where the term extended came from. I don't use it at all because in order to show the difference I would say my 'immediate family' which takes in my husband and my son; and when I talk about 'family' I'm talking about my sisters, my mother, my nieces, my nephews. So I don't like the term 'extended', and particularly how we operate, because if something is wrong with my nephew it could well be wrong with my son (There would be no difference) ... in the way I'll go about dealing with it ... So I just see us as one big family, and that's how we'll act around you ... (Hylton 1997, p 14)

Jones and Butt (1995) found that intervention strategies for working with Black families were underdeveloped. In our study (Barn, Sinclair and Ferdinand 1997), we found that in one of our three local authorities, family oriented practice was proving to be effective in the case of Asian families and adolescents where social workers acted as mediators to achieve consensual goals and objectives. Research also point to a higher success rate where such methods of intervention are employed with Black families (Ho 1987; Paniagua 1994). The concept and meaning of family, and its hegemonic framework require attention. The current polarisation between the 'deficit model', and the 'strength model' is unhelpful in the development of social work theory and practice.

Conclusion

The experiences of African-Caribbean families paint a complex picture of multiple disadvantage and discrimination in housing, employment, education, health. Demographic data on the number of African-Caribbean children and young people, and household and family structure are, however, insufficient to conceptualise the high numbers of African-Caribbean children in the care system. The racial discrimination faced by African-Caribbean families increases the social and familial vulnerability of many. Although many African-Caribbean families would and do survive such difficult circumstances, there are others who require help and assistance from public agencies such as social services. Our research suggests that the majority of African-Caribbean families who come into contact with social services departments are lone mothers. The social work focus upon Caribbean family structure as pathological and dysfunctional or, alternatively, as 'abundantly resourceful', de-emphasises structural discrimination and heightens family relationships as problematic. Although, social services cannot ameliorate all ills in society, they can play a significant role in combating racial discrimination within the personal social services. The high rates of entry into care of African-Caribbean children, their subsequent experiences in care, and the role of social work theory, practice and provision require serious and urgent attention.

13 Ageing in Babylon: elderly Caribbeans in Britain

Dwaine Plaza

Introduction

> Grandparents like me are vital in the development of the younger ones in this society. We are part of the coping strategy that helps out the family. Some of our younger children in this society are missing that. It was a very sad time in my life when I saw my best friend decide to move back to Jamaica. Not only was he leaving me but he was leaving his grands who would not have the benefit of his knowledge and his stories. It's now been five years since he has seen them and I know that his memory is fading in their minds as they reach into adolescents. It's not right…Grandparents are needed for nurturing and without them well you can see the results in the society today (JF 021/1/Tape 2/Side A).

Based on data from the Living Arrangements, Family Structure and Social Change of Caribbeans in Britain project outlined in the Preface and Introduction to the present volume, this chapter explores a number of issues arising from the social, economic and psychological adaptations faced by the ageing cohort of African Caribbeans in Britain. These problems are relatively new (see, Goulbourne, 1998b, Ch 4), because only recently have the 1950s cohorts of Caribbean migrants to Britain been noticeably part of the elderly population of the country, as David Owen has demonstrated in Chapter 5 above. However, from the 1980s a number of scholars and policy makers have been aware of several issues relating to the elderly in Britain's new minority ethnic communities (see, Blakemore, et al. 1994; Patel, 1990; Fenton, 1985; Jackson, et al. 1982). Returns from the 1991 national census of population (see, Table 13.1) show that Caribbeans over sixty years of age now constitute the largest new minority ethnic elderly population, and they are one of the most vulnerable groups within the Caribbean communities.

Table 13.1　Population aged 60 and over by ethnic origin and sex

Ethnic Origin	Males Aged 60 and Over	Females Aged 60 and Over
White	4,800,009	6,659,513
Black – Caribbean	30,169	24,139
Black – African	3,490	2,192
Black – Other	1,840	1,856
Indian	29,655	27,741
Pakistani	10,924	6,644
Bangladesh	4,083	1,215
Chinese	4,117	4,787
Other – Asian	3,633	4,414
Other – Other	7,116	7,450
Total (Ethnic Minorities)	95,027	80,438
Total	4,895,036	6,739,951

Source: The 1991 Census.

In the Caribbean, seniors had a role in maintaining the family structure, keeping links with the past alive, and socialising the young (Eldemire, 1994; Braithwaite, 1986). With migration and acculturation to British norms and values this important function has been transformed for both the younger and older generations. Retirement has also robbed many Caribbean elders of a sense of usefulness in British society, and when this is accompanied by decreased income and a limited role in their family some suffer from the added loss of self-esteem. There are, however, gender differences in impact and response. Caribbean-born women living in Britain have for the most part retained strong social networks based on emotional bonds with their children, family, extended kin, and friends. For them, the transition to old age seems to be a much less painful process than for many Caribbean-born men for whom the transition to old age has not been as positive. Many have not maintained the strong supportive social networks with family, kin and extended kin over the years. Living arrangements have also been such that some men have not kept close links with their children or partners. As a result, more Caribbean born men than women voice a serious concern for their well being in old age.

Traditional grandmother and grandfather roles in the Caribbean

The typical grandchild-grandparent relationship in the Caribbean is one of affectionate indulgence, and a kind of equality. As RT Smith

(1956, p 144) observed, 'It is commonly said that grandparents spoil their grandchildren and old men certainly display far greater affection for their grandchildren than they ever do towards their own children.' Equally, a grandmother, in particular, will often identify herself with her grandchildren and take their part in any quarrel they may have with their own mother.

The majority of the Caribbean born informants in the *Living Arrangements, Family Structure and Social Change of Caribbeans in Britain Project* recall that their grandmothers played an important part in the lives of their families and extended households. Many maternal grandmothers, for instance, were often looked upon to take on childcare responsibilities for their grandchildren, typically from their daughters. Such 'child shifting'[1] would often occur when a daughter migrated to some other part of the country or internationally in search of work, leaving her child(ren) in the care of her mother. A grandmother's readiness to assume responsibility for her grandchildren is a central aspect of the pattern of childrearing in Caribbean society. While it may be the intention that the children should spend only a limited period with the grandmother, in most cases, the child(ren) remained in the grand-mother's home for very long periods (Roberts & Sinclair, 1978:161) and the process of reuniting with children sometimes proved slow and incremental. This 'child shifting' practice recurred in a number of the interviews especially among those who arrived in Britain as teenagers. Henry[2], for instance, who grew up with his grandmother and 27 cousins in Black River, Jamaica, said of his grandmother:

> Yeh, she [mother] left me with my grandmother, when I was about, I think, a couple of months, or something like that. When she first arrived here, she arrive by herself ... then she send for one of her brother, and then she sent for her sister. Then she sent for her next brother. She sent for about, maybe about five of them, and they all come up here and start their own life over here. All the rest of we stayed with my grand-mother. And growing up in a big family, maybe of about 26, 27. Grannie she had a lot of responsibility, and she had to really prepare things for us, and make sure everything was all right. She was very hard working, a very hard-working woman. I can remember her very well, and then my mother she sent for each of us...She first sent for my bigger brother and my big, eldest sister and eventually she sent for me (JO 161/2/ Tape 1/ Side A).

In some families, grandmothers lived in the homes of their children, and often contributed, in cash or kind, to the household economy. John, for instance, recalled that in his Barbadian childhood in the 1940s his grandmother Elsie worked as a servant at a local plantation in order to supplement her son's (his father's) income. Elsie's contribution to the family savings was important because ultimately it allowed John's father to open up a small village rum shop. As John recalls:

> My grandmother, I mean, she lived in the house for all the years that I've known ... although my mother was present, you could still see her as a surrogate mother, as such, because she was very caring and very religious, and really, you could say, supplemented, initially, my father's income. I remember her working as a servant on the plantation. She had my father, and then his father went off to America, and she never had another man since. So she spent most of her time in the church and with us (BA 005/1/Tape1/Side A).

Grandmothers assisted in other ways. Even if not resident in the home of their children, they nevertheless constituted part of the wider household. Most lived close by and offered affection, nurture and sometimes accommodation to their grandchildren. All were acknowledged as participating in and contributing to the life of the wider family, and in return were cared for (and expected to be cared for) by their children and grandchildren. The grandmother's role appeared to be well defined and acknowledged, and grandmothers, particularly maternal grandmothers, were remembered as central figures in childhood.

Grandfathers, however, solicited a more mixed response. Many of our interviewees recalled these elderly men as being kind and loving. Some grandfathers were also recognised for making a significant economic contribution to the family through, for instance, 'working the land'. Beulah's grandfather, Matthew maintained a full-time job, worked a parcel of land and had a small shop to support his family in Trinidad. As Beulah explained,

> My grandfather. Very very strong, again, personality. Quietly strong, quietly assertive. So, he would be very hard working. He had a formal job, I'm not sure what it was, but I know they said he would go on his bicycle to his job. So maybe he was like an inspector of some sort, I don't know if it's inspecting at a farm, or whatever, but he definitely had a paid job, a formal job. And when he came back in the evenings, he would sort of work on his land. And so it was really his income that was the main thing. But also they had the little shop. But they were really hard-working, to do a lot of

different things for the betterment of their children…. He never, as far as I know, never drank … so wasn't into the rum shop crowd, playing cards. He's very sort of moral, upstanding member of the community. And so, in a way, he didn't need to sort of shout loud about what he is, because people could see that in the way he lived…. A lot of his family, and people have died, and he's still there, so, you know, he still has a lot of respect in that area, which I would value and respect as well (TJ 072/1/Tape1/Side A).

At the same time, some of the informants noted that their grandfathers were distant and at times unreliable. Some, for instance, had migrated and never returned. Others did not live with their grandmothers and could not receive the day to day contact which was a familiar feature of grandmother care. Others were remembered for playing a more ambivalent role in the lives of their families. Albert, for instance, recalled his grandfather in Jamaica, a farmer as:

a bit of a drunkard. He just seemed to constantly be drinking all the time. Even if, even if he'd wanted to marry my gran, I don't think she could have dealt with that. I don't think she could equate having a man like that … she seemed to have been brought up that way, to accept that kind of thing. Mmm. Mmm. And, as I said, he was a, he was a womaniser … (JQ 067/1/Tape1/Side A).

Nevertheless, Albert also conceded that:

he was also a very hard worker, and he provided for all his children. Mmm, he provided for all of them. In Jamaica, he's left land to … he's left family land that can't be sold or anything, it's family land (JQ 067/1/Tape1/Side A).

While some grandfathers may not have played a central role in the care or upbringing of their grandchildren, recent research by for instance Barrow (1998) suggests that men did perform important economic and socialising functions towards consanguineal kin which, we must assume, extended across the generations. In cases where grandfathers were not resident in the family of creation, their presence, and that of their kin, were known and acknowledged by most of our informants. Equally, elders in the community could command the respect due to superior age and experience.

It would appear that the experience of migration to Britain, outlined by Chamberlain in Chapter 3 and their settlement experiences described by Goulbourne (1991, 1998b), affected the traditional living arrangements and family structures of Caribbeans. These changes seem to have had an effect on the long-term variations to the traditional roles and status for the elderly in Caribbean households in Britain.

Issues of adaptation for Caribbean elderly in Britain

A common feature reported by our informants related to the atomisation of the family unit, which had implications for the establishment of family structures, and/or was a contributory factor in break-up. The low pay, and often anti-social hours which needed to be worked (through, for instance, shift work) required a major adjustment in the working lives of many Caribbean migrants. The constraints of both men and women having to work odd hours put added pressure on the family and were also given by some informants as the cause of domestic break-ups. Having to work alternative shifts in order to manage childcare duties meant that many couples went for weeks without seeing one another or having time to 'just share a little intimacy' as one informant put it. In many Caribbean families in Britain it seems that the women continue to be responsible for the triple duty of working full-time, maintaining the primary responsibility for the care and welfare of the children, and the household, and being a supportive wife. Men, on the other hand, were often burdened with having to hold down more than one job in order to meet household expenses. The effect of these economic and social pressures are reflected on Table 13.2, which shows that those Caribbean-born elders who are now over 60 have a high rate of divorce. This trend is especially evident for Caribbean-born women over 60 years old who have a (20 per cent) divorce rate compared to the overall average of (13 per cent) for British-born women of the same age. As a result of this, there are more single elderly Caribbean males.

Finally, one of the effects of long-term exposure to racism is that many Caribbeans have come to regard themselves as outsiders from the

Table 13.2   Marital status of Caribbean elders

	Male	Female	Total
Single	11.7	12.3	218
Married	59.8	47.7	989
Remarried	10.4	4.3	139
Divorced	12.1	19.9	286
Widowed	5.9	15.8	191

Source: 1991 Census of Population 1% Household Sample of Anonymised Records.

mainstream of British society. From the interviews it seems that Caribbean males in particular have a different experience with respect to the racism they are exposed to compared to their female counterparts. The women interviewed in the study did not seem to experience the same physically hostile acts or racial taunting, as Raymond, a 55-year-old Trinidad-born resident of London, explained:

> ... White men did not see our women as a threat in the same way as he saw us ... our women were their nurses and helpers ... we black men however, threatened his jobs and more importantly we threatened to take away and spoil his women (TL 089/1/Tape2/Side A).

Feeling marginalised in British society was a common theme repeated in the interviews with Caribbean-born men. Raymond's narrative captured the feelings that some of the male informants had about Britain and how they saw themselves fitting into British society; he said:

> I'll be frank with you, I don't feel comfortable in this country, I still do not feel relaxed among White people ... I don't see myself as British, no. I have a British Passport ... and my body is here, but I am still in the Caribbean. I'm very very Caribbean, whereas Gail my wife is, more or less British. She likes here and all this sort of thing. But I don't see myself as British. If people ask me where I'm from, I usually say Trinidad. Or the Caribbean, or Afro-Caribbean .... Definitely not British (TL 089/1/Tape2/Side A).

This is partly the result of the structural problems involved in replicating the proximity of family networks. It is also partly the result of generational change. However strong the family values, children of Caribbean-born migrants have necessarily been influenced by British as well as Caribbean values. This sense of isolation from the family takes two forms. In the first instance, the men and women from this sample felt acutely that their role as grandparents had been displaced within Britain. In the second, the grandchildren living in Britain also seemed to express less importance for the role of grandparents in the British/Caribbean family.

While many children of migrants were growing up, their own grandparents were still in the Caribbean, as a consequence they were not socialised (except at long distance) into recognising the centrality of the role of grandparents in the rearing of children. The pioneer elderly migrants in this sample are essentially the first-generation of Caribbean-born grandparents living in Britain. Although they can fondly recall their own grandparents, this recollection is often denied to their children and grandchildren because of the settlement patterns and acculturation to British norms and values. This has resulted in the role of grandparents being made somewhat redundant. In Britain, relatives sometimes live considerable distances apart and the opportunities for getting together are limited by the pressures of a modern lifestyle. In contrast, in the Caribbean, informants recalled living on family land and being close enough to extended kin that they could freely walk in and out of each others' houses. For children born in Britain during the 1960s or 1970s many were raised without ever knowing their grandparents. Information about family history, cultural reference points, and aspects of the families oral culture were for many children of this generation dependent on the willingness of the migrant generation to share their experiences.

Becoming accustomed to the British norms and values it is little surprise therefore, that when the next generation began to have their own children in the 1980s and 1990s many downgraded the importance of grandmothers or grandfathers in the socialisation and care of children. In many ways, this reflected British social norms which also relegated grandmothers and grandfathers as peripheral members of the family who are visited only on holidays like Christmas, Mothers' Day, and Easter. At the same time, however, many of the elders also wished to maintain some distance between themselves and their children's families. This counter intuitive pattern suggests that having lived and worked in Britain for some 30 years or longer this has had an effect on the way that African Caribbean elders regard their role in the family. Although many complain about not having enough time or control over how their grandchildren are brought up, many also seemed happy to know that they lived far enough away from them that they would not be used by their children as an unappreciated baby sitter. This pattern contrasts strongly with that which pertained in the memories of those born in the Caribbean.

The social, economic and psychological issues of ageing

Growing old in Britain has not been easy for Caribbeans. All of our elderly interviewees had serious concerns for their future. This related to their role and position within their families and also to an anxiety about the future of state provision, and the restructuring of social provision. With respect to their families, both the men and women were concerned about being neglected by their children as they become more frail and sickly. Many felt that acculturation to British traditions and values have resulted in their children adopting an attitude that the seniors would be happier if they live autonomous and separate lives, reflecting in some ways the more common British patterns. The interviewees in our study voiced a concern of not wanting to be left alone and vulnerable in a foreign society. At the same time, many also expressed a wish to remain independent for as long as possible. This is not as paradoxical as it may seem, for the model of ageing from the Caribbean suggested both independence and family support. Roland, Peter and Ralph all provide individual and insightful perspectives on the situation. Roland begins by saying:

> Getting old in this country is something that I hate. Yes I am afraid of it because I will not get the treatment that I am entitled to. Basically what they are trying to do now is if you're Black before you get hospital treatment you must carry a passport and things like that. Can you imagine I have a heart attack and I go in the hospital and they say 'Where is your passport? We cannot treat you'. How do expect me to feel when I have lived here over 40 years for some 25 year old nurse or doctor comes to me and says 'I am sorry but can you produce your passport before I can attend to you'. Did they ask me to produce my passport when they were taking out my taxes? No they took it out. My face and my colour did not matter, they took it out willingly. You are telling me at my old age now when I need help the most I have to carry a passport ... I am not begging for it that's what I paid for. This is what I am scared of. I am not scared of dying. Don't get me wrong (JRO 142/1/Tape 2/Side B).

Roland s concern for being treated differently by the state because of his skin colour was a sentiment also heard in a number of the interviews. Although he felt that it was possible to cope with differential incorporation and racism during his younger days, in old age, Roland felt more vulnerable to the state because he would no longer be able to fight back with the same energy or determination that he might have had in the past.

The importance of reminiscence for the elderly is now a recognised practice in geriatric care, and vital in the process of countering geriatric depression and forms of dementia. Yet one of the concerns voiced by our informants was that their particular needs – within the broad area of isolation – are not being addressed within the institutional provision for elderly Caribbeans in Britain. Those who do or can make use of residential and day care centres continue to experience degrees of institutional and systemic racism which compounds the sense of rejection and isolation which many have experienced throughout their lives in Britain. The importance of being able to reminisce in old age for Caribbeans is made by Peter:

> People cannot reminisce here in Britain which is very important. I feel its taken people a long time to decide to go home, because as they are getting older its about reminisces. When you are young you are saying that you are still making plans. After saying when are we going to go home, by the time I reach 60 I will revert back to talk about family history and the importance of childhood in the Caribbean, you cannot have those reminiscences in an old peoples home in this country. The people in these homes never talk to you. People are not going to listen to you (BK 079/2/Tape/Side B).

Ralph's concern for his own future well being summarises the ambivalent feelings that ageing Caribbeans seem to be experiencing in Britain today. These individuals would like to return to the Caribbean but many do not have the financial resources to make such a move. Indeed, many have little but their state pension to support them in old age, supplemented if they are lucky by an occupational pension. As a result, many Caribbean elders express concern about the future and fulfilling their dream of return, and building a home on family land in the Caribbean. As Ralph argued:

> Getting older in this society is very bad news. I got to the stage where I wanted to get away from this place before I considered myself old. Looking around here, it's not the kind of climate I want to get old in. I have seen old people moving around, I seen old people not moving around I dread to be in those situations....I am planning on getting away from here ...What I don't think that I could not do is keep myself going in a community like this which does not care. Although you think that you can financially prepare for some of these issues they are not interested in you in this country. If you run out of money in this country you are on the scrap heap (BI 071/2/Tape2/Side B).

The sense of isolation for elderly Caribbeans is often exacerbated by the fact that many have never become accustomed to living in a society that holds them as 'outsiders'. The sense of isolation means that for those being placed in institutions like old-age homes it can be an alienating and depressing experience. As Mary, a second generation geriatric nurse at a London residential old age home, observed:

> The sense of isolation for elderly Caribbeans is often exacer-
> bated by the fact that there's a lot of elderly people here who
> have never lived with white people, but they get to eighties,
> seventies, they end up in a residential home, one of forty.
> And I think a lot of those people would actually like to go
> back, but there's no welfare system in Jamaica, they can only
> take their pension with them.

> I've been in situations where I've gone to a residential
> home, and it was near Christmas, and they were having
> entertainment, and there was this black man sitting there all
> on his own, you know, while everybody else was having
> these sing-along. He's not used to that kind of sing-along.
> He doesn't even know what they're saying, because he's
> never had to be in that position before, you know (BK
> 079/2/Tape 2/SideB)

Her experience highlights the potential difficulties that some Caribbeans may begin to face, and raises important policy issues relating to incorporation and inclusion in a system which appears to pay little regard to the social requirements of ethnic minorities.

The sense of isolation does not seem to be experienced by women to the same degree. In old age Caribbean women are more likely to become what I have called 'transnational flying grannies'. These are women who spend their days, travelling between children and grandchildren in the international Caribbean Diaspora (London, New York, Toronto, and the Caribbean). Their responsibilities include maintaining the flow of communication about the addition of new family members, or the social and economic circumstances of individual family members. Some of these grandmothers may also be called upon to provide temporary foster care or child minding services for individual members of the extended family. An awareness and a respect for these 'flying grannies' was provided by Margaret a sixty-eight-year-old Jamaican living in Birmingham as she reflected on the lifestyle of her best friend Patricia:

> The flying granny is more networked into the family. She
> tends to be more mobile than her male counterpart. Women
> have children spread out...Men are more drawn into them-
> selves. You do find that happening to men. Women when
> they came to this country became more accustomed to the

system. They were the ones who became involved. Women seemed to be more able to get out there and fight it out in the system. Women are always fighting it out in this society. Traditionally that's the role that women do best (JL 035/2/Tape 3/Side A).

Some of the major social, economic and psychological adaptation issues Caribbean elders in Britain will have to face include the fact that they are reaching retirement age at a period in time when their pensions are low. Because of the occupational profile of this generation, (determined often by the structural and individual discrimination) not all will have their state pension supplemented with an occupational pension. At the same time, many Caribbean elders find themselves dependent on a system of health care which does not cater to their particular health care needs, or who may find that their health in old age has been compromised by the physical demands or environmental hazards experienced in their working lives. Racism will undoubtedly continue to be an unresolved and festering issue that makes Caribbean elders feel alienated in a country which they have lived and contributed to for most of their lives. The divisiveness of racism will also likely continue to make Caribbean elders wish that they could just return to the constructed island 'paradise' they departed from some 30 or more years ago. Finally, the fact that many Caribbean elders may find themselves placed in old age homes in the future with limited family and kin contacts, while at the same time they are denied the dignity of being surrounded by individuals like themselves to reminisce about the 'good old days' may present itself as a psychologically depressing reality for many. In many respects the ageing cohort of Caribbeans were pioneers in arriving in Britain in the early 1950s and many will be pioneers once again in the new millennium because they will be the first large non-white ethnic cohort to reach old age in the United Kingdom.

British government policy makers need to work more closely with the Caribbean community and more specifically with the elders to plan and implement new enabling and targeted programmes that meet the particular health and geriatric needs of this group rather than being incorporated into existing generic provision. The Caribbean community has its own wants, needs, desires, customs and traditions and many feel that as taxpayers and contributors to the national insurance scheme, they are entitled to a return more sensitively attuned to their particular needs.

David's sentiment about the situation seems to capture the overall feelings of many elders about their future in Britain. The greatest fear for many seems to be living in 'Babylon' as a frail elderly person where no one seems to care. David tells us:

> If left England I would miss theatres, shopping, and things like that ... I do think that I could do without them. What I don't think that I could do is keep myself going in a community like this which does not care. Although you think that you can financially prepare for some of these issues they are not interested in you in this country (TF 045/1/Tape 1/ Side B).

Conclusion

Ageing in British society has not been an easy transition for Caribbean immigrants. Most Caribbeans who are now elderly originally hoped to be in Britain for no more than five years. Many did not foresee that thirty or forty years later they would still be in Britain. Most assumed that they would accumulate sufficient savings to return to the Caribbean. This was the dream that many had constructed for themselves based partly on the experience of older family members or friends who may have migrated previously to Panama or the United States to work and returned a few years later with enough savings to make a better life for themselves and their families. The reality for many Caribbean elders in Britain today however, is that they are stuck in 'Babylon' and made to feel like 'foreigners'.

Notes

1　Sally Gordon (1987) describes child-shifting as fostering, involving the reallocation of dependent or minor children to a household not including a natural parent. In her sample of 49 households in Antigua, she finds 41 cases of child-shifting spread over 21 households (42.9 percent). The reasons that children are moved from one household to another are varied and include the child wanting to live with X, or X asked for the child, as well as singular events such as the migration of a natural parent. Gordon notes that child-shifting is perceived as a domestic responsive strategy to economic circumstances whereby the costs and benefits of child rearing are relocated among households by shifting children from those less economically secure and less able to support them to those who are better off.

2　In this discussion, all original names of respondents have been anonymised.

Conclusion

14 | Trans-Atlantic Caribbean futures

Harry Goulbourne

Introduction

Each of the 13 contributions to this volume raises important questions about Caribbean families within a generally understood Atlantic context, particularly the British and Caribbean zones within the far larger world of the North Atlantic. A major strength of the volume is that it draws on a number of disciplines in order to give a comprehensive coverage of Caribbean families in Britain and the Commonwealth Caribbean. While some chapters have focused on family matters in Britain and others have placed emphasis on Caribbean sites, together the collection is offered as a contribution to developing a broad understanding of family life within what many are describing as the Caribbean Diaspora. Given this general aim, it is appropriate in these concluding remarks to point to aspects of what potential futures there may be for the transnational communities that Caribbean people have established across the Atlantic and within which we must understand their family and kinship dynamics.

Changing Caribbean identities and families

In several of the chapters in this volume it has been assumed that Caribbean communities, having been established in Europe and maintaining close links with the Caribbean and North America, will continue into the foreseeable future. Some of the data presented in the chapters suggest that we might expect the persistence of both patterns of continuity and change in the kinds of futures envisaged for a multicultural Britain. For example, some of the data presented here suggest that Caribbean living arrangements in Britain and the Caribbean are remarkably similar and therefore reveal patterns of continuity. The historical emergence and development of patterns of low rates of marriage, and the correspondingly high level of female-headed households with high female participation in the workforce are features with strong Caribbean antecedents and a powerful contemporary social reality for Caribbeans as well as other communities.

While, however, the fact of a strong Caribbean presence in Britain is presently not in doubt, it has been suggested that:

> ...the Afro-British population of Caribbean ancestry will have been nearly completely absorbed into the mainstream British population within the next forty to fifty years. Britain will have solved its 'racial problem' by simply breeding it away. In doing so, the nation will have remained true to its past (Patterson, 1999, p 27).

Orlando Patterson came to this conclusion after observing the decline in the Caribbean-born population and the tendency for Caribbean men and women to have partners from the majority White population. Although he does not take into account factors such as deaths and return migration, as do Peach (1991), Byron & Condon (1996) and Goulbourne (1999b), Patterson does raise an important point. The high rate of exogenous partnerships (marriages, living together) and the growth in the numbers of people of mixed Caribbean and White British heritage, have been a matter of some concern to spokespersons in the African Caribbean communities in Britain in recent years. Whilst Patterson sees this as a sociological process with deep historic roots in British culture going back to the Celts – that is, the British capacity to absorb newcomers – there are those in the Caribbean communities in Britain who express concern about the loss of ethnic (or cultural) and of racial (or colour) identities. Were this imagined scenario to become reality by the middle of this new century, then the confidence with which contributors to this volume have written about Caribbean families in Britain will indeed be misplaced and misleading. It is an intriguing speculation, therefore, whether there is a future for Caribbean communities, identities and families in Britain so soon after being undisputedly established on European shores following several false starts since the fates of Europe and West Africa first became closely intertwined in the sixteenth century.

This question may also be asked within the context of a different set of issues: are people of Caribbean backgrounds in Britain likely to lose their identities as a result of the majority communities becoming more like Caribbean people in terms of family patterns and living arrangements? It is usual to pose the problem of acculturation to which this question relates, in terms of the new minority adopting the values of the indigenous majority population. But, at least in this respect, it is important to consider whether we do not have a situation in which the patterns of Caribbean families and living arrangements are not becoming the generalised patterns for the majority community. This calls for an explanation.

It was asserted in Chapter 1 of this volume that Caribbean families and living arrangements are best understood within the context of the development of modernity over traditionalism. But this must not be taken to mean that Caribbean families are merely responding or adjusting to contemporary social change, in the way that journalists and some sociologists would speak about groups in Britain becoming Westernised, that is, the young imbibing the mores, values and general practices of Western secular society and abandoning the values of traditional society.

For example, in early September 1999 the news of the day was dominated by reports about the increase in crime by young Muslim men in British cities, and while there was mention of these young men's age profile, their strong response to racist attacks, and rebellion against parental control, the principal reason given for the perceived dramatic change in this Asian community was the influence of 'Western values' (see, for example, *The Times*, 3 September 1999; 1, 6; also leader; 23). The four or so pieces in *The Times* newspaper explaining the situation were replete with statements such as '...Western influence has been a catalyst for change' (p 6); the journalist and Asian spokesperson, Yasmin Alibhai-Brown, was reported to say that unemployment and lack of education were making some young Asian men feel excluded from society, but there was '. . . also a lot of concern in Asian families that they are losing some of these young men to more Western values' (p 6); and the writer of one of one piece entitled 'Western values help to send young astray', Richard Ford, reported that:

> Within British Asian communities it has been clear for some time that the social, cultural and sexual mores that controlled the lives of an older generation were being undermined by Western values. The traditional extended family, integral to the life of first generation Asians, is slowly giving way to the immediate family with young men enjoying a social life that centres on friends rather than family (ibid.; 6).

Harry Fletcher, assistant general secretary of the National Association of Probation Officers declared that his colleagues '... have seen the gradual breakdown of strong Asian families' (p 6), and *The Times* leader article on the subject saw the situation in much the same terms, stressing that '. . . these young people, growing up in conservative homes but in a surrounding culture that prizes individualism, are shaking off the strong sense of family discipline and respect for authority which once bound their communities' (p 23).

The reason for referring at length to this account of a perfectly natural change in the Asian communities in Britain is to illustrate my general point that whilst it may be true that there are changes in cultural values, and structural forms may be exerting strong influences on some of Britain's new communities, in the case of Caribbeans in Britain (as in the Caribbean) the values pointed to have long been integral parts of their cultural baggage. The striving of young Asian men to exercise a degree of autonomy is not new to Caribbean men or women, nor did they acquire this value in Britain. Caribbean societies have been modern societies from their very inception in the seventeenth century, in the sense that these societies started on a *tabula rasa*. This is to say that on the whole the indigenous populations died (or at best pushed to the margins) and with them their cultures and civilisations also died; West Europeans and West Africans arrived with different social values and institutions. The encounters marked the most glaring inequality in modern times: Europeans were conquerors, settlers and masters, who initially determined the patterns of entry and settlement; Africans were slaves, captives or defeated groups from a turbulent West Africa who had to make do as best they could; the indigenous peoples simply disappeared and played no significant part in subsequent developments. However, the society that emerged was not merely the re-making of Europe; nor was it a reconstitution of Africa. Rather, the societal order fashioned by the social encounters of Africa and Europe (and later groups from Asia) resulted in the creation of a new social and cultural order. Significantly, this was an inclusive cultural order, as compared to the social and cultural plural societies found in several other parts of the former imperial world in Africa and Asia where indigenous cultures significantly continued to exhibit patterns of continuity, and where slavery was not instituted on a generalised scale.

This historical encounter has led to some important features that are perhaps uniquely Caribbean. The fundamental feature of the value system of these societies is an extremely high level of individualism based on the notion that each individual must be seen and accepted on the basis of being an autonomous conscious being. Consequently, whilst a person's colour/race is important, social action is judged according to a person's individual virtues rather than those purported to be exhibited by a whole group. It is not surprising, therefore, that Caribbean societies more than most outside advanced industrial societies are distinguished by high levels of social and political tolerance of racial/colour and political difference.

These patterns are also illustrated by another feature: Caribbean Creole societies have been able to absorb and equitably incorporate otherness or new cultures. For example, while communities and families in the South Asian Diaspora have been distinguished by their determination to maintain traditional customs, religion, kinship, language, etc., in the Caribbean they have not been able to do so to the same extent that they have in other parts of the world. This is because the Caribbean social and cultural order is sufficiently open to embrace rather than threaten or exclude. The experience here suggests that tolerance makes it less necessary for individuals and groups to want to defend and promote their cultural differences with the majority population or the hegemonic culture. Of course, this could be turned upon its head to show that the culturally tolerant society has the effect of disarming new cultural communities and thereby either absorbing or ejecting them into the outer sphere occupied by pariah or marginalised groups.

This returns us to the question of whether Caribbean identity in Britain is likely to disappear by the middle of the new century. In the first place, it needs to be acknowledged that there is at least one sense in which this assertion is very likely to become true. After all, in the past when Africa and Europe came into close contact (the sixteenth to eighteenth centuries and again in the nineteenth century and the early part of the present century) Africans were indeed absorbed by the majority population or expelled, as in the Elizabethan era and during the 1920s (see, Shyllon, 1974; Fryer, 1989; Cohen & May, 1975; Phillips, 1974). Racially mixed families, births and migration could very well effect much the same result, as Patterson and others envisage.

More significantly, however, the people of Caribbean heritage are themselves likely to continue what began with migration to Britain, namely, the search for an identity. In the 1950s and 1960s Caribbean communities perceived themselves, and were perceived by others, to be West Indians, and within this broad category they were (to themselves) Antiguans, Barbadians, Jamaicans, St Lucians, Trinidadians, and so forth. In the 1970s, radicals emphasised the fact of being West Indians as a collective category, or Afro-Caribbeans. Still later in the 1980s and in the last decade of the century, Caribbeans came to see themselves in terms of being African Caribbeans, following Jessie Jackson's call for Black America to describe itself as African without an hyphen to their present identity as Americans in line with other groups in the country.

It is not unlikely that in the next half century people of Caribbean backgrounds in Britain will undergo a number of other changes in self-description as well as description by the wider White and Asian communities. Consider, for example, how for a considerable time the identity forged by people of mixed European and African ancestry in the Caribbean ('coloureds') came to be universally used to describe people other than White people. Moreover, contemporary America has revived this nomenclature in the last decade of this century and they speak, unabashedly, about 'people of colour', as if there are some people who lack colour. The more things change, the more they remain the same; it appears that we have come full circle since the 1960s: in America people moved from being coloureds to being blacks to being Afro-Americans and currently to being African Americans and also members of a wider category called 'people of colour'. A similar process has occurred in Britain over the same period, and presently the 'politically correct' nomenclature is African Caribbean, which seeks to distinguish people of African and Caribbean heritage from others, including Africans and Caribbeans with Asian (South Asian, Chinese) European and Middle-Eastern backgrounds. In other words, it may be a waste of time to speculate about how the Caribbean presence in Britain and the Atlantic world will be described either by groups with legitimate links to Africa and the Caribbean and by the wider society in the next four or five decades. The ability to integrate with others – to look outwards from the group – is likely to continue to make the question of identity an abiding question amongst people of Caribbean backgrounds, Africans as well as others, but perhaps particularly so with respect to those of African backgrounds.

My main concern, however, is to suggest that there are several reasons to believe that in the next four or five decades people of Caribbean backgrounds are more likely than not to maintain some distinctive features of their identity or presence in Britain. This identity will not necessarily be the one they now proclaim; just as in the past their sense of who they were changed with events and other circumstances, so in the future that sense of who Caribbean people outside the region are is likely to change. But such changes may not necessarily significantly shift or disturb a perception of being Caribbean. The colour and other physical characteristics of members may change or become varied as a result of mixed partnerships and births, but the notion of being of Caribbean heritage may continue well into the future, depending on broader developments in Europe as well as North America. The situation may be compared to the experiences that Jewish people have undergone over two thousand years, depending on what parts of the world to which they migrated, following the great dispersal of AD 70, when the future Roman princeps, Titus, destroyed Jerusalem.

So, how can my supposition of a continuing Caribbean awareness be maintained? In the first place, the observation that African Caribbean families in Britain are far more racially and ethnically mixed than any other community is not only simplistic but also ignores the social construction of Caribbean societies themselves. In other words, these societies as I have suggested above, are comprised of families which embrace mixture and difference; life is not seen to be dependent on the maintenance of centuries-old traditions and unchanging customs. Families welcome or embrace the potential richness of what others (who are themselves in the process of change) may bring. There is curiosity about other persons' differences, rather than perceiving others as threats to existing values. There is a predisposition to take cogniscience of the fact that one's own cultural assumptions and practices are subject to change. In short, Caribbean families and communities are societies caught up in and cognisant of difference, they are certain of their own peaceful identities and therefore can understand or appreciate the differences of others.

Second, the Caribbean sense of identity in Europe, particularly in Britain, may continue in the midst of change, because it is very likely that other new communities (Southern and Eastern Europeans, various Asian communities) will continue to maintain their senses of difference from their most immediate historical neighbours as well as the majority indigenous populations. For example, the concern in some quarters to construct and celebrate a model of Asian families and communities as self-reliant and unified and to contrast this with its supposed anti-thesis – Caribbean families and communities – might very well have the effect of stimulating a strengthening of the nuclear family form in Caribbean communities in Britain. To a degree, this response occurred in the 1960s when Caribbean immigrants joined in the British celebration of the nuclear family as the universal and ideal model, and formal marriage rates increased in the immigrant community.

The developing context of the Atlantic world

Perhaps, however, the most powerful reason for asserting that Caribbeans in Britain are likely to maintain a visible and recognisable identity over the next few decades, is that the Atlantic world in which they live is dynamic, not anachronistic. Most of the history of the Atlantic world has been dominated by the spread of Europeans in a western expansion. While the role of people of African backgrounds is not entirely ignored, in the main, their role and presence have been muted, and one of the challenges of the first decades of the new millennium may be to reassess the contributions of Africa to the Atlantic world. After all, as Patterson noted, the spread of Africans outside Africa has been generally restricted to the Atlantic world; this is unlike Europeans and East and South Asians, who during the last centuries have spread out across several continents and island of the seas. When this reassessment is made there will be need to consider the place and role of the hitherto relatively silent voices of Africans in Central and South America, particularly Brazil, but there must also be a critical appraisal of the movement of Caribbeans within the wider Atlantic world.

In this reassessment certain distinctive features of the Caribbean presence in the Atlantic world must be addressed. First, as stressed in this volume and as others have variously noted (see, for example, Patterson 1999; Thomas-Hope, 1980) Caribbean people are great travellers, particularly within the Atlantic world bounded by North and Central America, the Caribbean itself and, during the last half century, West Europe, where their forebears made their transit (at ports such as Bordeaux, Antwerp, Bristol and Liverpool) en route from Africa to the New World.

Second, within this broad framework, particular attention is deserved by those Africans who have made the Caribbean islands of slavery their homes and have, slowly from the nineteenth century, made that part of the sub-region their own in demographic, cultural and political terms (though not economically so), and spreading outward to Central and North America and Europe. In this respect, attention must be given to the influence of the different groups of people from the Britain Isles (English, Scots, Welsh, Irish) – themselves great exemplars of peoples engaged in movement from one place to another whilst laying down (like landmarks) their cultural-marks and value-marks which had the capacity, over time, to absorb and integrate, although initially aggressively exclusivist.

There is a third dimension here. This is the deep concern of Caribbeans to heal the breaches forced by slavery, indenture and colonialism between peoples and cultures spread out across the seas of the Atlantic and beyond. With respect to Caribbeans of South Asian backgrounds, there has been a growing awareness of their historic roots, much the same as there has been such an awareness of Africa among African Caribbeans since the 1960s. Settlement in the Britain by these groups provides an important opportunity for them to renew closer links with the Indian sub-continent directly as well as *via* the East African and Asian communities who are directly from those regions.

Conclusion

These assertions raise at least two important questions for the research agenda. The first of these is the question of the forms that the continuing relations between Britain's communities of Caribbean heritage will take. Whilst, for example, Asian families continue to find partners for their offspring in their historic homelands, the ability of Caribbeans to find partners from the majority population would suggest that as far as families are concerned marriage or partnership may not be a site for maintaining close links with the Caribbean. There is a need, however, to research this question, rather than make an assertion a certainty. The second research question is that regarding the nature of the links there are between Indo-Caribbeans and African-Caribbeans with their respective earlier homelands in Asia and Africa. Third, there is a significant volume of Caribbeans returning to the region, strengthening the close dynamic links with Britain and by extension Europe. This process raises both research and policy questions for the relevant communities on both sides of the Atlantic. Fourth, there are continuing patterns of kinship which stretches across the Atlantic, including North America which requires further research in order that we can better appreciate the links that are being constructed in the Caribbean Atlantic Diaspora. Finally, within Britain – our point of departure within Europe – there are problems arising from the very processes of migration and transnationality, which require greater empirical attention. Physical disability, mental illness, and family well-being, are examples of some of the issues which have not been directly addressed in this volume, but will require careful consideration in the immediate future. There is, however, enough here to show that the presence of Caribbeans across the Atlantic is a necessary area of investigation by the academic and policy communities on all sides of the waters.

Bibliography

Abdulah, Nonma (1991) 'Ethnicity, Mating Patterns and Fertility', *Social and Occupational Stratification in Contemporary Trinidad and Tobago*, St Augustine, Institute of Social and Economic Research, Trinidad and Tobago.

Abenaty, F. (1998) 'The dynamics of return migration to St Lucia', paper presented to the 22nd Annual Conference of the Society for Caribbean Studies, University of Warwick, July.

Agrosino, M. (1976) 'Sexual Politics in the East Indian Family in Trinidad', *Caribbean Studies*, Vol. 16, No. 1, p 44–66.

Alexander, C. (1996) *The art of being black*, Oxford: Clarendon Press.

Alexander, J. (1976) 'A study of the cultural domain of "relatives" (Jamaica)' *American Ethnologist*, 3(1), 17–38.

Almond, G & Verba, S (eds), (1963) *The civic culture: political attitudes and democracy in five nations*, New Jersey: Princeton University Press.

Almond, G & Powell, GB. (1966) *Comparative politics: a developmental approach*, Boston & Toronto: Little Brown & Co Ltd.

Anwar, M. (1994) *Race and elections: the participation of ethnic minorities in politics*, Monographs in Ethnic Relations, No 9, Coventry: ESRC Centre for Research in Ethnic Relations, University of Warwick

Anwar, M. (1979) *The Myth of Return: Pakistanis in Britain*, London: Heinemann.

Appignanesi, L & Maitland, S (eds.) (1989) *The Rushdie file*, London: Fourth Estate Ltd.

Arnold, E. (1982) 'Finding Black Families for Black Children in Britain', in Cheetham, J. (ed.), *Social Work and Ethnicity*, London: Allen and Unwin.

Aschenbrenner, J. (1975) *Lifelines: Black Families in Chicago*, New York: Holt, Rinehart and Winston.

Augustus, P. (1994) *Babyfather*, London: X Press Publishing.

Austin-Broos, D. (1998) 'Women and Jamaican Pentecostalism' in Barrow, C (ed.) *Caribbean Portraits: Essays on Gender Ideologies and Identities*, Kingston: Ian Randle Publishers.

Back, L. (1996) *New ethnicities and urban culture: Racism and multi-culture in young lives*, London: UCL Press.

Backett, K. (1988) *Mothers and Fathers: A study of the development and negotiation of parental behaviour*, London: Macmillan.

Ballard, R. (ed.) (1994) *Desh Pardesh: the South Asian presence in Britain*, London: Hurst & Company.

Barber, HB and Jeffrey (1986) *Guyana: Politics, Economics and Society*, London: Francis Pinter

Barn, R. (1993) *Black Children in the Public Care System*, London: Batsford.

Barn, R. (1997) 'Race and Racism: Can Minority Ethnic Groups Benefit from Social Work', in J Edwards and JP Revauger, (eds.) *Discourse on Inequality in France and Britain*, Aldershot: Ashgate.

Barn, R. (1999) 'White Mothers, Mixed-Parentage Children and Child Welfare', *British Journal of Social Work*, 29(2).

Barn, R, Sinclair, R and Ferdinand, D. (1997) *Acting on Principle: An Examination of Race and Ethnicity in Social Services Provision for Children and Families*, London: British Agencies for Adoption and Fostering.

Barrow, C. (1986) 'Finding the Support: Strategies for Survival' in *Social and Economic Studies*, 35(2).

Barrow, C. (1988) 'Anthropology, The Family and Women in the Caribbean', in Mohammed, P & Shepherd C (eds.) *Gender in Caribbean Development*, Mona, Jamaica: Women and Development Project, University of the West Indies.

Barrow, C. (1992) *Family Land and Development in St Lucia*, Institute of Social and Economic Research, University of the West Indies, Cave Hill, Barbados.

Barrow, C. (1996) *Family in the Caribbean: Themes and Perspectives*, Kingston: Ian Randle Publishers/Oxford: James Currey Publishers.

Barrow, C. (1998) 'Caribbean Masculinity and Family: revisiting 'Marginality' and 'Reputation' in Barrow, C (ed.) *Caribbean Portraits. Essays on Gender Ideologies and Identities*, Kingston: Ian Randle Publishers.

Barrow, J. (1982) 'West Indian families: an insider's perspective', in RN Rapoport, MP Fogerty & R Rapoport *Families in Britain*, London: Routledge.

Bartholomew, R, Hibbett, A and Sidaway, J. (1992) 'Lone Parents and the Labour Market: Evidence from the LFS', *Employment Gazette*, November, pp 559–77.

Basch, L, Glick Schiller, N and Szanton Blanc C. (1994) *Nations Unbound. Transnational Projects, Postcolonial Predicaments and Deterritorialized Nation States*, Pennsylvania: Gordon and Breach.

Bebbington, AC and Miles, JB. (1989) 'The Background of Children who enter Local Authority Care', *British Journal of Social Work*, 19(5), pp 349–368.

Bell-Scott, P. (1988) [eds.] *Double-stitch: Black women writing about mothers and daughters*, Boston: Beacon Press.

Benjamin, W. (1997) *One Way Street*, London: Verso.

Bennett, L. (1983) *Selected Poems*, Kingston: Sangster's Book Stores.

Berrington, A. (1996) 'Marriage patterns and inter-ethnic unions' in Coleman D & Salt J (eds.) *Ethnicity in the 1991 Census: Demographic Characteristics of the Ethnic Minority Population*, Vol 1, London: OPCS.

Berrington, A. (1994) Marriage and Family Formation among the White and Ethnic Minority Populations in Britain, *Ethnic and Racial Studies*, 17(3), pp 517–46.

Bertaux, D and Thompson, P. (1993) *Between Generations. Family Models, Myths and Memories International Yearbook of Oral History and Life Stories Vol. II*, Oxford: Oxford University Press.

Bhachu, P. (1986) *Twice immigrants*, London: Tavistock Publications Limited

Bhavnani, R. (1994) *Black women in the labour market: A research review*, London: Equal Opportunities Commission

Birch, AH. (1993) *The concepts and theories of modern democracy*, London: Routledge.

Black, ML. (1995) 'My Mother Never Fathered Me: Rethinking Kinship and the Governing of Families', *Social and Economic Studies*, 44(3).

Blakemore, K and Boneham, M. (1994) *Age, Race and Ethnicity: A Comparative Approach*, Buckingham: Open University Press.

Blount, M and Cunningham, G. (1996) *Representing Black Men*, London: Routledge.

Bornat, J. (1994) *Reminiscence Reviewed: Evaluations, Achievements, Perspectives*, Buckingham: Open University Press.

Boss, P and Homeshaw, J. (1974) 'Britain's Black Citizens: A Comparative Study of Social Work with Coloured Families and their White Indigenous Neighbours', *Social Work Today*, 6(12).

Bott, E. (1957) *Family and Social Network: Roles, Norms, and External Relationships in Ordinary Urban Families*, London: Tavistock Publications Limited.

Bourdieu, P. (1990) *The logic of practice*, Translated by Richard Nice. Stanford: Stanford University Press.

Bowman, P and Forman, T. (1997) 'Instrumental and expressive family roles among African-American fathers', in Taylor, R Jackson, S and Chatters, L [eds.], *Family life in black America*, California: Sage.

Boyce Davies, C. (1994) *Black Women, Writing and Identity. Migrations of the Subject*, London and New York: Routledge.

Brackette F Williams and Drexel G *Woodson*, Madison: The University of Wisconsin Press.

Bradshaw, J and Millar, J. (1991) Lone Parent Families in the UK, Department of Social Security Report 6. London: HMSO.

Braithwaite, F. (1986) *The Elderly in Barbados*, Bridgetown: Caribbean and Research Publications Inc.

Brana-Shute, R and Brana-Shute, G. (1982) 'The Magnitude and Impact of Remittances in the Eastern Caribbean' in Stinner, WF, de Albuquerque, K & Bryce-Laporte, RS (eds.) *Return Migration and Remittances: Developing a Caribbean Perspective*, Research Institute on Immigration and Ethnic Studies, Occasional Papers No 3 Smithsonian Institution.

Brockman, CT. (1987) 'The Western Family and individualisation: convergence with Caribbean patterns', *Journal of Comparative Family Studies*, 18(3).

Brown, G. (1984) *Black and White Britain*, London: Policy Studies Institute/ Heinemann.

Brown, JM & Foot, R (eds.) (1994) *Migration: the Asian experience*, London: Macmillan.

Bryan, P. (1990) *Philanthropy and Social Welfare in Jamaica: An Historical Survey*, Mona: Institute of Social and Economic Research, University of the West Indies.

Bulmer, M. (1996) 'The ethnic group question in the 1991 Census of Population', in, Coleman & Salt (eds.) *Ethnicity in the 1991 Census: demographic characteristics of the ethnic minority populations*, Vol 1. London, OPCS

Burke, A. (1986) 'Racism, Prejudice and Mental Illness', in J Cox (ed.) Transcultural Psychiatry, London: Croom Helm.

Byron, M. (1994) *Post-War Caribbean Migration to Britain: the Unfinished Cycle*, Aldershot: Avebury

Byron, M. (1998) 'Migration, work and gender: the case of post-war labour migration from the Caribbean to Britain' in Chamberlain, M *Caribbean Migration. Globalised Identities*, London and New York: Routledge

Byron, M and Condon, S (1996) 'A comparative study of Caribbean return migration from Britain and France: Towards a context-dependent explanation' *Transactions, Institute of British Geographers* 21(1)

Calley, M. (1965) *God's people*, Oxford: Oxford University Press.

Caribbean Insight, passim

Carillo Roxanne, 'Battered Dreams'. *Violence Against Women as Obstacles to Development*, UNIFEM n.d.

Castells, M. (1996) *The rise of the network society*, Vol 1, Oxford: Blackwell.

Cazenave, N. (1981) *Black men in America: The 'Quest for Manhood'*, *California:* Sage.

Chamberlain, G. (1997) 'St Lucia: The Economic and Business Report' in *The Americas Review*, 16th Ed., Essex: Walden Publishing Ltd.

Chamberlain, M. (1995) 'Family and Identity: Barbadian Migrants to Britain' in Benmayor, R and Skotnes A (eds.) *Migration and Identity International Yearbook of Oral history and Life Stories*, Vol III, Oxford: Oxford University Press.

Chamberlain, M. (1997) *Narratives of exile and return*, London: Macmillan.

Chamberlain, M. (1998) 'Brothers and sisters, uncles and aunts: a lateral perspective on Caribbean families in Britain' in Silva, E and Smart, C (eds.) *The New Family*, London: Sage

Chamberlain, M. (1998) (ed.) *Caribbean Migration. Globalised Identities*, London/New York: Routledge

Chamberlain, M. (2000) 'The Global Self. Narratives of Caribbean Migrant Women' in Coslett, T and Summerfield, P *Feminism and Autobiography*, London: Routledge.

Chamberlain, M and Thompson, P. (1998) 'Narrative and Genre' in Chamberlain, M and Thompson, P *Narrative and Genre. Routledge Studies in Memory and Narrative*, London/New York: Routledge

Chamberlain, M and Goulbourne, H (forthcoming) *Caribbean Families in Perspective*.

Chambers, Claudia & B Chevannes (1991) *Sexual Decision-making among women and men in Jamaica: Report on six focus group discussions*, ISER., University of the West Indies, Mona.

Chamoiseau, P. (1997) *Texaco*, New York: Pantheon.

Chapman, R. (1988) Introduction, in Chapman, R and Rutherford J (eds.) *Male. Order: Unwrapping Masculinity*, London: Lawrence and Wishart.

Charbit, Y. (1980) 'Union patterns and family structure in Guadeloupe and Martinique' *International Journal of Sociology and the Family*, 10(1) 41–66.

Cheetham, J. (1988) 'Ethnic associations in Britain' in Jenkins (ed.) *Ethnic Associations and the Welfare State*, New York: Columbia University Press, pp 107–154.

Clarke, E. (1957) *My Mother Who Fathered Me: A Study of the Family in Three Selected Communities in Jamaica*, London: Allen & Unwin.

Cohen, R. and May, R. (1975) 'The Interaction between Race and Colonialisation: a Case Study of the Liverpool Race Riots of 1919' *Race and Class* Vol 16: No 2

Cohen, R. (1987) *The New Helots. Migrants in the International Division of Labour*, Aldershot: Avebury Press.

Cohen, R. (1994) *Frontiers of identity: the British and others*, London: Longman.

Cohen, R. (1997) *Global Diasporas: Introduction*, London: UCL Press.

Cohen, YA. (1956) 'Structure and function: family organisation and socialisation in a Jamaican community', *American Anthropologist*, pp 664–686.

Coleman, D & Salt, J (eds). (1996) *Ethnicity in the 1991 census: demographic characteristics of the ethnic minority populations*, Vol 1, London: OPCS.

Comitas, L and Lowenthal, D (eds) (1973) *Work and family life: West Indian perspectives*, New York: Anchor Press/Doubleday 1973.

Commission for Racial Equality (1990a) *Britain: a plural society, report of a seminar, Discussion papers No. 3*, London: Commission for Racial Equality.

Commission for Racial Equality (1990b) *Law, blasphemy and the multi-faith society, report of a seminar, Discussion papers No 1*, London: Commission for Racial Equality.

Commission for Racial Equality (1992) *The Social Security Persons Abroad Regulations: An Analysis of the Conditions Governing Continued Entitlement to Disability Benefits of Persons Going Abroad and Their Implications for Ethnic Minorities*, London: Commission for Racial Equality.

Commission for Racial Equality (1997) *Employment and Unemployment Factsheets*, London: Commission for Racial Equality.

Conway, D. (1988) 'Conceptualising contemporary patterns of Caribbean international mobility', *Caribbean Geography*, 2(3).

Craig-James, S. (1992) 'Intertwining roots' in *Journal of Caribbean History*, 26(2).

Cross M, Entzinger H. (1988) *Lost Illusions: Caribbean Minorities in Britain and the Netherlands*, London: Routledge.

Cross, M, Johnson MRD. (1988) 'Mobility Denied: Caribbean minorities in the UK labour market' in Cross M, Entzinger H (eds.). *Lost Illusions.*

Dabydeen, D. (1987) *Hogarths Blacks: Images of Blacks in Eighteenth-Century English Art*, Manchester: Manchester University Press.

Dahya, B. (1973) 'Pakistanis in Britain: Transients or Settlers?' *Race*, 14(3) p 241–277.

Dahya, B. (1974) 'The Nature of Pakistani Ethnicity in Industrial Cities in Britain', in Cohen, (ed.), *Urban Ethnicity*, London: Tavistock.

Daly-Hill, O & Zaba, B. (1981) *Preliminary Analysis of 1980 Census Data*, Georgetown: Caribbean Community (Caricom).

Daniel, WW. (1968) *Racial Discrimination in England*, London: Penguin.

Dann, G. (1987) *The Barbadian Male: Sexual Attitudes and Practice*, London: Macmillian.

Daro, D and McCurdy K. (1991) *Current trends in child abuse reporting and fatalities: The results of the 1990 annual fifty state survey*, Working Paper No. 808, Chicago: National Center on Child Abuse Prevention Research, National Committee for Prevention of Child Abuse.

Davenport, W. (1961) 'The family system of Jamaica' in *Social and Economic Studies*, pp 383–396.

Davidson, L. (1962) 'The East Indian Family Overseas' in *Social & Economic Studies*, 13(3).

Davis, A. (1981) *Women, race and class*, London: Women's Press Ltd.

Davis, A, Burleigh, B Gardner and Gardner, M. (1941) *Deep South: a Social Anthropological Study of Caste and Class*, Chicago: University of Chicago Press.

Davison, RB. (1962) *West Indian Migrants*, London. Oxford University Press.

De la Motta, C. (1984) *Blacks in the Criminal Justice System*, Unpublished MSc thesis, University of Aston.

Dench, G. (1986) *Minorities in the open society: prisoners of ambivalence*, London: Routledge & Kegan Paul.

Dench, G. (1992) *From extended family to state dependency*, London Middlesex University CCS.

Dench, G. (1996) *The place of men in changing family cultures*, London: Institute of Community Studies.

Department of Health (1991) *The Children Act 1989 Guidance and Regulations*, London: HMSO.

Department of the Environment (1993) *Housing in England: Housing Trailers to the 1988 and 1991 Labour Force Surveys*, London: HMSO.

DeVeer, H. (1979) *Sex Roles and Social Stratification in a Rapidly Growing Urban Area – May Pen, Jamaica*, Chicago: University of Chicago Ph.D. Dissertation.

Donzelot, J. (1979) *The Policing of Families*, New York: Pantheon Books.

Draaijer, N. (1988) *Intrafamiliar sexual abuse of girls*, Ministry of Social Affairs and Labour, The Hague: Vrije Universiteit van Amsterdam.

Drew, D. (1992) *Against All Odds: The Education and Labour Market Experiences of Black Young People*, England and Wales: Department of Employment.

Driver, G. (1982) 'West Indian Families: An Anthropological Perspective', in Rapoport, RN, Fogarty, MP and Raporport, R (eds.) *Families in Britain*, London: Routledge & Kegan Paul.

Du Bois, WEB. (1961) [1903]. *The Souls of Black Folk*, New York: Fawcett Publications.

Dubreuil, G. (1965) 'La Famille Martiniquaise: analyse et dynamique', *Anthropologica*, 7(1).

Duncan, S and Edwards, R. (1998) *Lone-mothers and paid work: Content, discourse and action*, London: Macmillan.

Duncan, S and Edwards, R. (1997) (eds.) *Single Mothers in an International Context: Mothers or Workers*, London: UCLA Press.

Duncan, S and Edwards, R. (1997) '*Lone Mothers and paid Work: Rational or Economic Man or Gendered Moral Rationalities'*, Feminist Economics, no: 3:(2).

Dutt, R and Phillips, M. (1996) 'Race, Culture and the Prevention of Child Abuse, Childhood Matters', Vol 2, *National Commission of Inquiry into the Prevention of Child Abuse*, London: The Stationery Office.

Ebanks, GE, George, PM & Nobbe, CE. (1974) 'Patterns of sex-union formation in Barbados' in *Canadian Review of Sociology and Anthropology*.

Ebanks, GE, George PM and Nobbe, CE. (1974) 'Fertility and Number of Partnerships in Barbados', Population Studies, Vol. 28, No. 3, p 449–461.

Edwards, J. (ed.) (1992) *Let's praise him again*, London: Kingsway Publications Ltd.

Eggleston, J Dunn, DK Anjali, M and Wright, CY (eds.) (1986) *Education for some*, Staffs: Trentham Books.

Eikaas, FH. (1979) 'You Can't Go Home Again? Culture Shock and Patterns of Adaptation of Norwegian Returnees' in *Papers in Antropology*, 20(1), pp 105–115.

Eldermire, D. (1986a) 'Sexual abuse of children: Case studies of incest in an urban Jamaica Population' *West Indian Medical Journal*, 35:175–179.

Eldermire, D. (1986b) 'Sexual abuse of children in Kingston and St Andrew, Jamaica', *West Indian Medical Journal*, 35:38–43.

Eldermire, D. (1994) 'The Elderly and the Family: The Jamaican Experience' *Bulletin of Eastern Caribbean Affairs*, 10(3).

Family Welfare Association (1960) *The West Indian Comes to England*, London: FWA.

Fenton, S. (1985) *Race Health and Welfare: Afro-Caribbean and South Asian People in Central Bristol*, Bristol: University of Bristol Press.

Fernando, S. (1988) *Race and Culture in Psychiatry*, London: Croom Helm.

Fernando, S. (1991) *Mental Health, Race and Culture*, London: Macmillan.

Festinger, L. (1957) *A Theory of Cognitive Dissonance*, New York: Harper.

Finkelhor, D and Dzuiba-Leatherman, J. (1994) 'Victimization of children' in *American Psychologist*, 49(3):1173–183.

Finkelhor, DG, Hotaling, I, Lewis J, Smith, C. (1990) 'Sexual abuse in a national survey of adult men and women: Prevalence, characteristics, and risk factors', *Child Abuse and Neglect*, 14:19–28.

Firth, R. (1956) *Two Studies of Kinship in London*, London: Athlone Press.

Firth, R. Hubert, J & Forge, A. (1970) *Families and their Relatives*, London: Routledge and Kegan Paul.

Fitzgerald, M. (1984) *Political parties and black people*, London: Runnymede Trust.

Fitzherbert, K. (1967) West Indian Children in London, London: Bell and Sons.

Foner, E. (1988) *Reconstruction: America's Unfinished Revolution 1863–1877*, New York: Harper and Row.

Foner, N. (1979) 'West Indians in New York City and London: A Comparative Analysis' in *International Migration Review*, 13(2)

Foner, N. (1979) *Jamaica Farewell*, London: Routledge & Kega Paul.

Foner, N. (1998) 'Towards a comparative perspective on Caribbean migration' in Chamberlain, M (ed.) *Caribbean Migration: Globalized Identities*.

Foot, P. (1969) *The rise of Enoch Powell*, Harmondsworth: Penguin.

Foren, R and Batta, I. (1970) 'Colour as a Variable in the use made of a Local Authority Child Care Department', *Social Work*, 27(3), 10–15.

Forte, Alyson, G. (1996) *National Census Report: Barbados 1990*, Caribbean Community Secretariat.

Foucault, M. (1978) *The History of Sexuality*: Vol. I, An Introduction, New York: Pantheon Books.

Frazier, EF. (1948) *The Negro Family in the United States*, Chicago: University of Chicago Press.

Fryer, P (1984) *Staying Power: The History of Black People in Britain*, London, Pluto Press.

Furstenburg, F. (1988) 'Good dads – bad dads: Two faces of fatherhood', in Cherlin, A (ed.) *The changing American family and policy*, Washington D. C: Urban Institute Press.

Gambe, D Gomes, J Kapur, V Rangal, M and Stubbs, P. (1992) *Improving Practice with Children and Families*, Leeds CCETSW.

Gardner, RE, Podolefsky, AM. (1977) 'Some further considerations on West Indian conjugal patterns' in *Ethnology*, 16(3).

Gay, P & Young, K. (1988) *Community Relations Councils: roles and objectives*, London: Policy Studies Institute.

Gerloff, R. (1992) *A plea for British black theologies*, London: Verso.

Gillborn, D. (1995) *Racism and anti-racism in real schools*, Buckingham: Open University Press.

Gilroy, P. (1993) *The Black Atlantic. Modernity and Double Consciousness*, London: Verso

Glass, R. (1961) *London's Newcomers*, Cambridge, Mass: Harvard University Press.

Glendinning, C and Millar, J. (1987) *Women's poverty in Britain*, Brighton: Wheatsheaf.

Gmelch, G. (1983) 'Who Returns and Why: Return Migration Behaviour in Two North Atlantic Societies' *Human Organisation*, 42(1) Spring, 46–54.

Gmelch, G. (1992) *Double Passage: The Lives of Caribbean Migrants Abroad and Back Home*, Ann Arbor: University of Michigan Press.

Goldthorpe, J. (1987) *Social Mobility and Class Structure in Modern Britain*, Oxford: Clarendon Press.

Gomez, C Kelsie, DK and Gibson, N. (1996) *National Census Report: The Bahamas 1990*, Caribbean Community Secretariat.

Goode, WJ. (1960) 'Illegitimacy in the Caribbean Social Structure', *American Sociological Review*, 25(1).

Gopaul-McNicol, S. (1993) *Working with West Indian Families*, New York: Guildford Press.

Gordon, S. (1987) 'I Go To Tanties: The Economic Significance of Child-shifting in Antigua', West Indies', *Journal of Comparative Family Studies*, 18, (3).

Gorell Barnes, G, Thompson, P, Daniel, G & Burchardt, N. (1998) *Growing Up In Stepfamilies*, Oxford: Clarendon Press.

Goulbourne, H. (1990) 'The contribution of West Indian groups to British politics' In Goulbourne, H (ed.) *Black Politics in Britain*, Aldershot: Avebury.

Goulbourne, H. (1991a) *Ethnicity and nationalism in post-imperial Britain*, Cambridge: Cambridge University Press.

Goulbourne, H. (1991b) 'The offence of the West Indian: political leadership and the communal option', in, Anwar M & Werbner P (eds.), *Black and ethnic leaderships: the cultural dimensions of political action*, London: Routledge.

Goulbourne, H. (1998a) 'The participation of new minority ethnic groups in British politics', in Tessa Blackstone, Bhikhu Parekh & Peter Sanders (eds.), *Race relations in Britain: a developing agenda*, London: Routledge.

Goulbourne, H. (1998b) *Race relations in Britain since 1945*, London: Macmillan.

Goulbourne, H. (1999a) 'The transnational character of Caribbean kinship in Britain', in McRae S (ed), *Kinship in Britain in the 1990s*, Oxford: Oxford University Press.

Goulbourne, H. (1999b) 'Exodus?: some social and policy implications of return migration to the Caribbean Commonwealth in the 1990s', *Social Policy*, Vol. 20, No. 3.

Government of St. Lucia (1991) *Population and Housing Statistics* Castries, St. Lucia.

Government of St. Lucia (1991) *Vital Statistics Report*, Statistics Department, St. Lucia.

Green, Robert-Jay & Werner Paul (1996) 'Intrusiveness and Closeness – Caregiving: Rethinking the Concept of 'Enmeshment', *Family Process*, Vol. 35 No. 2.

Greene, EJ. (1984) 'Challenges and Responses in Social Science Research in the English speaking Caribbean' in *Social & Economic Studies*, 33(1).

Greenfield, SM. (1962) 'Households families and Kinship systems in the West Indies' in *Anthropological Quarterly*, 35, 3.

Grosfoguel, R. (1998) 'Modes of incorporation: colonial Caribbean migrants in Western Europe and the United States' in Chamberlain, M (ed.) *Caribbean Migration. Globalised Identities*.

Groves Chris & Soothill K. (1996) 'A Murderous Underclass? The Press reporting of Sexually Motivated Murder'. *The Sociological Review*, Vol. 44(3), pp 398–415.

Halbwachs, M. (1980) *The Collective Memory*, New York: Harper and Row.

Hall, S et al. (1978) *Policing the crisis: mugging, the state and law and order*, London: Macmillan Press.

Hall, S. (1988) 'Migration from the English Speaking Caribbean to the United Kingdom, 1950–1980', in Appleyard, R *International Migration Today* Vol. 1, Paris: UNESCO Publication.

Handwerker, P. (1993) 'Gender power differences between parents and high-risk sexual behavior by their children: AIDS/STD risk factors extend to a prior generation'. *Journal of Women's Health*, 2(3):301.

Harewood, J. (1984) 'Mating and Fertility: Results from Three WFS Surveys in Guyana, Jamaica and Trinidad and Tobago' *WFS Scientific Reports* No. 67, Voorburg, Netherlands, International Statistical Institute.

Harrison, P. (1983) *Inside the Inner City: Life Under the Cutting Edge*, Harmondsworth: Penguin.

Haskell, L & Randall M. (1993) *The women's safety project: Summary of key statistical findings*, Ottowa: Canadian Panel on Violence against Women.

Haskey, J. (1989) *Families and households of the ethnic minority and white populations of Great Britain*, Population Trends, 57, 8–19.

Haugaard, JJ and Emery RE. (1989) 'Methodological issues in child sexual abuse research.' *Child Abuse and Neglect*, 13:89–100.

Health Education Authority (1994) *Survey of Black and Minority Ethnic Health*, London: HEA.

Heath, R. (1990) *Shadows Round the Moon*, London: Collins.

Heath, K. (1996) *National Census Report: S Vincent and the Grenadines 1991*, Caribbean Community Secretariat.

Heise, L, Pitanguy J and Germain A. (1994) *Violence Against Women: The Hidden Health Burden*, Washington, D.C: The World Bank.

Heise, L, Moore, K, Toubia N. (1995) *Sexual Coercion and Reproductive Health: A Focus on Research*, New York: The Population Council.

Henrard, JC. (1996) 'Cultural problems of ageing, especially regarding gender and intergenerational equity'. *Social Science and Medicine*, 43(5).

Henriques, F. (1949) 'West Indian family organisation', *American Journal of Sociology*, 55(1).

Henriques, F. (1953) *Family and Colour in Jamaica*, London: Eyre and Spottiswoode.

Herskovits, M. (1958) [1941] *The Myth of the Negro Past*, Boston: Beacon Press.

Herskovits, MJ. (1960) 'The Historical Approach to Afro-American Studies: A Critique' in *American Anthropologist*, 62.

Hewitt, L. (1996) *National Census Report: Trinidad and Tobago 1990*, Caribbean Community Secretariat.

Higman, B. (1973) 'Household Structure and Fertility on Jamaican Slave Plantations: A Nineteenth-Century Example'. *Population Studies*, 27(3).

Higman, BW. (1984) *Slave Populations of the British Caribbean, 1807–1834*, Baltimore: Johns Hopkins Press.

Hill-Collins, P. (1991) *Black feminist thought*, London: Routledge.

Hill-Collins, P. (1994) 'Shifting the centre: Race, class and feminist theorizing about motherhood', in Glenn, E et al. (eds.) *Mothering: Ideology, experience and agency*, California: Routledge.

Hinds, A. (1992) *Report on Organisations Serving the Afro-Caribbean Community*, London: West Indian Standing Conference.

Hintjens, H. (1995) *Alternatives to Independence: Explorations in Post-Colonial Relations*, Aldershot: Dartmouth Publishing Company.

Hintjens, H. (1997) 'Governance options in Europe's Caribbean dependencies: the end of independence', *The Round Table*, Vol 344.

Ho, C. (1993) 'The Internationalization of Kinship and the Feminization of Caribbean Migration: The Case of Afro-Trinidadian Immigrants in Los Angeles', *Human Organization*, 52(1).

Ho, MK. (1987) *Family Therapy with Ethnic Minorities*, Sage Publications.

Hodge, M. (1974) 'The Shadow of the Whip: A Comment on Male-Female Relations in the Caribbean' in Coombs E (ed.). *Is Massa Day Dead?*, London: Doubleday.

Hoetink, H. (1961) 'Family structures in the Caribbean' in *Mens en Maatschappi*, 36, 2.

Hooks, B. (1997) *Bone Black: Memories of my childhood*, London: The Women's Press.

Howe David, (1992) 'Child Abuse and the Bureaucratisation of Social Work'. *Sociological Review*, Vol. 40(3), pp 491–508.

Humphry, D and John, G. (1971) *Because they're black*, Harmondsworth: Penguin.

Huxley, E. (1964) *Back Streets, New Worlds*, London: Chatto and Windus.

Hylton, C. (1997) *Caribbean Community Organisations in Leeds*, Unpublished PhD Thesis, Department of Sociology, University of Leeds.

Hylton, C. (1997) *Family Survival Strategies: Moyenda Black Families Talking*, York: Joseph Roundtree Foundation.

Hyman, R. (1961) 'Marital relationship in a Trinidad village', *Marriage and Family Living*, 23(2).

Ince, L. (1998) *Making it Alone*, London: BAAF.

Ingman, T. (1996) *The English legal process*, London: Blackstone Press Limited.

Jackson, M and Kolody, B. (1982) 'To be Old and Black: The Case for Double Jeopardy on Income and Health', in Manuel, RC (ed.) *Minority Aging*, Westport, Connecticut: Greenwood Press.

Jamaica Information Service, (1996) *National Industrial Policy: A Strategic Plan for Growth and development*, Kingston: Jamaica Information Service.

Jayawardena, C. (1960) 'Marital Stability in two Guianese sugar estate communities', *Social & Economic Studies*, 9(1).

Jayawardena, C. (1962) 'Family organisation in plantations in British Guiana', *International Journal of Comparative Sociology*, 3(1) pp 43–64.

Jencks, C. (1992) *Rethinking Social Policy: Race, Poverty, and the Underclass*, Cambridge, Mass: Harvard University Press.

Jenkins, R. (1967) 'Racial equality in Britain' in Lester, A (ed.), *Essays and speeches by Roy Jenkins*, London: Collins.

Jenkins, S (ed.) (1988) *Ethnic associations and the welfare state*, New York: Columbia University Press.

Johnson, H (ed.) (1988) *After the Crossing: Immigrants and Minorities in Caribbean Creole Society*, London: Cass.

Jones, A and Butt, J. (1995) *Taking the initiative: The Report of a National Study Assessing Service Provision to Black Families and Children*, London: NSPCC.

Jones, J. (1992) *The Dispossessed: America's Underclasses from the Civil War to the Present*, New York: Basic Books.

Jones, T. (1993) *Britain's Ethnic Minorities: An Analysis of the Labour Force Survey*, London: Policy Studies Institute.

Joseph, G and Lewis, G. (1980) *Common differences: Conflicts in black and white feminist perspectives*, NY: Anchor Books Ltd.

Kasinitz, P. (1992) *Caribbean New York: Black Immigrants and the Politics of Race*, Ithaca: Cornell University Press.

Keith, M. (1993) *Race, riots and policing: lore and disorder in a multi-racist society*, London: UCL Press.

Kerns, V. (1997) (1984) *Women and the Ancestors. Black Carib Kinship and Ritual*, Urbana and Chicago: University of Illinois Press.

Kerr, M. (1952) *Personality and Conflict in Jamaica*, Liverpool: Liverpool University Press.

Kerr, M. (1958) *The People of Ship Street*, London: Routledge and Kegan Paul.

Keung Ho, M. (1992) *Minority Children and Adolescents in Therapy*, London: Sage.

Khan, VS. (1977) 'The Pakistanis: Mirpuri Villages at home in Bradford', in Watson JL (ed.) *Between Two Cultures: Migrants and Minorities in Britain*, London: Blackwell.

Kopijn, Y. (1998) 'Constructions of ethnicity in the diaspora: the case of three generations of Surinamese-Javanese women in the Netherlands' in Chamberlain, M (ed.) *Caribbean Migration. Globalised Identities*.

Lakey, J. (1997) 'Neighbourhood and Housing', in T Modood et al., *Ethnic Minorities in Britain*, London: Policy Studies Institute.

Lasswell, H. (1958) (1936) *Politics: who gets what, when, how*, Cleveland/New York: Meridian Books.

Lasswell, H & Kaplan, A. (1950) *Power and society*, New Haven/London: Yale University Press.

Lau, A. (1988) 'Family Therapy and Ethnic Minorities', in Street E and Dryden W and (eds.) *Family Therapy in Britain*, Milton Keynes: Open University Press.

Lau, A. (1988) 'Family Therapy and Ethnic Minorities', in Dwivedi, KN and Varma VP, (eds.) *Meeting the Needs of Ethnic Minority Children*, London: Jessica Kingsley Publishers.

Laurence, KO. (1994) *A Question of Labour. Indentured Immigration into Trinidad and British Guiana*, Kingston: Ian Randle Publishers/Oxford: James Currey Publishers.

Lawrence, E. (1982) 'In the Abundance of Water: the Fool is Thirsty', in Centre for Contemporary Cultural Studies, *The Empire Strikes Back*, London: Hutchinson.

Laws of Jamaica (1952) Jamaica Government Printing Office, Kingston, Chapter 155, pp 1–3.

Layton-Henry, Z. (1992) *The politics of immigration*, Oxford: Blackwell.

Lazarus-Black, M. (1994) *Legitimate Acts and Illegitimate Encounters: Law and Society in Antigua and Barbuda*, Washington & London: Smithsonian Institution Press.

Le Franc, E Wyatt, GE, Chambers, Eldermire, C, Bain, D, Ricketts, B&H. (1996) 'Working women's sexual risk taking in Jamaica' *Social Science and Medicine*, 42, (10).

Leo-Rhynie, (1993) *The Jamaican Family: Continuity and Change* Grace Kennedy Foundation Lecture, Institute of Jamaica.

Levi-Strauss, C. (1977) *Structural Anthropology*, London: Penguin Books.

Lewis, C and O'Brien, M. (1988) *Reassessing fatherhood: New observations on fathers and the modern family life*, London: Sage.

Lewis, J. (1984) *The Politics of Motherhood*, London/New York: Routledge.

Lightbourne, Robert and Susheela Singh (1982) 'Fertility, Union Status and Partners in the WFS Guyana and Jamaica Surveys, 1975–1976', *Population Studies*, Vol. 36, No. 2, pp 201–225.

Littlewood, R and Lipsedge, M. (1989) *Aliens and Alienists*, London: Unwin Hyman.

Liverpool, V (1986) 'When backgrounds clash', *Community Care*, 2 October, 19–21.

London Borough of Lambeth (1987) *Whose Child: The Report of the Panel Appointed to Inquire into the Death of Tyra Henry*, London Borough of Lambeth.

Long, Edward (1774) [1972]. *The History of Jamaica*, 3 Vols London: T Lowndes in Fleet Street [New York: Arno Press].

Look Lai, W. (1993) *Indentured Labor, Caribbean Sugar: Chinese and Indian Migrants to the British West Indies*, Baltimore: Johns Hopkins University Press.

Lord Chancellor's Advisory Committee on Legal Education and Conduct (1997).

Lowenthal, D. (1972) *West Indian Societies*, London: Oxford University Press.

Lutz, H. (1998) 'The Legacy of migration: immigrant mothers and daughters and the process of intergenerational transmission' in Chamberlain, M (ed.) *Caribbean Migration. Globalised Identities*.

Macdonald, JS & Macdonald, LD. (1973) 'Transformation of African and Indian Family traditions in the Southern Caribbean', *Comparative Studies in Society and History*, 15(2),

Malinowski, B. (1961) *The Dynamics of Culture Change*, Westport: Greenwood Press.

Mama A. (1990) *The Hidden Struggle: Statutory and Sector Responses to Violence against Black Women in the Home*, Institute of Social Studies. The Hague.

Mama, A. (1993) 'Woman abuse in London's black communities', in James, W and Harris, C [eds] *Inside Babylon: The Caribbean Diaspora in Britain*, London: Verso.

Manyoni, JR. (1977) 'Legitimacy and Illegitimacy: misplaced polarities in Caribbean Family Studies', *Canadian Review of Sociology and Anthropology*, 14(4).

Manyoni, JR. (1980) 'Extra-marital mating patterns in Caribbean family studies – a methodological excursus', *Anthropologica*, 22(1).

Marshall, D. (1979) 'The International Politics of Caribbean Migration' in Millett R and Will, MR *The Restless Caribbean: Changing Patterns of International Relations*, New York: Praegar.

Martin, J, Anderson, J, Romans, S, Mullen, P, O'Shea M. (1993) 'Asking about child sexual abuse: Methodological implications of a two-stage survey'. *Child Abuse and Neglect*, 17:383–392.

Massiah, J. (1983) *Women as heads of households in the Caribbean: family structure and feminine status*, New York: UNESCO.

Massiah, J. (1991) 'The Vulnerability of Female Headed Households: Paradoxes and Paradigms – A Caribbean Perspective', Paper prepared for ISER Staff Seminar June 19, 1991.

Maunder, WF. (1955) 'New Jamaican Emigration', (in *Social and Economic Studies* (4).

McAdoo, HP (eds.) (1996) 2nd edition, *Black families*, California: Sage.

McAdoo, J. (1986) 'Black fathers' relationship with their preschool children and the children's development of ethnic identity', in Lewis, R and Salt, R [eds.] *Men in families*, California: Sage.

McAdoo, J. (1988b) 'Changing perspectives on the role of the black fathers', in Bronstein, P and Cowan, C [eds.] *Fatherhood today: Men's changing role in the family*, New York: John Riley.

McAdoo, J. (1993) 'The role of African-American fathers: An ecological perspective', in *Families in Society*, No. 74, pp 28–35.

McArthur, HJ. (1979) 'The Effects of Overseas Work on Return Migrants and Their Home Communities: A Philippine Case', *Papers in Geography*, Spring 20(1), pp 85–101.

McCulloch, J Batta, I and Smith, N. (1979) 'Colour as a Variable in the Children's Section of a Local Authority Social Services Department', *New Community*, 7, 78–84.

McGlynn, F and Drescher, S (eds.) (1992) *The Meaning of Freedom: Economics, Politics, and Culture After Slavery*, Pittsburgh and London: University of Pittsburgh Press.

Melbourn, Pauline (1991) *Child Abuse: A Collaborative Study in Jamaica 1988 & 1989*, Kingston: Child Guidance Clinic, Comprehensive Health Center, Ministry of Health.

Mercer, K and Julien, I. (1988) 'Race, sexual politics and black masculinity', in Chapman, R and Rutherford, J [eds.] *Male order: Unwrapping masculinity*, London: Lawrence and Wishart.

Messina, AM. (1989) *Race and party competition in Britain*, Oxford: The Clarendon Press.

Midgett, DK. (1977) *West Indian Migration and Adaptation in St Lucia and London*, unpublished PhD. thesis, University of Illinois.

Milbrath, L. (1965) *Political participation*, Chicago: Rand McNally.

Miller, L. (1990) 'Violent Families and the Rhetoric of Harmony', *The British Journal of Sociology*, Vol. 41(2), pp 263–288.

Ministry of Social Development, 1996: *The Determination and Measurement of Poverty in Trinidad and Tobago: Indicators from the 1992 Survey of Living Conditions*, Port of Spain: Ministry of Social Development.

Mintz, S (1993) 'Goodbye, Columbus: Second thoughts on the Caribbean region at Mid-Millenium' *Walker Rodney Memorial Lecture*, Coventry: Centre for Caribbean Studies, University of Warmick.

Mintz, S and Price, R (1992) *The Birth of African American Culture: an anthropological perspective*, Boston: Beacon Press.

Mirza, H. (1992) *Young, female and black*, London: Routledge.

Modood T, Berthoud R, Lakey J, Nazroo J, Smith P, Virdee S, Beishon S. (1997) *Ethnic Minorities in Britain: Diversity and Disadvantage*, PSI Report 843, London: Policy Studies Institute,

Monagan, AP. (1985) 'Rethinking 'matrifocality', *Phylon*, 46(4).

Morgan, DH. (1975) *Social Theory and the Family*, London: Routledge and Kegan Paul.

Moynihan, D. (1965) *The Moynihan Report: The Negro Family, the case for national action*, Washington, DC: Government and Printing Office.

Murphy M (1996) 'Household and Family Structure among Ethnic Minority Groups', in Coleman D and Salt J, (eds.), *Ethnicity in the 1991 Census*, London: HMSO.

Murray, C. (1985) *Losing ground: American social policy, 1950–1980*, New York: Basic Books.

Murray, U, Brown, D. (1998) *They look after their own, don't they?: Inspection of Community Care services for black and minority older people*, London: Department of Health Social Care Group and Social Services Inspectorate.

National Association for the Care and Resettlement of Offenders (1989) *Race and Criminal Justice: A Way Forward, A Second Report of the NACRO Race Issues National Advisory Committee*, London: NACRO.

National Children's Home (1954) 'The Problem of the Coloured Child: The Experience of the National Children's Home', *Child Care Quarterly*, 8(2).

Navidi, U. (1997) *The tables are bare*, London: MSF.

Nazaroo J, 'Uncovering Gender Differences in the Use of Marital Violence: The Effect of Methodology' in *Sociology*, Vol. 29(3), pp 475–494.

Neale, B and Smart, C. (1997) 'Experiments with Parenthood', in *Sociology*, Vol. 31, No. 2, pp 201–219.

Nevadomsky, J. (1980) 'Changes in Hindu Institutions in an Alien Environment', *The Eastern Anthropologist*, Vol. 33, No. 1, pp 39–53.

Nevadomsky, J. (1982) 'Changing Conceptions of Family Regulation among the Hindu East Indian in Rural Trinidad', *Anthropological Quarterly*, Vol. 55, No. 4, pp 189–198.

Nevadomsky, J. (1985) 'Developmental sequences; domestic groups in an East Indian communities on rural Trinidad', *Ethnology*, 24(1).

Newton, V. (1984) *The Silver Men. West Indian Labour Migration to Panama 1850–1914*, Kingston: University of the West Indies, Institute of Social and Economic Studies.

Nichols, G. (1986) *The Whole of a Morning Sky*, London Virago.

Niehoff, A. (1959) 'The Survival of Hindu Institutions in an Alien Environment', *The Eastern Anthropologist*, Vol. 12, No. 3, pp 171–187.

Noble, T. (1991) 'Guyana and the Demographic Transition', *Transition*, 18.

O'Donoghue, D. (1984) 'A Hidden Epidemic, Special Report', *Newsweek*, May 14:32.

Olwig, K Fog. (1993) 'The Migration Experience: Nevisian Women at Home and Abroad', in Momsen, J. (ed.) *Women and Change in the Caribbean*, London: James Currey.

Olwig, K Fog. (1998) 'Constructing Lives: migration narratives and life stories among Nevisians' in Chamberlain, M (ed.) *Caribbean Migration, Globalised Identities*.

Oostindie, G. (1998) 'The delusive continuities of the Dutch Caribbean diaspora' in Chamberlain, M. *Caribbean Migration, Globalised Identities*.

Oppenheim, C and Harker, L. (1996) *Poverty: The facts*, London: CPAG.

Osler, A. (1997) *Exclusion from School and Racial Equality*, London: Commission for Racial Equality.

Otterbein, KF. (1965) 'Caribbean family organisation: a comparative analysis', *American Anthropologist*, 67(1).

Owen, D. (1993a) *Ethnic Minorities in Great Britain: Housing and Family Characteristics*, Coventry: University of Warwick Centre for Research in Ethnic Relations, 1991 Census Statistical Paper No. 4.

Owen, D. (1993b) *Ethnic Minorities in Great Britain: Age and Gender Structure*, Coventry: University of Warwick Centre for Research in Ethnic Relations, 1991 Census Statistical Paper No. 2.

Owen, D. (1993c) *Ethnic Minorities in Great Britain: Economic Characteristics*, Coventry: University of Warwick Centre for Research in Ethnic Relations, 1991 Census Statistical Paper No. 3.

Owen, D. (1994) *Black People in Great Britain: Social and Economic Circumstances*, 1991 Census Statistical paper No. 6, Coventry: University of Warwick: Centre for Research in Ethnic Relations.

Owen, D. (1994a) *Ethnic Minority Women and the Labour Market* Manchester: Equal Opportunities Commission.

Owen, D. (1994b) *Black people in Great Britain: Social and Economic Circumstances*, Coventry: National Ethnic Minority Data Archive Census Statistical Paper 6.

Owen, D. (1996) '*A demographic profile of Caribbean households and families in Great Britain*', in Living Arrangements, Family Structure and Social Change of Caribbeans in Britain ESRC populations and household change research programs.

Owen, D. (1996) 'Size, structure and the growth of ethnic minority populations', in, Coleman & Salt (eds). *Ethnicity in the 1991 Census: Demographic Characteristics of the Ethnic Minority Populations*, London: OPCS.

Owen, D. (1998) 'Marital Status and Families in the Caribbean and Great Britain Compared', *Working paper 1/98, Living arrangements, family structure and social change of Caribbeans in Britain*, ESRC Population and Household Change Research Programme.

Palmer, R (ed) (1990) *In Search of a Better Life. Perspectives on Migration from the Caribbean*, New York: Praeger.

Paniagua, FA. (1994) *Assessing and Treating Culturally Diverse Clients*, Sage Publications,

Patel, N. (1990) *A 'Race' Against Time? Social Services Provision to Black Elders*, London: Runnymead Race and Policy Series, No. 1.

Patterson, O (1999) 'The Afro-Atlantic Diaspora: a sociological overview of "race" and ethnicity in the UK and America', Paper presented at *Race, Ethnicity and Mobility Conference*, Bath 24–27 June.

Patterson, O. (1967) *The Sociology of Slavery: An Analysis of the Origins, Development and Structure of Negro Slave Society in Jamaica*, Rutherford: Fairleigh Dickinson University Press.

Patterson, S. (1965) *Dark strangers: a study of West Indians in London*, Harmondsworth; Penguin.

Payne, T. (1994) *Politics in Jamaica*, Kingston: Ian Randle Publications.

Peach, C. (1968) *West Indian Migration to Britain: A Social Geography*, London: Oxford University Press.

Peach, C. (1991) *The Caribbean in Europe: contrasting patterns of migration and settlement in Britain, France and the Netherlands,* Research Paper in Ethnic Relations No. 15, Coventry: Centre for Research in Ethnic Relations, University of Warwick.

Pensions & Overseas Benefits Directorate (1997) *Overseas Pensions and Benefits*, Newcastle.

Pensions & Overseas Benefits Directorate (1998) *Overseas Pensions and Benefits*, Newcastle.

Pensions & Overseas Benefits Directorate (1996/97) *Overseas Pensions and Benefits*, Newcastle.

Petras, EM. (1980) 'The Role of National Boundaries in a Cross-National Labour Market', *International Journal of Urban and Regional* Research 4(2).

Petras, EM. (1988) *Jamaican Labor Migration: White Capital and Black Labor 1850–1930*, Boulder and London: Westview Press.

Phillips, D. (1987) 'Searching for a Decent Home: Ethnic Minority Progress in the Post-War Housing Market', *New Community*, 14 (1/2), 105–117.

Phillips, D. (1996) 'Medical professional dominance and client dissatisfaction', *Social Science and Medicine*, 42(10).

Phillips, M (1974) 'Landfall' *The Listener*, 21 November.

Phillips, M & Phillips, T. (1998) *Windrush: The Irresistible Rise of Multi-Racial Britain*, London: HarperCollins Publishers.

Phillips, R. (1996) *National Census Report: British Virgin Islands 1991*, Caribbean Community Secretariat.

Phoenix, A. (1988) The Afro-Caribbean Myth', *New Society*, 4 March, 11–14.

Pilkington, E. (1988) *Beyond the mother country: West Indians and the Notting Hill Riots.*

Plaza, D. (1996) 'Frequent Flier Grannies' paper presented to the *Caribbean Studies, Association,* Puerto Rico.

Portelli, A. (1990) 'Uchronic dreams: working class memory and possible worlds' in Samuel R and Thompson, P (eds.) *The Myths We Live By,* London: Routledge.

Portelli, A. (1998) 'Oral History as Genre' in Chamberlain, M and Thompson, P. (eds.) *Narrative and Genre, Routledge Studies in Memory and Narrative,* London/New York: Routledge.

Portes, A. (1998) 'Globalisation from Below: The Rise of Transnational Communities', *Transnational Communities Working Paper,* WPTC-98–01, University of Oxford.

Powdermaker, H. (1993) *After Freedom: A Cultural Study in the Deep South,* with an introductory essay Hortense Powdermaker in the Deep South by Brackette F Williams and Drexel G Woodson Madison: The University of Wisconsin Press.

Powell, D. (1982) 'Network Analysis: A Suggested Model for the Study of Women and the Family in the Caribbean', in Massiah, J (ed.) *Women in the Family,* Cave Hill, Barbados: Institute of Social and Economic Research, University of the West Indies.

Powell, D. (1984) 'The Role of Women in the Caribbean', *Social and Economic Studies,* 33(3).

Pryce, K. (1990) 'Culture from below: politics, resistance and leadership in The Notting Hill Gate Carnival 1976–1978' in Goulbourne (ed.) *Black Politics in Britain,* Aldershot: Avebury.

Pryce, K. (1979) *Endless Pressure: A Study of West Indian Life-style in Bristol,* Harmondsworth: Penguin Books.

Pulsipher, L. (1993) 'Changing roles in the traditional West Indian houseyards', in Momsen, J [eds.] *Women and change in the Caribbean,* London: James Currey Publishing.

Ram, B. (1990) *New Trends in the Family: Demographic Facts and Features,* Ministry of supply and Services Canada.

Rampton, A. (1981) *West Indian Children in Our Schools: Interim Report of the Committee of Inquiry into the Education of Children From* (sic) *Ethnic Groups,* Cmnd. 8273, London: HMSO.

Rapoport, RN, Fogarty MP and Rapoport, R (eds.) *Families in Britain,* London: Routledge and Kegan Paul.

Reay, D. (1998) *Class Work: Mothers Involvement in their Children's Primary Schooling,* London: Taylor and Francis.

Renvoize, J. (1981) *Child Sexual Abuse,* London: Bascapan Publishers, pp 1–13.

Report of the consultative seminar on standards and regulation of immigrant advice, London: Millbank Tower.

Rex, J & Mason, D (eds.) (1988) *Theories of race and ethnic relations,* Cambridge: Cambridge University Press.

Rex, J & Tomlinson, S. (1979) *Colonial immigrants in a British city,* London: Routledge & Kegan Paul.

Rex, J and Mason, D (eds.) *Theories of Race and Ethnic Relations,* Cambridge: Cambridge University Press.

Reyes, A. (1996) 'From a Lineage of Southern Women', in Etter Lewis, G and Foster, M *Unrelated Kin: Race and Gender in Women's Personal Narratives,* London/New York: Routledge.

Reynolds, T. (1997a) '(Mis)Representing the Black (Super)Woman', in Mirza, H [ed.] *Black British Feminism,* London: Routledge.

Reynolds, T. (1998) *African-Caribbean mothering: Reconstructing a 'new' identity*, unpublished PhD, South Bank University, London.

Richardson, B. (1983) *Caribbean Migrants, Environment and Human Survival on St Kitts and Nevis*, Knoxville: University of Tennessee Press.

Richardson, B. (1985) *Panama Money in Barbados 1900–1920*, Knoxville: University of Tennessee Press.

Roberts, GW and Braithwaite, L. (1962) 'Mating among East Indian and Non-Indian Women in Trinidad', *Social and Economic Studies*, Vol. 11, No. 3, pp 203–240.

Roberts G and Braithwaite, L. (1967) 'Fertility Differentials by Family Type in Trinidad', *CSO Research Papers No. 4*, pp 102–119.

Roberts, GW and Sinclair, SA. (1978) *Women in Jamaica: Patterns of Reproduction and Family*, Millwood New York: KTO Press.

Roberts, G and Mills, D. (1958) 'Study of External Migration Affecting Jamaica 1953–1955', *Social and Economic Studies. Supplement*, 7(2).

Roberts, G and Sinclair, S. (1978) *Women in Jamaica: Patterns of Reproduction and Family*, New York: KTO Press.

Roberts, GW. (1975) *Fertility and Mating in Four West Indian Populations*, Kingston: Institute of Social and Economic Research, University of the West Indies.

Roberts, GW. (1955) 'Emigration from the Island of Barbados' in *Social and Economic Studies*, 4(3).

Roberts, S, Palacio, PS, Arnold, E and Hobo, E. (1996) *National Census Report: Belize 1991*, Caribbean Community Secretariat.

Robinson, P. (1970) 'The Social Structure of Guyana' pp 57–76 in Searwar L (ed.) *Co-op Republic: Guyana 1970*, Georgetown: Ministry of Education.

Rodman, H. (1966) 'Illegitimacy in the Caribbean Social Structure, a reconsideration', *American Sociological Review*, 31, 5.

Rodman, H. (1971) *Lower Class Families: The Culture of Poverty in Negro Trinidad*, London, Oxford University Press.

Rodney, W. (1969) *Groundings with my brothers*, London: Bogle L'Ouverture Publications.

Rodriquez, R. (1995) Returning to St Lucia, paper presented at the Eastern Caribbean Commission, London, 2 December.

Roschelle, A. (1997) *No more kin: Exploring class, race and gender in family networks*, California: Sage.

Rosser, C & Harris, CC. (1965) *The Family and Social Change*, London: Routledge and Kegan Paul.

Rowe, J and Lambert, L. (1973) *Children Who Wait*, London: Association of British Adoption Agencies.

Rowe, J, Hundleby, M and Garnett, L. (1989) *Child Care Now*, London: BAAF, Research Series 6.

Rubenstein, H. (1977) 'Diachronic inference and the pattern of lower class Afro-Caribbean marriage', *Social & Economic Studies*, 26(2).

Rubenstein, H. (1980) 'Conjugal behaviour and parental role flexibility in an Afro-Caribbean village', *Canadian Revue of Sociology and Anthropology*, 17, 4.

Rubenstein, H. (1982)(a) 'The Impact of Remittances in the Rural English-speaking Caribbean, in Stinner, WF and de Albuquerque, K (eds.) *Return Migration and Remittances: Developing a Caribbean Perspective*, Washington D.C: Smithsonian Institution.

Rubenstein, H. (1982)(b) 'Return Migration to the Caribbean', in Stinner, WF and de Albuquerque, K (eds.) *Return Migration and Remittances: Developing a Caribbean Perspective*, Washington D.C: Smithsonian Institution.

Rubenstein, H. (1983) 'Caribbean family and households organisation – some conceptual clarifications', *Journal of Comparative Family Studies*, 14(3).

Russell, DEH. (1983) 'The incidence and prevalence of intrafamilial and extrafamilial sexual abuse of female children, *Child Abuse and Neglect*', 7:133–146.

Saggar, S. (1992) *Race and politics in Britain*, London: Harvester Wheatsheaf.

Samuel, R and Thompson, P (eds.) (1990) *The Myths We Live By*, London: Routledge.

Sarre, P. (1986) 'Choice and Constraint in Ethnic Minority Housing', *Housing Studies*, 1, 71–86.

Scarman, Lord Justice (1975) *The Red Lion Square Disorders of 15 June 1974*, Cmnd. 5919, London: HMSO.

Scarman, Rt Hon Lord Leslie (1982) *The Brixton disorders 10–12 April 1981*, Cmnd. 8427, London: HMSO

Schei, B. (1990) 'Prevalence of sexual abuse history in a random sample of Norweigan women', *Scandinavian Social Medicine*, 18(1):63–68.

Schlesinger, B. (1968a) 'Family patterns in Jamaica', *Journal of Marriage and the Family*, 30, (1).

Schlesinger, B. (1968b) 'Family patterns in the English speaking Caribbean', *Journal of Marriage and the Family*, 30(1).

Schuler M. (1992) *Violence Against Women: The International Perspective. in Freedom From Violence: Strategies around the World*, UNIFEM.

Schwartz, B. (1964) 'Caste and Endogamy in Trinidad', *Southwestern Journal of Anthropology*, Vol. 20, pp 58–66.

Schwartz, BM. (1965) 'Patterns of East Indian family organisation in Trinidad', *Caribbean Studies*, 5(1).

Schwarz, B. (1996) 'Black Metropolis, White England' in Nava, M and O'Shea A (eds.) *Modern Times. Reflections on a century of English Modernity*, London: Routledge.

Searwar, L (ed) (1970) *Co-op Republic: Guyana 1970*, Georgetown: Ministry of Education.

Segal, A. (1987) 'The Caribbean Exodus in a global context: Comparative migration experiences' in Levine B. (ed.) *The Caribbean Exodus*, New York: Praeger.

Senior, O. (1991) *Working miracles: Women's lives in the English speaking Caribbean*, London: James Currey Publishers.

Sewell, T. (1993) *Black tribunes: black political participation in Britain*, London: Lawrence & Wishart.

Sewell, T. (1997) *Black masculinities and schooling: How black boys survive modern schooling*, London: Trentham Books.

Sharma, KN. (1986) 'Changing Forms of East Indian Marriage and Family in the Caribbean', *Journal of Sociological Studies*, pp 20–58.

Sharpe, S. (1994) *Fathers and daughters*, Harmondsworth: Penguin Books.

Sheldon, B. (1994) 'The Social and Biological Components of Mental Disorder: Implications for Services', in *International Journal of Social Psychiatry*, 40:2, 87–105.

Shepherd, V. (1998) 'Indians, Jamaica and the emergence of a modern migration culture' in Chamberlain, M *Caribbean Migration. Globalised Identities*.

Shepherd, V, Brereton, B, & Bailey, B (eds.) (1995) *Engendering History: Caribbean Women in Historical Perspective*, Jamaica: Ian Randle Publishers.

Shukra, K. (1990) 'Black Sections in the Labour party', Goulbourne H, (ed.), *Black politics in Britain*, Aldershot: Avebury.

Shyllon, FO (1974) *Black Slaves in Britain*, London: Oxford University Press.

Sillitoe, K and White, P. (1992) 'Ethnic Group and the British Census: the Search for a Question', *Journal of the Royal Statistical Society A*, 155, 141–163.

Simey, TS. (1946) *Welfare and Planning in the West Indies*, London: Oxford University Press.

Singh, S. (1979) 'Demographic Variables and the Recent Trend in Fertility in Guyana 1960–71', *Population Studies*, 33, 2: 313–317.

Smart, C and Neale, B. (1997) 'Good enough morality? Divorce and postmodernity', in *Critical Social Policy*, Vol. 17, No. 4: 3–27.

Smith, DJ. (1977) *Racial Disadvantage in Britain*, London: Penguin.

Smith, MG. (1962) *The Plural Society in the British West Indies*, Los Angeles: University of California Press.

Smith, MG. (1962) *West Indian Family Structure*, Seattle and London: University of Washington Press.

Smith, MG. (1974) *Corporations and society*, London: Duckworth.

Smith, MG. (1988) 'Pluralism, race and ethnicity in selected African countries' in Rex. J and Mason D (eds.) *Theories of Race and Ethnic Relations*, Cambridge: Cambridge University Press.

Smith, MG. (1984) *Culture, Race and Class in the Commonwealth Caribbean*, Kingston: University of the West Indies School of Continuing Studies.

Smith, RT. (1953) 'Aspects of Family organisation in a coastal negro commnity in British Guiana', *Timehri*, 1, 32.

Smith, RT. (1955) 'Land tenure in three negro villages in British Guiana', *Social and Economic Studies*, 4(1).

Smith, RT. (1956) *The Negro Family in British Guiana: Family Structure and Social Status in the Villages*, London: Routledge and Kegan Paul.

Smith, RT & Jayarwardena, C. (1958) 'Hindu marriage customs in British Guiana', *Social and Economic Studies*, 7(2).

Smith, RT and Jayawardena, C. (1959) 'Marriage and the Family Amongst East Indians in British Guiana', *Social and Economic Studies*, Vol. 8, No. 4, pp 321–376.

Smith, RT & Jayarwardena, C. (1959) 'Marriage and the family amongst East Indians in British Guiana', *Population Studies*, 13(1).

Smith, RT. (1963) 'Culture and social structure in the Caribbean: some recent work on family and kinship studies', *Comparative Studies in Society and History*, 6(1).

Smith, RT. (1974) 'The matrilocal family', in Goodey, J. (ed.) *The Character of Kinship*, Cambridge: Cambridge University Press.

Smith, RT. (1978) 'The family and the modern world system: some observations from the Caribbean', *Journal of Family History*, 13(4).

Smith, RT. (1982) 'Family, Social Change and Social Policy in the West Indies', *Nieuwe West-Indische Gids*, 56(3/4):111–142. [Reprinted as Chapter 6 in RT Smith (1996)].

Smith, RT. (1987a). 'Kinship and Class in Chicago', in Mullings L. (ed.), *Cities of the United States: Studies in Urban Anthropology*, New York: Columbia University Press.

Smith, RT. (1987b). 'Hierarchy and the dual marriage system in West Indian society', in Collier, J and Yanagisako, SJ *Gender and kinship: essays toward a unified analysis*, Stanford: Stanford University Press. [Reprinted as Chapter 5 in RT Smith (1996)].

Smith, RT. (1988) *Kinship and class in the West Indies: a genealogical study of Jamaica and Guyana*, Cambridge: Cambridge University Press.

Smith, RT. (1996) *The Matrifocal Family: Power, Pluralism and Politics*, New York and London: Routledge.

Smith, RT (forthcoming). 'The Caribbean Family: Continuity and Transformation', Chapter XVI of Volume 5, *UNESCO General History of the Caribbean*.

Solien, NL. (1960) 'Household and family in the Caribbean', *Social & Economic Studies*, 9(1).

Song M and Edwards, R (1997) 'Comment: raising questions about perspectives in Black lone motherhood', *Journal of Social Policy*, Vol 26, No 2 (233–244)

St Bernard, G. (1997a) *The Family and Society in Trinidad and Tobago: The Findings of the National Survey of Family Life* (Draft Copy), The Ministry of Social Development, The Government of Trinidad and Tobago.

St Bernard, G. (1997b). 'Kinship and Family Dynamics in Laventille' in Ryan, S, Mc Cree R and St Bernard G *Behind the Bridge: Poverty, Politics and Patronage in Laventille, Trinidad*, The Institute of Social and Economic Research St Augustine, Trinidad and Tobago.

St Bernard, G. (1994) 'Ethnicity and Attitudes Towards Inter-Racial Marriages in Trinidad and Tobago – An Exploration of Preliminary Findings', *Caribbean Quarterly*, Vol. 40, Nos. 3 & 4, pp 109–124.

St Bernard, G. (1996) *National Census Report: St Lucia 1991*, Caribbean Community Secretariat.

Stacey, M. (1960) *Tradition and Change*, Oxford: Oxford University Press.

Stack, C. (1974) *All our kin: Strategies for survival in black community*, New York: Harper and Row.

Stack, C and Burton, L. (1994) 'Kinscripts: Reflections on family, generation and culture', in Glenn, E et al. [eds.] *Mothering: Ideology, experience and agency*, California: Routledge.

Staples, R. (1985) 'The myth of the black matriarchy', in Steady, F [eds.] *The black woman cross-culturally*, New York: Schenkmann Books Inc.

The Star (St Lucia), 10 October, 1992.

The Star (St Lucia), 5 October, 1996.

Stark, O & Lucas, R. (1988) 'Migration, Remittances and the Family', *Economic Development and Cultural Change*, 36.

Stewart, M. (1983) 'Racial Discrimination and Occupational Attainment in Britain', *Economic Journal*, 93(4).

Stinner, WF, de Albuquerque, K & Bryce-Laporte, RS (eds.) *Return Migration and Remittances: Developing a Caribbean Perspective*, Research Institute on Immigration and Ethnic Studies, Occasional Papers No 3 Smithsonian Institution.

Strauss, MA (1979) 'Measuring intra-family conflict and violence: The Conflict Tactics Scale', *Journal of Marriage and the Family*, 38(1) 15–28.

Stubbs, P. (1988) *The Reproduction of Racism in State Social Work*, Unpublished PhD thesis, University of Bath.

Supperstone, M & O'Dempsey, D. (1996) *On Immigration and Asylum*, London: FT Law & Tax.

Sutton, C (1997) 'Introduction', Kerns, V *Women and the Ancestors*: Black Carib Kinship and Ritual, Urbana and Chicago: University of Chicago Press.

Sutton, C and Chaney E (eds.) (1994) *Caribbean Life in New York City: Sociocultural Dimensions*, New York: Center for Migration Studies of New York.

Sutton, C and Makeisky-Barrow, S (1985) 'Social inequality and sexual status in Barbados', in Steady, F [ed.] *The black woman cross-culturally*, New York: Schenkmann Books Inc.

Swann, Lord Michael (1985) Education for all: Report of the Committee of Inquiry into the Education of Children of Ethnic Minority Groups, Cmnd. 9453 London: HMSO.

Talburt, T (forthcoming) *'The Lomé Conventions' rum protocol and Jamaica's development policies'*, PhD Thesis, South Bank University, London.

Taylor, R Jackson, S and Chatters, L (eds.) (1997) *Black family life in America*, California: Sage.

Thomas, CY. (1988) *The Poor and the Powerless*, New York: Monthly Review Press.

Thomas-Hope, E. (1980) 'Hopes and reality in West Indian migration to Britain', *Oral History Journal*, Vol 8, No 1.

Thomas-Hope, E. (1992) *Explanation in Caribbean Migration*, London: Macmillan.

Thomas-Hope E. (1978) 'The establishment of a migration tradition: British West Indian movements to the Hispanic Caribbean in the century after emancipation', in Clarke, CG (ed.) *Caribbean Relations*, Monograph Series No. 8, Centre for Latin American Studies, University of Liverpool.

Tidrick, G. (1966) 'Some Aspects of Jamaican Emigration to the United Kingdom 1953–1962', *Social and Economic Studies*, (15).

Tipler, J. (1986) *Is Justice Colour-Blind? A Study of the Impact of Race in the Juvenile Justice System in Hackney*, Social Services Research Note 6.

Todaro, MP. (1976) *International Migration in Developing Countries*, Geneva: International Labour Organisation.

Tomlinson, S. (1983) *Ethnic Minorities in British Schools*, London: Heineman Educational Books.

Tonkin, E. (1992) *Narrating Our Past*, Cambridge: Cambridge University Press.

Trouillaut, M. (1992) 'The Caribbean region: an open frontier in anthropological theory', *Annual Review of Anthropology*, 21.

United Nations, (1987) *Report on the Retrospective Demographic Survey in Guyana 1986*.

Valee, L. (1965) 'La legitimite et de la matrifocalite: tentative de re interpretation' *Anthropologica*, 7, 2.

Vertovec, S. (1992) *Hindu Trinidad: Religion, Ethnicity and Socio-Economic Change*, London, Macmillan Caribbean, Warwick University Caribbean Studies.

Walby, S. (1990) *Theorizing patriarchy*, Oxford: Blackwell.

Walker, MA. (1988) 'The Court Disposal of Young Males by Race in London in 1983', *British Journal of Criminology*, 28(4), 441–460.

Walkerdine, V. (1997) *Daddy's Girl: young girls and popular culture*, London: Macmillan.

Wallace, M. (1978) *Black macho and the myth of the superwoman*, New York: Dial Press.

Wallerstein, L. (1979) *The Capitalist World Economy*, Cambridge: Cambridge University Press.

Walvin, J. (1997) *Questioning Slavery*, Kingston: Ian Randle Publishers.

Watson, H. (1982) 'Theoretical and Methodological Problems in Commonwealth Caribbean Research: Conditions and Causality' *Social and Economic Studies*, 31(1).

Weber, Max (1968) [1918–20] *Economy and Society: An Outline of Interpretive Sociology*, Edited by Guenther Roth and Claus Wittich, New York: Bedminster Press, 3 Vols.

Webster, W. (1998) *Imagining Home. Gender 'Race and National Identity 1945–64*, London: University College London Press.

Weinberg, DH *Fighting poverty: What works and what doesn't*, Cambridge, Mass: Harvard University Press.

White, A. (1986) 'Profiles: Women in the Caribbean Project' in Joycelin Massiah (ed.) *Women in the Caribbean* (Part 1), *Social and Economic Studies*, Vol. 35, No. 2 – Special Issue, pp 59–81.

Whitehead, TL. (1978) 'Residence, kinship and mating as survival strategies – a West Indian example', *Journal of Marriage and the Family*, 40(4).

Williams, C, Soydan H Johnson MRD (eds.) (1998) *Social Work and Minorities: European Perspectives*, London: Routledge.

Wilson, WJ. (1987) *The truly disadvantaged: the inner city, the underclass and public policy*, Chicago: University of Chicago Press.

Wilson, WJ. (1996) *When work disappears: The work of the new urban poor*, New York: Random House.

Wilson WJ. (1987) *The truly disadvantaged: The inner city, the underclass and public policy*, Chicago: University of Chicago Press.

Wiltshire-Brodber, R. (1988) 'The Caribbean Transnational Family', paper presented to UNESCO/ISER Eastern Caribbean Sub-regional Seminar, University of the West Indies, Cave Hill.

World Bank, (1996) *Poverty Reduction and Human Resource Development in the Caribbean*, Washington, DC: Government and Printing Office.

Wyatt, GE. (1985) 'The sexual abuse of Afro-American and white American women in childhood', *Child Abuse and Neglect*, 9:507–519.

Wyatt, GE and SD Peters (1986) 'Issues in the definition of child sexual abuse in prevalence research', *Child Abuse and Neglect*, 10:231–240.

Young, M and Wilmott, P (1957) *Family and Kinship in East London*: Routledge and Kegan Paul.

Index

Numbers in *italics* indicate Figures, those in **bold** Tables.